*I Travel by Train*

By ROLLO WALTER BROWN

Emergence
    THE FIREMAKERS
    TOWARD ROMANCE
    THE HILLIKIN
    AS OF THE GODS

LONELY AMERICANS
DEAN BRIGGS
ON WRITING THE BIOGRAPHY OF A MODEST
    MAN
NEXT DOOR TO A POET

THE CREATIVE SPIRIT: AN INQUIRY INTO
    AMERICAN LIFE

I TRAVEL BY TRAIN

—"*seeing what kind of country it is that I live in.*"

*Rollo Walter Brown*

# I TRAVEL BY TRAIN

ILLUSTRATIONS BY GRANT REYNARD

D. *Appleton*-*Century* *Company*
INCORPORATED

*New York*           *London*

1939

COPYRIGHT, 1939, BY
D. APPLETON-CENTURY COMPANY, INC.

*All rights reserved. This book, or parts thereof, must not be reproduced in any form without permission of the publisher.*

PRINTED IN THE UNITED STATES OF AMERICA

# *Preface*
[TO BE READ]

IN THE dead of night in the Oklahoma Panhandle country, I climbed aboard a long train from the Pacific Coast that had generously offered to stop at a small town for a solitary passenger. I was still much awake from a busy evening, and while the porter made down a berth for me, I wandered back through the train—through two or three darkened sleeping-cars where passengers snug behind green curtains were sound asleep, then through four or five others that were almost as dark, but not made down for the night, and without passengers. In the rear section of the last of these a brakeman—a man of forty or forty-five with an active face—sat musing in the dim light of the berth-lamp. The unoccupied cars, he explained, had carried a company of youngsters to a Conservation Camp farther southwest, and were now going "deadhead" back to Kansas City.

For five minutes I stood and talked with him.

"Sit down," at last he begged of me. "I haven't talked to anybody all day."

He seemed a trifle loquacious, and it was late, but I complied. As soon as I was seated, he laughed a little. "I wanted to get you down so as I could ask you a question. If you don't mind, I'd just like to know what you work at. When you came walking back here I hardly thought you looked like a business man."

I let him guess. Then I told him.

"Well, say! A writer? I don't often meet any of them—that is, that I know of. But I know a book you or somebody ought to write—about trains and railroads and the excitement of them."

I told him that I was soon to go to work on a volume that might not be altogether unlike what he had in mind; that for more than a dozen years I had had to cover much of the United States three or four times each year, and that I meant to write about what I had seen—about a trip here and there out of many.

"But you'll be sure to say plenty about trains, won't you? Anybody that ever saw as much water as the Cimarron River has got in it in August writes about ships. And trains are lots more thrilling. Ever stand in the Union Station at Cincinnati or St. Louis, or in one of the big stations at Chicago or Minneapolis, at night maybe, when the big boys with their names on their tails are all lined up to go —the Bluebonnet, the Chief, the Corn King Limited, the Katy Flyer, the Viking, the Meteor, the F.F.V., the Flamingo, the Wolverine, the Zephyr, the Columbine, the Golden Arrow? You see, I know some of them, all right.

"And boy! You don't go to sleep while you're working on a train. Can you imagine what it's like jumping off the pilot of a freight engine to run ahead to open a switch, and your feet slip out from under you where there's some smooth ice under the snow, and you fall smack across the rail with the old engine creeping along only about eight feet behind you? Or when everything is covered with ice, slipping down *ka-plump* between two flat-cars when they're moving? I did that once starting on a night run to Omaha. I had sense enough to keep on running, down in there between the two sets of trucks, but she was already going too fast for me to dodge out across the rails, and I didn't know how long I was going to be able to keep on running, with the engine picking up a little all the time. Then she began to slow down, and finally stopped! Boy, oh, boy! The engineer said his engine didn't feel as if she was pulling just right, and he thought he'd better stop and find out what was wrong before he got going.

"Now isn't that good enough for a book?"

"Yes, but you are the person to write that one. Mine will be about the people I see on trains—what they are up to, and—"

He interrupted: "Say, I could write one like that, too—if I knew how. I talked once with fourteen movie actresses on this run. And sometimes I see something along the way. There! in that little town the agent's wife is a sour-looking devil—I know that much."

I tried to pull him back to my point of view. I told him that I was interested in the people I saw when I got off trains, too: in the people who produce food, in the people who must go hungry, in what people endure, in what they dream, in what comes true—and in what it all seems to mean when you try to put it together.

"I get you!" he said. "The low-down on about everybody."

No, I protested; it would not be a book of such pretensions. But it would at least be about the United States which one long-distance train traveler had eventually come to see and think about.

R. W. B.

# Contents

| | | PAGE |
|---|---|---|
| Foreword | | vii |

| CHAPTER | | |
|---|---|---|
| I. | Color | 1 |
| II. | Discovery | 20 |
| III. | Sustenance | 36 |
| IV. | Southbound | 55 |
| V. | Hunger | 65 |
| VI. | Parasite | 85 |
| VII. | Heat | 107 |
| VIII. | Evergreen | 128 |
| IX. | Smoke | 141 |
| X. | Dust | 157 |
| XI. | Waste | 170 |
| XII. | Creole | 189 |
| XIII. | Home | 203 |
| XIV. | Rain | 217 |
| XV. | Detour | 237 |
| XVI. | Ferment | 248 |
| XVII. | Sunlight | 267 |
| XVIII. | Novelty | 282 |
| XIX. | Panorama | 299 |

*I Travel by Train*

# i

## Color

WHENEVER I think of traveling, I see the United States as merging areas of color. For I always begin my travels in the autumn. It was so a dozen years ago; it was so the year before last; it was so last year.

The day of departure carried its own announcement. Chill winds swept across the New Hampshire hills from Mount Monadnock and whirled the showering maple-leaves everywhere. The last lingering bluebirds sought the protected side of the barn and chirred regretfully in the afternoon sun. Shining pheasants, a dozen strong, marched boldly into the open meadow, stopped, and while the wind almost blew them off their feet, looked toward the house as if to say, "What? You still here?" By the next morning I was without regrets at going. For the wind had left the hills only dull, colorless pinnacles that were rendered all the more desolate by occasional areas of evergreen and clumps of birches the least bit too white in their fresh nakedness.

Down in the edge of Massachusetts the maples still provided a little color—until you came too near—and in Concord and Arlington and Cambridge there were almost as many yellowing leaves on the elms as in the streets beneath them.

There was much to be done in Cambridge in two short hours—if I were to catch the noon train. As I hurried to the haberdasher's I was reminded—at the end of the summer I never fail to be—that I had reverted to type. For when all sorts of persons looked at me as though there were a reason for doing so, I began to wonder what was wrong. Did I have shaving cream in my ear? Did my last year's hat look worse than I had thought? Or was I merely looking in general like the provincial that I was? But when one man stopped me on the sunny side of Harvard Square, introduced himself, and told me that he had read my latest book, I felt so immeasurably better that as soon as I had visited the barber's I ventured over into the Harvard Yard—just for one brief minute, to see how it felt. I met many old friends, and I snatched a second from all thought of unwaiting trains to survey the trees. After the sight of natural woodland all summer, these trees in the Yard looked carefully pruned, a trifle overcivilized, as if they lived too constantly in an intellectual air.

Just when I was about to rush away and take a taxi to the house, a stranger came up to me and timidly wondered if I would be good enough to tell him how to get to the new chapel. There it was in plain view, but many distant, impersonal smiles along the paths had made him hesitant. I glanced at the clock to see if I had still a precious minute or two that I could spare. "But perhaps I shouldn't have troubled you—either," he began. I protested that it was no trouble; that I was only thinking of a train that I had to catch; that I should have just time enough to go with him.

Inside, while he stood and looked awesomely about, I enjoyed the quiet. It is a white and sterilized quiet, but quiet none the less. I once came upon the architect of the building sitting in there alone. He told me that he never knew how he happened to produce that great sense of quiet, but that it was there, and that he sometimes came and sat for fifteen minutes just to enjoy it. When the stranger at last regained speech, he felt a little better toward the people in the Yard. We said good-bye, and I sped to the house to rediscover a half-dozen things after our six months' absence—things that I had suddenly thought of in the quiet of the chapel.

Nobody of consequence in Boston ever takes his train in South Station. It is not so much of a station, as stations come and go, and it is surrounded by an atmosphere of leather, wool, roasting coffee, and dank sea water. But the traveler who is not too much in social bondage knows that it has its advantages. The sleeping-car is there in readiness—twenty minutes before leaving time. It immediately quiets the nerves to go into a car that is standing as if it meant to stay. And it increases a man's self-respect to walk to his space, see his luggage slipped under the berth, and then sit in the calm of green upholstery for ten minutes just as if only a half-hour before he had not been raging at everybody because his shirts had been smudged in the laundry. I had done pretty well in packing up—and so had my wife. I could think of nothing at all that I had left behind. Yet I pretended that I thought of something. Yes, it was something that would justify me in going to the rear of the train to telephone back to the house. I wanted my wife to hear me say in perfectly restrained voice that I was there and settled and all ready to go.

Even if it does sound like writing a testimonial for somebody, I must confess that I enjoy this traveling on a train. For a journey, as I like to think of it, consists not only of getting there, but of going. In the course of a week, a month, I shall be able to use all my spare time in seeing what kind of country it is that I live in.

Immediately, too, I began to see it. For within five minutes after the engineer had given us the none-too-gentle jerk which assured us that we were on our way, we were coming into the Back Bay Station. Crowds of competently dressed men and women with dogs and children were saying good-bye on the platform. No fringes of any other classes of people were in sight. It was—and always is—America's best cross-section of a Brahmin population. In a crisp atmosphere that is a blending of the acquisitive and the intellectual, they are at perfect ease among themselves. Their language on such occasions, when they speak a little excitedly as if they were doing something unusual, has a flavoring that is more European than American. It is not precisely British—the British would be the first to tell you so—yet there is in it something that is more like Charing Cross or Bowness than Broad Street or Mackinac.

Only a few of them came into the car. They usually stick so close to the Atlantic seaboard that it is unnecessary for them to take a sleeper—except on those rare occasions when they go to Washington, and those rarer ones when they go to Miami. When they are sailing from New York they can ride down in a parlor-car. Yet when the last redcap had rushed from the starting train, our passenger list in the sleeper had been increased. In front of me was a little girl of four with her mother. They were going to Elizabeth,

## Color

New Jersey, and thought a section in the sleeping-car would be more comfortable for so long a journey Across the aisle a boy of six and his mother adjusted their belongings for a trip as far as Newark, Ohio. The mother was not a Bostonian; she had only married one.

I felt perturbed. I had had in mind looking over some jottings. There might not be great quiet. But I fortified myself. I like children. I recalled proudly how I had always been able to work with children playing—though not fighting—right beneath my window in Cambridge. And the little girl smiled at me with great blue eyes round the corner of her high-backed seat.

The boy saw her smile, and felt that he must participate. But he was less subtle. He walked over and wanted to know what my name was, and where I was going. His mother, who tried to look unadorned and sheer, very mildly reprimanded him. Then he asked the little girl. Soon they were playing in the aisle and looking out at my window, and the two mothers were discussing education—or rather, schools. The boy began a demonstration of what his school had already done for him by swinging between his seat and mine and turning flipflops to the constantly accelerated accompaniment of a school chant. Then he began to yell very rhythmically as if he had learned that through teaching, also. I began to feel the least bit caged in. Instead of looking at my jottings, I concentrated on what was outside my window. The blueberry bushes were clumps of scarlet, the oaks beyond them were a brown that still somehow suggested life. It seemed a long hour before we had passed enough factories to be at Providence. I was on the state-house side of the train, and spent the five minutes allowed for the stop in wondering why Providence, with all its many attractive spires and towers, would let somebody erect a great square hulk of a yellow building just across from the state-house and dwarf the graceful older building until it seemed to be shouldered off its hill.

At Westerly a little dried-leaf of an old lady who must have been at least eighty-five came shakily into the car. As the train started, it tottered her into a seat on the wrong side of the aisle.

"Oh," she exclaimed with a startling clearness, and rather eagerly, as if she were not always heard attentively, "I didn't mean to do that. I want over there, on that side—where I belong."

The very courteous, very black porter helped her over.

"Now!" she said. "Now! Now I can see them when we pass. It is so comfortable, too. So if it wants to storm now" —the sky was a little heavy—"we'll just let it storm."

The boy had watched her. He gave his upper lip a twitch of contempt. "She's an old devil, that's what she is!"

"Why, sweetheart, dearest!" his mother protested softly. "You shouldn't say that. Don't you see, she might be your own nice grandmother."

"I don't want any grandmother!" he shouted at the top of his voice.

A waiter came through from the dining-car hammering out some musical notes every so often and announcing that this was the last call for luncheon. I remembered that I had meant to eat a bite after I got aboard. Could there be a more appropriate hour?

A man can put in a lot of time in a dining-car if he is experienced. He can order item by item as he eats, and then eat very slowly, with full pauses now and then to read two or three consecutive pages in some interesting book, and with other pauses for the passing landscape. So for an hour and a half I sat and ate lettuce salad, and belated blueberry pie, and ice-cream, and read a little, and reordered coffee that was hot, and looked out at the sea, and heard, without trying, the conversation of the two youths at the other side of the table who professed ardently to believe that their prep. school had more class than either Groton or St. Mark's. One of them had just bought a yacht for which he had paid more than I in an entire lifetime had ever earned—or at least had ever received. He felt sure that his father would be able to stampede somebody into buying several blocks of stock at a good fat advance and by so doing pay for the boat without any drain whatever upon the established treasury.

Back in the sleeping-car I grew weary of the rhythmic jungle cries, and decided to seek out a place in the observation-car. I have made the test through a dozen years, but I made it yet again—with the same result: on these Boston–New York trains, as one walks through, there are more people reading books than on any other trains in the United States. It must be said also that there are more feet stuck out in the aisle, more people who glance up in disgust at you when you wish to put the aisle to other use.

There were no unoccupied chairs in the observation-car, and I immediately walked the full length of the train in the other direction. In the coach smoker close up against the section devoted to baggage I sat on the sleek oilcloth upholstery all the rest of the way to New York and enjoyed the bronzed reds of the Connecticut hills, the lighthouses on rocky points, the gulls flying everywhere, and listened with approval from some vague emotional depth of myself to two battered old pugs with heavy cauliflower ears while they declared with many variations that it was the good old sock right on the corner of the chin that made the world go round—at least for the other fellow in the ring.

Somewhere in the region of Hell Gate Bridge the train

moved hesitantly for a time, and then made a broad sweep to the southward as if it were trying to find a way of getting around New York. It was exploring as it sped along. As it circled into open space, one of the fighters—they had both been silent for a time—looked off to the westward with a puzzled, interested stare as though he were seeing something that was beyond his understanding. Then I saw. The whole of New York from the region of Forty-second Street on downtown stood up in a leaden sunset sky like the dream of some brilliant madman. In a moment everybody in the car was silent and looking. It was something pagan, yet something unearthly. What had men been celebrating when they built it? A moment later when the train carried us along slowly where a veil of smoke in the foreground subdued the fading sunlight even more subtly than the clouds in the background had, the gray of the towers was less of the earth still. Soon afterward the train came to a full stop. There was no confusion near us outside, and everybody in the car for the moment was as silent as if he slept. We participated in something fantastic.

Evidently the train decided that there was no way of getting around. The only thing left to do was to go under. It gave us a violent jerk, swerved sharply to the right, and made a dive into a roaring tunnel which eventually brought us into the bowels of the Pennsylvania Station.

I went up for air. I bought the latest edition of three or four papers. I bought a magazine or two. I bought a book. And I received the welcome reassurance that New Yorkers are just as childlike as anybody else, by watching hundreds of them solemnly ride a newly opened escalator down, since they were not going at the end of the day in the direction that would enable them to ride it up.

But it is never a journey until one is beyond New York.

From New York it is still possible to telephone back home in a jiffy. And always among the pushing millions there are some of your friends. When I take a bedtime train in this direction I always find a vague inappropriateness in going to bed until we are past New York at two o'clock or so. And if I do go, I do not feel that I can settle down to solid sleep until after the long stop and the quick coming of the tingling pressure in the ears as the train drops swiftly beneath the Hudson. But when we are beyond the Hudson we are away—regardless of the hour. We have left behind everything peninsular and known. We are facing something vastly expansive. The train moves as if it had plenty of room.

The next morning when I awoke the light was squeezing in at my window. I pushed the shade up to see where we were. We were racing along a winding river among rounded hills, and two old women in sunbonnets fished from a flat-boat. The maple trees on the hillsides beyond the river were as much green as yellow or red. When the train sliced off a piece of corn-field to save the trouble of keeping to the river, the ground from which the corn had been cut was matted with white and pink and purple morning-glories—and the fences were covered.

We swung out into more open country. Far in the distance I saw a dark train as long as our own, and racing as swiftly. I could tell by the design of the cars that they were sleepers. As day grew bright, today and every day, how many of them were there, racing everywhere in the United States, carrying whole towns of people along in their beds—and preparing breakfast for them? I tried to visualize a map of the United States with every long-distance train designated, as we mark the daily location of ships on the Atlantic. There they were, speeding everywhere—up from the South, across the Alleghenies, along the Great Lakes, down the Mississippi, across the Great Plains, through the Rockies, across the sands, up and down the Pacific coast.

When I was up and dressed and fed and ready to leave the breakfast table, our train slowed down and was cut over to the eastbound track. A moment later we passed scores of foreign-looking laborers who were busy putting down new steel on the track that normally would have been ours. Almost before we were at full speed again there were wild shrieks of the whistle, and a jolting, shuddering grind of brakes which brought us to such an abrupt stop that tableware crashed to the floor.

Since I had finished eating, anyhow, I went to the nearest open vestibule to lean out and see what had happened. There were fifteen cars or so in the train, and the diner was in the middle. I saw the conductor hurrying along on the ground from far in the rear, looking intently under the train as he ran. Far forward, the engineer in clean-looking striped overalls was coming back, looking under a bit more deliberately. Three or four porters had swung down and were standing back on the turf so that they might see farther alongside.

I swung down and walked forward toward the engineer. Before I came quite up to him, he stopped, looked back toward the conductor, and with a single easy lift of his stout arm signaled for him to come on up.

The conductor was there as soon as I was.

"There he is, under the front trucks of that baggage-car," the engineer said, without being quite able to be wholly matter-of-fact.

The conductor steadied himself by putting one hand against the lower edge of the car's body—which stood high above the road-bed—and looked under. A very black-headed Italian boy of about fourteen lay there limp and almost completely nude from having been dragged and rolled over the rough limestone ballast.

"He's not cut up to speak of," the conductor said. "We ought to get him out of there and be on our way in no time."

From somewhere a representative of the railroad company appeared. He glanced under. "That's easy. I'll look out for everything. You can scoot right along."

From somewhere also—from the houses on the hillside just above the right-of-way—a number of dark-eyed children came running to see why the train had stopped.

"Any of you kids know who that boy was that was walking on the tracks bringing groceries home from the store?"

A cloud swept the faces of the entire group, as if they thought the boy had been arrested for something that he should not have done.

"Do you?"

"Yes," the oldest boy in the group said. "It was Fortunato."

"Fortunato? Your brother?"

"No, just my—friend."

"Well, he was walking on the tracks, and the train killed him."

In terror and helplessness the boy looked about at the rest of us as if we ought not to be there, twisted slowly away without moving his feet, lifted his hands to his face and then sank to the earth sobbing, "Oh, Fortunato!"

The other children stood speechless, except one boy who said half to the rest, half to the conductor, "The train was running on the wrong track."

"Yes, I know it was. But you see, he shouldn't have been walking on either track. He should have walked in the road."

"But there are automobiles."

I wandered back along the train. As I passed the dining-car it was still crowded with people who were obliviously enjoying their breakfasts and the bright morning.

I swung onto the train and walked all the way back to the observation-car.

There was only one person back there—a stout woman all freshly made up for the day, who was busy with a story in the *Delineator*.

She glanced up. "Can you tell me why this train is standing so long?" she asked. "We don't seem to be in any town."

"Oh," I replied, "we killed an Italian boy—up ahead."

"Why, how perfectly terrible!" she said in a voice so well modulated that she might have been reading from the story.

The train gave a little shrug of a lurch forward. "But I guess we must be going now."

Passengers began to come in from breakfast. Soon they had filled all the comfortable chairs. For two hours I sat with my back to the window and read. Periodically I let the book drop to the arm of the chair and looked out at the windows on the other side of the car past the heads of the solid row of those who sat across the aisle and did their own reading or smoked as if for once it would do no good to be impatient. Groves of maples, numerous in the hills and on the flat land alike, were splashed with fire. Occasionally some tree was solid yellow. Why had nobody ever said anything about the beauty of the hills between Coshocton, Ohio—or Athens—and St. Louis? Only Brown County, Indiana, has received any part of the praise due the entire region. And Brown County became known chiefly because a group of painters found it paradise when the genteel population of neighboring cities laughed at it because it was short on railroads and plumbing.

Within the train, too, a change had taken place since yesterday. Most of the New Englanders had gone on to Washington—if they had not taken a boat at New York—and the transcontinental passengers had already been outnumbered by energetic Buckeyes, who are always going somewhere, and who are not troubled in the least by getting up and taking a train at five or five-thirty in the morning. They sat wherever there was room, smoked cigars, talked pleasantly with some half-recognizable remnant of New England or Virginia in their speech, and felt that the world was not such a bad place, after all.

One of them left the chair next to mine. It was promptly taken by a rangy, bony man whose heavy dark hair was loosely combed over to the side, and whose brows were shaggy. "Did you ever think," he began rather promptly as if he were in great need of expression, "of taking a straw vote of all the people who travel on a train like this to find out how many of them are running away from something—the same as we are?" He gave a single ha of a silent laugh. "They might not tell you what they were running from, but they might be willing to say whether they were running."

I twisted a little in my chair to look him in the face. His eyes were very wide open, like those of a maniac occupied with his favorite hallucination. But there was a trace of a smile close round his lips and under his eyes and in front of his ears. It spread till it covered his face.

"Maybe you think I'm crazy," he said as he tried to make out the expression on my own face. "And who knows, maybe I am."

"And maybe you are only another Hoosier poet."

He laughed his single ha of a silent laugh again.

"Maybe I am that, too. You know, there's a mighty thin shade of difference. And I come from Kokomo, if there's anything in a name."

His face spread in a new smile. "And I'll be coming back from St. Louis by way of Paris."

I must have seemed puzzled. "Paris, Illinois," he added. "Don't you remember? That's where lots of American girls have got their French."

We talked about Booth Tarkington, Meredith Nicholson, James Whitcomb Riley, Lew Wallace, Theodore Dreiser, George Barr McCutcheon, Gene Stratton Porter, and a dozen others of the older generation of Hoosier writers. Of course, he had known them all. He paused sometimes to speak of the sumac in the ravines in southern Illinois, or nod for my benefit toward the men in small towns who were selling late roasting-ears, and apples fresh from the tree.

As we came into the smoke of East St. Louis, the train moved cautiously. It was above the housetops. It seemed to be getting ready for something important.

"Old Man River!" the man from Kokomo announced. "I find something to come over here for every once in a while just to see this."

He glanced at the man opposite us who had his face buried in a copy of *Liberty*. "It must be a hell of a good story he's reading if he means to pass this up for it. Or maybe he's just afraid he'll fall short three seconds of the prescribed reading time."

There was quiet as we moved deliberately above the last houses—frowsy affairs of tarred paper, corrugated iron, and oddments of boards—and out over the east bank of the spreading river, over the resistless, eddying, boiling middle of it where we could look down through the steel of the bridge into it just as if nothing much supported the train, and at last over steamboats moving in to the western waterfront. Then everybody scrambled forward to be ready by the time we were in the station.

But for me St. Louis was only a pause—not long enough to rob me of my sense of motion. My next train stood ready. I was on it so soon, and it was so soon away, that I had difficulty in feeling that I had made a change.

After a late luncheon I sat in the lounge half of the café-car and studied the world outside. Without effort, even in spite of myself, I heard the conversation of two men who had lingered, after everyone else, at the luncheon table nearest me. One had a heavy roll under his chin; the other, on the back of his neck. They talked and ate and drank time away.

Within two or three hours we were climbing toward a ridge of the Ozarks—over sharp curves and counter-curves, on and on, up and up. Close beside the long train, which moved a little below speed yet resistlessly, thin-looking cows picked grass from steep rocky hillsides under good-sized papaw bushes that were just beginning to lose their greenish yellow leaves and reveal fat clumps of green fruit not yet quite ready to fall. The only bright color anywhere was the red of some gum or persimmon tree.

How many railroads are there in the world that spurn the valleys, as this one does, and follow low mountain ridges for a hundred or a hundred and fifty miles? In these ancient worn-off hills the valleys were too complicated, too stuffy, for some dreaming surveyor, and he took to the hills. Now, after the engine's long steady climb that seemed to be taking us across a county or two, we were up on them ourselves. We swept round long curves from which we could look down over ranges of hills on both sides of the train; we took long straight-of-ways on the comb of watersheds; we described letter S's; we made sharp hair-pin turns—all in an effort to keep to the ridges. Once we passed a freight train that was taking water at a tank and filling the air with surplus steam. Several minutes later I saw the same train not more than a mile or two from us across a wooded valley. We had followed a wide round horseshoe in order to get where we were.

The two men had been drinking steadily while they discussed the economic ills of the country, and their eyeballs were getting pretty yellow. But they could still see what the train was doing.

"I bet you, by God," one of them began easily as if he were established in a point of view that enabled him to see whatever was wrong, "that the fellow who had the contract for building this railroad got paid by the mile. Just look there, will you? There's that same damned freight train that we passed a half-hour ago. Why didn't they come straight across there? It wouldn't have required a trestle more than three or four hundred feet high—or maybe five hundred. If we were building her today, that's the way we'd do her."

Once, to the southeast and east, as far as eyes could see detail, the sun was on billowing woodland; and at the horizon there were dark, indistinguishable ridges. There seemed to be no houses. One felt a thinning-out of telepathic ties. Man had not yet done enough to the region to make his kind feel at home in it. Once, to the west, for a memorable second, the red sun shone full in our faces through a gaunt and abandoned old log tobacco-house just above us.

All the while, the steward, a slender youngish man whose

hair was thinning, stood at the buffet end of the car, neat and official in his blue suit and white vest, and looked at the floor as if nothing of grandeur were to be seen. Only occasionally did he glance up to learn if the two men were signaling for further drinks.

The two talked on—in cumulative friendliness. One of them was interested in oil. The other was the head of a dozen factories. They talked in millions—regardless of what they discussed. One of them said the most valued thing he possessed was his acquaintance with nice people. "If there are any nice people in town, we know them. I wouldn't take five million for that—just that. Honest to God, I wouldn't."

They grew confidential. They discussed their wives. For ten minutes their wives would have been in heaven if they could have heard. Then one of them set forth a list of his wife's deficiencies that would have made her stick her fingers in her ears and run if she had been secretly present. The other admitted that his was sometimes a little hard to manage. But he was gleeful over the birthday present she wanted. He was getting off with nothing more than a trinket of a ten-thousand-dollar necklace. "I said, 'All right, if that's what you want, you shall have it.' " He chuckled. "The jeweler is making it up."

They returned to the state of the nation. "The real trouble with this God-damned government," the man with the roll on the back of his neck said finally, "is that there's too much extravagance among the higher-ups." He was now in the stage of inclusive, graceful gestures, and set out to discuss the matter in detail. But something interrupted the flow of his thought, and he ended up by insisting that he pay for the luncheon—now four hours agone—and for the drinks.

His friend would hear nothing of the kind. "Or at least we'll go Dutch." But the other was insistent, and held on to the slips which the steward had very tactfully presented face downward. He looked at the bills. Then he fumbled for his large-style reading glasses. The luncheons were $3.50; the drinks thus far, $14.25. After swallowing once in consternation he said, "You see, I'll just put it on my expense account."

The other showed a ready acquiescence. "Oh, well! That's different. If you want to let the stockholders pay it, O.K. But I won't let you pay it yourself—wouldn't think of it."

One of them begged the other to see the gorgeous sunset. It was not gorgeous. In fact, it was a washed-out, pale blue-green affair hardly deserving of a glance. But it was a sunset. The sun was going down. So the two of them decided just to stay right on where they were and eat their suppers. They ordered sirloin steaks and French fried potatoes and apple pie and cheese and ice-cream and coffee. An hour later, when I had finished my own meal and was thinking that I might go early to bed, they were having a little drink together as an aid to digestion.

The next morning I was awakened by inescapable early risers. I am sure they never get up early at home. They probably are very lazy. But on a train they talk across the aisle to each other about whether they should set their watch forward an hour, or back an hour, or leave it just where it is. Then after they have awakened everybody in their end of the car, they call to the porter to come and make up their berths right away so that they may sit in them. One of the upper berths sticks, and the porter has to do some hammering. But eventually he has all in readiness for them, and they then sit dumb for two hours. In the wakefulness that these on our train brought to me, I had a drowsy memory that we had stood still for a long time in the middle of the night. Then I heard a porter explaining in subdued tones why we were hours late.

But when I lifted the shade to see where we were, I was glad we were nowhere else. A clear sun was coming up over low wooded mountains somewhere in eastern or southeastern Oklahoma. There were no accompaniments—no clouds, no mottled skies, no romantic haze; just hard outlines of gray-green flecked with settlers' unpainted low houses, and a great stark ball of deep red. I was blinded to the band of evergreen and white birches on bleak hills that stretched a thousand miles westward from New Hampshire, to the bronzing reds westward from Massachusetts and Connecticut, to the living brightness of Ohio and Indiana, to the billowing green merely touched with bright tips of red that extended from the Ozarks back eastward across Kentucky and Virginia. Here one was in the presence of nothing but fundamentals.

By noon I was off the train in northern Texas where the world bore yet another face. Cattle roamed in limitless fields, and the trees were still green.

"I'm mighty glad to see you," the hotel manager assured me as if he meant it. "I sure am." And Jake the black "boy," who according to his own testimony was just old enough to remember seeing soldiers coming back from the Civil War, remarked pleasantly as he shuffled along with my luggage: "Mus' a' been 'bout two years ago that you was here the last time, ain't it—Doctah?"

## ii

## Discovery

SOMETHING had happened to this little Oklahoma city since my last visit there a year and a half before. At that time it was a serenely active community of a few thousand people, with wide streets, plenty of small shade-trees, a young college, and brand-new churches—all on low rolling hills where thirty years or so before there had been no town at all. But this morning I knew before I arrived at the hotel that a change had taken place—some fundamental change in the community's thought. It was

## Discovery 21

in the air. The people moved along the street as if life had at last straightened away toward a definite purpose that made the going worth-while.

Always the hotel had seemed so new and shining that it gave the impression of being little used. A man could loaf around in the lobby and talk to the manager, and to the girl at the cigar counter or switchboard, or to a traveling salesman or two who came there regularly, and feel that he was more or less of the family. I had expected to find the same kind of quiet this time. But when the bell-boy who shuffled my luggage kicked the door around so that I could enter, a babel of voices caught me full in the face. The lobby was crowded—with short men and tall men in khaki breeches, flannel shirts, broad-brimmed hats, and high laced boots, puttees, or smart riding boots. I could scarcely push my way through to the desk.

"Your telegram came all right yesterday," the room clerk explained as if he were not doing anything unusual, "but there wasn't a room in the house at the time—and there isn't one now. But if you'll just have the boy check your bags, and 'll stick around for a while, I think maybe we'll be able to fix you up."

"What has happened?" I asked a bit sourly. I had hoped to supplement a short night on the train by stretching out for an hour or two.

"Oh! Haven't you heard? Oil. About twelve or fourteen miles down south here. It may turn out to be the richest field in the mid-continent area."

In the coffee shop I had to stand for fifteen minutes before I could get a stool at the counter. Others waited. The man close against my elbow was a trim fellow of thirty-eight or forty who would have made the perfect smashing lieutenant-colonel in a movie.

I saw him looking me over. Then he asked: "Did you have anything down there where they found it?" He had decided that I had just arrived from New York to cash in on my holdings.

"No, nothing at all."

"Neither did I. I got in wrong right at the beginning. When they got to talking about oil down this way, everybody I knew thought it would be out east—or northeast. I went to a geologist—one of the highest-priced rock hounds I know—and paid him real money and said, 'Now I want the low-down on this Ada field. Is there anything down there? And if there is, where is it?'

"He told me that there ought to be something down here, all right. Then he said, 'As for where it is, just do a little thinking. Did you ever hear of these big shots in the game looking for chances to throw their money at birds? Of course not. They're in the game for what they are going to get out of it. Well, where are they sticking theirs?'

"Well, that's where I stuck mine—not so much, but around sixty thousand. And now, by God, they go and find the oil somewhere else. Oh, well! I didn't lose half as much as some people I know."

Two stools side by side were vacated at the same time, and we sat together. After he had picked up his first great sweet roll and taken a huge bite or two out of the edge of it, and had swallowed his first cup of coffee, he seemed calm again. He laughed a faint little laugh at himself—a little sadly, but with a bit of "What difference does it make?" in his manner more than his voice. "The hell of it is, this fellow who got somebody to sink a well down south here tried to interest me once. He believed the formation of the old mountains farther south was just right to make a pool where they found it. He had a nice theory. But I figured that the fellow was half-cracked. And so did a lot of other people, so far as that goes. God!"

He talked on. To me, what he said seemed to have come from a storybook. He spoke casually of such and such wells that flowed nine thousand barrels a day—or would if they were not choked down; and no less casually of a man at Tulsa who had made three millions in a deal that he put through in two days.

He observed the difficulty with which I believed. "Why, there's a fellow here in this town," he said in an effort to provide cool evidence right at hand, and mentioned a name, "who cashed in for about five million just last month."

After breakfast I pushed in among the men in the lobby. They were cheerful. They were awakened and warmed by a sense of common enterprise. They were human beings together. I wanted to go into the oil business myself—or to join them in anything else that they might propose.

But all the figures they mentioned were too high. I had to get out into thinner air where somebody talked in sums that were within my range of comprehension. Since the clerk at the desk had no railroad time-tables on hand—he said he had been unable to keep any for three months now —I thought I might walk to the station a few blocks away and get my own supply.

Before I came within sight of the station I ran into a thin crowd strung along the sidewalk. "Now ladies and gentlemen," a man on an improvised platform on a vacant lot was saying, as he arranged a diversity of paraphernalia on a box that he had made into a table, "I am not only going to show you magic, but I'm going to show you how you can do something magical yourselves."

He noticed that nobody seemed to be inclined to draw nearer. "See here," he said, and cast his eye over the line of men in overalls, in khaki, in trim October suits, "I promised your police force when I talked with him last night"—he waited for them to laugh—"I promised that I would not let the crowds that gathered around to see my show block the sidewalks. So won't you please step in—just a little?"

A few moved off the sidewalk onto the autumn grass. He waited. Then he repeated his announcement; waited until others moved forward; repeated it to the new arrivals; waited again—until he had a good-sized crowd close around him.

He held a magic chain aloft. "See this chain? See that small link at the top? Now anybody can tell that that link is not large enough to slide down over the other links, can't they? All right, now watch. See it slide all the way right down to the bottom—like that?"

While they were intent and mystified he talked on as he put the chain down. "Now before I let you in on that one, I want to start you on my second piece of magic."

I glanced about. I expected to see O. Henry in the edge of the crowd somewhere making notes.

"See that?"

He exhibited a hot-dog. They laughed. "Do you know what's in them? I'll tell you. Whatever is not fit to be sold as a piece of meat is made into hot-dogs. It's all ground up so fine that you can't tell what's in it by the looks, and they put so much mustard on it for you that you can't tell by the taste. These big millionaire packing houses go around over the country and buy up every old bull and every old boar —and maybe an old mule once in a while, for all I know— and grind them up, gristle and all, into these hot-dogs. That's the way some people in this world make their money."

As he talked he cut the hot-dog up into bits and dropped them one by one into a good-sized ewer half filled with water. Then he put some bits of white bread in. "The bread is really not fit to eat, either. But we eat it, just the same. Now watch!"

Some of the crowd revealed signs of restlessness. He plunged ahead, still breaking up bread all the while. "Once when I was down on the Mexican border—down along the old Rio Grande—I had been eating so many of these hot-dogs and so much stale baker's bread that I thought I would die of stomach trouble. It was miles to a doctor. A pretty Mexican girl—you know, guitar and all that—that I had been trying to make myself solid with said she thought she could help me to a way. Well, sir, the first thing I knowed, I had hold of one end of a halter strap that had a horse on the other." Great laughter and better suspense. "Of course, I had not thought of keeping the horse —just borrowed it." Greater laughter still. "Well, they caught up with me, and somebody said he knew of just the right-sized tree. Another fellow—who was in love with the same girl—said, 'Let's not string him up just yet. Let's let him taste it awhile in advance.' So they bound me up tight like this"—and he began to string some rope over his shoulders. "They put the noose around my neck and stretched me up a little, with my toes just touching the ground, so that I could have something to think about while they went and had a drink. It was a long drink, too. But I knowed how to get loose!"

He played with the rope that hung over his shoulders and around his neck. "Now I want you to see what happens to that hot-dog and white bread when they've had a chance to become acquainted." He held the water bottle up. "You can see that something is happening, all right, all right. Now lots of people will tell you when things fight in your stomach like that, to take bicarbonate of soda—baking-soda. But you watch and decide for yourselves."

He put bicarbonate of soda in the ewer, and then carefully stretched the neck of a deflated toy balloon—a dirigible—over the top of it. "Now watch her!"

The balloon began to expand. "See her fill up with gas? Now watch her when I shake her a little." The balloon expanded until it began to assume the shape of a slender watermelon. "See the state you are in when you take bicarbonate of soda?

"I used to take it for my stomach trouble. And I got so bad that the doctors thought I was going to die of cancer of the stomach—and plenty of people do. They said I might live a year. Well, I thought if that was all there was going to be to it I'd see a bit of this world before I left it. I had a little money, so I started out. That's how I happened to get hold of this magic chain—from a Hindu wonder-worker —one of these dark-skinned guys in a yellow and black turban hat and a skirt, who can walk across a bed of live red-hot coals without getting burnt. I paid him to show me how to do this magic chain trick. But he couldn't do anything for my stomach, with all his wonder-working. Nobody could! Nobody could!

"Did you ever stop to think how a man feels when he knows that he has less than a year to live? Nothing ahead to be interested in, because it won't make any difference. I just drifted. I found myself in China.

"One day I talked with an old Chinaman—I had learned a little Chinese, like this" (and he rattled off something that sounded like the front room in a laundry) "and could make out. He was the oldest-looking man I ever saw on legs—honest to God, he was. He would have made old John

# Discovery 27

D. Rockefeller look like a pink little girl in primary school. But he was healthy. He said to me he had never been what you would call sick a day in his life. I begged him to tell me the secret. And gentlemen, believe it or not, he did. And I have never had stomach trouble from that day to this.

"And I am going to tell you the great secret—the master magic! Watch me!"

He poured some dark fluid in with the hot dog and white bread and slipped the neck of the balloon over the top of the water bottle again. Now where is all that gas?"

"You're not shaking her this time!" some man in the crowd called out. But the magician ignored him.

"Here you have the reason why the Chinese are a hardy race. And here you have the reason why I haven't had indigestion now for years. And you needn't, gentlemen. Here is a greater discovery than the one they've made down in the Fittstown oil field. For what is anything else worth to you if you have lost your precious health? Use ginseng, gentlemen! That's what the Chinese have done as long as anybody can remember. That's where we sold most of our ginseng for years. But now we are getting wise. We are taking it ourselves. One dollar a bottle, gentlemen, today as long as it lasts, before I move on to the next town! Face the future hopefully, gentlemen!"

He was busy passing out bottles and accepting dollars from men who now had dollars in their pockets.

"How about that magic chain?" somebody called.

He disregarded the question until he believed he had made his last sale. Then he picked up the chain. "The link really don't slide down. If you do that," and he gave the top end of the chain a slight fillip, "it just seems to slide down. That is what us scientists call optical eelusion."

I caught a little of the pleasant fever. Men had money in their pockets. They wanted to feel more secure still. They would pay out their money for any promise of good health that anybody who came along made to them. They wanted every possibility ahead to be a good one.

I found myself walking faster when I went back up the street from the station. I remembered a young poet whom I had once met in this town. By making a slight detour I was able to stop at the drug-store where he worked—from morning until eleven at night. When business was not too good—and it was not too good—he could devote himself to poetry. This morning, he had just been composing a poem —thus far held only in his mind—and would I accept a copy if he sat down and wrote it out?

While he wrote on some ruled paper at a white-topped round table where customarily bright, chaffing young ladies and gentlemen tried to encompass romance by not being too serious about anything, I wandered back and forth in a store that looked easy-going, read advertisements, studied shelves, noted a prayer above the desk that read, "O Lord, help me to keep my damned nose out of other people's business," and watched the automobiles and mule teams and pedestrians in the street. He finally handed me five stanzas—genuinely poetic ones, that have since been published.

We talked for an hour, ate luncheon together, talked for another hour. Yes, this discovery of oil was something. But he was more interested in the romantic discovery that had been going on in the region better than a half-century ago. He pictured it as it must have been. Man was worth something, life was worth something, when everybody was doing a little discovering. That was it—to discover.

I caught more of the pleasant fever. The next day when

a friend offered to take me out to the new field, I was eager to go. While we sped along over a road that was showing signs of extraordinary use, I learned that the region we were in was so rich in geologic variety that geologists came there for first-hand study from every corner of the earth. I learned something, too, of this "half-cracked" more or less self-educated geologist who had had to do with the development of the field. Some of the "big shots" in oil said they had not given more attention to what he said because he wasted so much of his time dabbling around with such trivialities as finding suitable camp sites for Boy Scouts, showing students and visiting geologists over the geologic wonderland of the Arbuckle mountain region, or making his backyard well produce liquid asphalt. What could such a man know about the hard, practical business of oil lands? They wanted to stake their money on somebody who was accredited. And most of them did.

We came within sight of a few steel derricks in what seemed to be a creek valley, and then others, very far apart on the hills, where exploratory wells were being put down to discover the field's limits. But there was something else worth seeing right at hand—a town that was not yet old enough to have any age. Nothing was yet finished. Stakes in meadowland marked proposed streets. Stakes along the roadside marked proposed buildings. Carpenters were using lumber as fast as it came. One grocer had a counter and shelves up and was doing business while the carpenters were putting the weather-boarding on the other side of his store. But there was already an abundance of one thing—oil casing. It was piled up everywhere—neat ricks of long dark tubes of two or three different sizes—miles of it.

I wanted to see a well that was about to be drilled in, but the first ones we went to were all quite new ones. Some of them were down twelve hundred feet, some two thousand, some three thousand—and they had to go from forty-two hundred to forty-four or forty-five hundred to reach the sand that produced the "real oil " Eventually we came to one that was down four thousand feet.

"If you had come a day or two later," the great, burly, red-faced good-natured boy of a man of thirty-eight or so shouted close against my ear so that I could hear him above the grinding roar of the chain-driven rotary drill, "you might have seen something."

The older method—which I still see used in many oil fields—consisted of lifting and letting fall a heavy slowly rotated drill with a thick, somewhat sharpened bit that hammered its way down through the layers of the earth's surface. From time to time the drill was drawn up and a bailer let down to bring up the result of the drill's work in the form of sandy, muddy water. The first well I ever watched drilled by this earlier method required an entire spring and part of the summer for its completion, and it was only nine hundred and fifty feet deep—and dry. On many days—and they were twenty-four-hour days—the progress downward was as little as five feet. The crews rejoiced when they made fifteen.

But putting down a well with rotary tools is quite another matter. A drill that has sharp, hard-tempered teeth—or whatever other style of bit a particular formation requires—is attached to the end of strong steel piping, and this is spun round at a good rate of speed by a powerful engine, and rapidly bites its way down through anything it may encounter. As it makes its way down, piping is added, section by section, so that when the well—in this region—is nearly completed, the column of spinning steel pipe that drives the hard bit still on downward is the better part of a mile long. There are perforations in the drill near its head, and water is constantly forced down into the well and back up, so that it carries to the surface a stream of the drill's leavings. These are all held in a slushy pool until the well is completed, so that if it should be dry and the well should be filled up—to protect water supplies and the like, I was told—the layers would go back exactly in their order.

The driller on duty showed me his log for this well. On one day he had made two hundred and eighty-six feet. That was his best day. His poorest had been fifteen feet— "just like going through solid iron," he commented as he followed the days down the pages of his book. But good days had been numerous enough to send the well down four thousand feet in little more than a month.

Driving downward at that rate, though, is hard on the teeth of a rotating drill, even if the steel is as hard and as tough as it can be made. After a certain number of hours— the number dependent on the resistance offered by the formation, of course—a fresh drill has to be substituted. This means that the entire length of the pipe must be lifted from the well by means of a crane attachment in the derrick, and, as it emerges above the derrick floor, unjointed in long sections by a jerk and a spin of a power-wrench, and leaned over slightly so that the upper part of a section touches the inner balcony of the derrick about eighty feet above the floor. Somebody has to be up there to see that the tops of these sections are steadied into place.

Often enough this man wears a safety-belt attached to the derrick up there, so that if he should be swung out of balance by the long, virtually perpendicular piece of heavy pipe—or by any other hazard—he would only be suspended in mid air, and could scramble back. But one man liked to work up there without the annoyance of any safety-belt. "I warned him," the driller shouted into my ear. " 'You'll be coming down some day.' And sure enough, one day he did. I just happened to be looking right at him when he started, and I knew it was instant death if ever he hit this solid plank floor. When he came into my arms we bounced clear off outside there. But I did save him."

He received a medal and, I was told, a sum of money.

"I can't see why it didn't kill you both," I shouted close against the side of his red face.

"I can't either," he shouted back. "It just happened that his head didn't strike mine, or anything like that."

"No ill effects?"

"No—nothing much. Oh, sometimes I wake up in the night with my shoulders hurting through here"—and he showed me where—"but that is about as much as I ever notice now. Sometimes I can't go back to sleep. I guess it strained the nerves."

He let me see the log book—but a little reluctantly, as if it were not the practice to do such a thing. I spoke of the excitement of going down through all those many diverse layers of the earth's crust.

"Go over here where they're all turned up edgeways in the mountains and you can see them spread out right on the surface as you go along."

But to me that was not half so interesting as going down through them just as they were put there by some inconceivably long cosmic sequence.

"I'll show you other wonders," my friend said smilingly. And he took me to the house of a man past eighty who had settled in the region more than fifty years ago. When the oil was discovered he leased some of his land, but reserved ten acres around his log house because he did not want the noise of the drilling close to where he lived. Stories of the huge amounts of money he had already received from the wells on his land were in easy circulation. But he would not lease the ten acres on which his log house stood. Just a short while before I was there he had received an offer of a hundred thousand dollars for the lease of the tract But he steadfastly refused. "I don't want to be bothered by the noise."

"But," the prospective buyers urged, "with that much money you can build a new house somewhere else—wherever you want to, and any kind you like."

"I've got money," he told them; "and I like this one. There's nowhere else I want to go."

His house was of two joined sections—of hewn logs and white mortar. There were plenty of trees, and the ones nearest the house were neatly whitewashed from the ground up three or four feet. Yes, he thought oil was interesting, but he didn't care to have it too close.

For days, and especially for nights, I saw Oklahoma oil fields. One night I saw a well that had caught fire before it could be brought under control. The light from it could be seen across an entire county.

I rode for miles quite out in the country through what seemed to be entire townships of great tanks that stood thick on the earth like gigantic silvered puffballs. I saw Tulsa for the twentieth time—the wonder city of oil that had started out years before with the discoverer's quickened mind to have the best of everything, including education and architecture, and was for a period so successful that she became the myth city of the nation, and a national symbol. But despite the good architecture I was never quite so much interested in what the Tulsans built as in their clarified state of mind—now already somewhat muddled by the belief that perhaps all the discovering has been done and that they might as well settle down.

And then one night, after I had made a long trip in the form of a reversed letter S down through oil fields in northern and eastern Texas, I sat on a train till long after midnight with a member of the Metropolitan Opera Company whose engagements were taking him from one coast to the other, and talked about a day I had spent in a Negro college town. In the morning I had gone for a walk and had come to a modest campus. A distinguished-looking tall Negro stopped me and asked me if I were not the man who was to lecture at the college in the evening; he thought he recognized me by pictures he had seen. He was, he told me, the head of the conservatory of music, and he offered to show me about.

We saw recitation halls, laboratories, a library, and the auditorium in which I was to speak. Then he said quite humbly, yet with the utmost self-respect, "Should you care to see my building? It is an old plantation house. We have put partitions in the large parlors and bedchambers and made plenty of practice rooms for the girls."

We went through the building and heard the pandemonium that one may hear in any conservatory. But this one had an interest for me that few have. For, two generations after Negroes were in slavery, the grandchildren of those slaves were using somebody's plantation house as their own center of artistic activity.

Before I lectured in the evening to an attentive, intelligently responsive audience in which there was not one white face, a slender dusky girl whose features were as sensitive as those of Chopin came out and played two numbers from his works. Then a sturdier young woman, with lung power so suggestive of Caruso's that she could fill an ordinary auditorium without any noticeable effort, sang two short songs. She sang with some great simple elemental new hope, with something of the sureness of the men who knew that the oil was there in the earth beneath them.

## iii

## Sustenance

"WELL, I notice you like our Texas grapefruits," said the swarthy stout man across the dining-car table.

"Yes, but how about seeing carloads of them on sale along the street at fifty cents a bushel and then getting on this train and paying fifty cents for the two halves of one fruit?"

"Say! By George! That is tough!" He had to laugh. "The railroad company must be finding out how good they are."

They were good. I went so far as to express the wish that we could have a more regular abundance of them up where I lived.

## Sustenance

And where did I live?

When I told him his eyes came wide open and he smiled as if he had thought of something that perhaps he had better not mention. He took another look at me and decided to go ahead. "Then maybe you know the woman up there in Boston whose niece married a young fellow down here in the cattle country. The niece wanted her to come down for a visit. After being coaxed long enough, she agreed. When she went to the station to make her reservation she said to the agent, 'I'm going way down to Texas next week, and I thought I'd better come over and arrange for my ticket.' 'By Buffalo?' the agent asked. 'By buffalo?' she said. 'Why, I want to go by train as far as I can!'"

He laughed as if he were the originator of the story. "Gad, can't you see the old gal snorting into Dallas from the north? I'll bet you ten bucks that she rode side-saddle, too."

He did not hesitate to declare openly that Texas was quite a state. "Ever take a map and cut Texas out of it with the point of a knife and then stick a pin in one corner of it after another and swing it around to see how far it reaches? Stick the pin in at El Paso and swing her around to the west and she reaches clear out into the Pacific Ocean; stick the pin in over east of Beaumont and then swing her the other way and she reaches into the Atlantic; swing her north and she just misses the Canadian border; swing her south and she reaches clear across Mexico past Guatemala into Honduras, so that if you were up high enough you could almost jump off into the Panama Canal."

He was fearful that he had not impressed me.

"Or take my own case. My job is to make several cities that happen to be out along the edges of the state—every so often I make the trip—and from the time I leave Dallas till I get back at the end of the grand swing-around, I travel twenty-nine hundred miles."

I gave my imagination a push. "Texas is larger than France, isn't it?"

"Can't say about that, for I don't know just how big France is. I saw only about ten acres of it along the edge of some woods when I was over. But I remember figuring it all up for the Chamber of Commerce once, and Texas is just a little bigger than all of New England and New York and New Jersey and Maryland and Virginia and Pennsylvania and Ohio.

"But remember it's not just our size. It's what we've got. Name anything you like—pretty nearly anything—and we've got more of it than any other state in the Union. Take oil. A little piddlin' state like Oklahoma up here thinks she's got a lot of it. But what has she got compared with Texas? And sulphur—don't we produce about three-quarters of all the sulphur in the country? And just about all the carbon black—what everybody used to call lampblack? And beef; and goats; and sheep; and cotton; and melons; and turkeys. We ship turkeys up to Boston and they sell them as choice Vermont turkeys, and nobody can tell the difference; to New York and they are special spoon-fed Upstate turkeys; to Washington, D.C. and they're Virginia turkeys. They stand the test."

As if he had almost forgotten something that he always included, he hurried on: "And of course you know that Texas has the largest spinach farm in the world."

"Isn't that where some little town voted bonds and erected a monument to Popeye the Sailor?"

"Sure! But haven't you heard of towns voting bonds for worse things than that?"

Of course I had.

Texas could boast of plenty of other things, too: the biggest rose farms ever heard of; more mountains than all of New England—and higher ones; and bluebonnets; and lots of good universities and colleges and museums and artists and writers—O. Henry, for instance.

"We think we have a pretty strong state spirit down here, too. You know we still believe in local self-government."

"Then why don't you divide Texas up into about a half-dozen good-sized states so that the people can have it?"

He glanced at me in consternation, but when he saw that my face was not so serious as my words had sounded, he shook his head and smiled. "Say, blowing the big bazoo almost took me too far, didn't it?"

Then he explained just how it was. If I had not forgotten my school history, I would recall that Texas had once been an independent nation—not for long, to be sure, but long enough to instil a great spirit of solidarity and independence in the people. They had never lost it. Texas was now a part of the United States, of course, and compared with Rhode Island, for instance, it was pretty large for administrative purposes. But he was afraid it would never be divided up. Anyhow, in that case, just who would run things for the rest of the country over at Washington?

When he noticed that the train was pulling into a station, he threw some money at the waiter, got off hastily, and left me alone to answer the question, and to look out at the window and know that he had not exaggerated about Texas. Texas was producing what people who knew nothing of the state could not get along without. And Texas was only the southernmost extra-large unit in a vast area devoted to the kind of production that enables all the rest of us to live.

The man's expansiveness awakened my own imagination. Two hours ago I had seen the long journey ahead of me up across the plains to the Canadian border as only a somewhat monotonous trip through the cattle belt, the wheat belt, the hog belt, the dairy belt. But with his effusive aid I began to see the region as it is: a great, bulging cornucopia with the southern extremity of Texas as its point, reaching up, spreading out northward, and tilting over eastward in Illinois, Indiana, and Ohio as it pours its plenitude out into the world. Where is there a more vital silent drama than this of millions of men plowing the ancient earth, watching the sky, deciding to plant, planting too early, planting too late, making the most of whatever results, having something to sell, selling by tiny family units all over the area until the grand total feeds Chicago, feeds New York, helps London to feel easier, helps Paris to feel easier, enables marching millions in a half-dozen foreign armies to feel surer that now they will be strong enough to face each other in battle, to kill each other off for a principle?

Eventually the steward seated a woman—a well-made-up gray-haired woman who still looked young—where the man had sat. She seemed interested in my intent watching of the landscape, asked me if I would be good enough to pass the salt, and continued by remarking: "Pretty desolate, isn't it?"

"Why, I had not thought of it as desolate. Perhaps it's a bit grim—but it's a fascinating drama."

"Drama! Goodness! And here I was wondering if something could not be done to get all these people out of these little coops of houses and away to where they could have some of the comforts of life. Why, don't they have to wade around in mud and dust the year round, with nothing else much to do?"

## Sustenance

"And I was wondering if they might not be providing the pattern on which we should have to rebuild our entire civilization—or pretty nearly—sooner or later."

"Really? Why, you startle me. I had never thought of this whole flat Middle West as good for much except to hold the two coasts together. It is always dismal enough when I have to cross it."

She said it all with so much of the casualness which frequently accompanies a superior point of view, that I suddenly experienced a slumping of my own sureness. Could it be that in the long interval since I had known farms by working on them I had idealized them into something better than they were? Or had farms and farmers experienced a deterioration that I had not felt?

I got off in a small town up in the Red River country where unshaven men sat round the court-house square in the late October sun and talked things over, and let their eyes slowly follow with a strange interest any men who had shaved. In front of many grocery stores neat ricks of watermelons were on display. Where did they come from? A friendly business manager who was not too much in a hurry took me out a few miles southeast to see.

A low little house that seemed to hug the earth stood close to the side road. The front door was tightly shut, as if it were to be used only on momentous occasions, and sand had swirled over the front yard and almost completely covered it. But the rosebushes had not minded the sand. Or somebody had watered them. For they were bending with heavy clusters of red.

The sturdy little gray-haired woman of sixty or so who came from the kitchen round the side of the house was pleased when I assured her that I was not selling anything. I only wanted to get two or three watermelons, cut the

solid hearts out of them and eat them out in the open.
She would call her husband.

"I was admiring your roses," I explained when she walked back to us as though it were not quite appropriate to leave us there unthought about in a strange place.

Yes, they were blooming now. But they had had a hard time of it in the summer. It had been very dry. She had been afraid to use much water. Their well had held out during the hot weather, but now when it was raining once in a while, the level of the water had dropped until there was only about a foot left, and that was white with sand. She let the bucket down into the well and drew up a little, so that I could see.

Her husband came. Would he sell two or three watermelons to be eaten on the premises? Well, he hadn't been selling many recently. The season was about over. Somehow people stopped eating watermelons at about a certain time, no matter how many melons were left, and began to eat something else. But there were plenty of them out there. They had grown and ripened on vines that the September rains had revived. They were scarcely worth money, though.

We went back into the depths of his farm a little, and there, surrounded by rows of corn so that boys along the roads would not think of anything to eat, was his patch. He parted the high leaves of the vines in a few places so that I could see. The melons were so thick on the ground that they almost covered it. We carried four or five heavy ones back to the barn, and with a couple of butcher knives that he brought from the kitchen we cut them on the back end of one of the farm wagons. They were so ripe and so crisp that at the first touch of the point of the knife, they split from end to end.

"That's why we never have any like these as far away as where I live," I suggested.

"You can't have anything good if you have to ship it far," he answered calmly. "No taste to it."

We talked about farming. "We can live," he assured me, "as long as we don't have too many hot winds. Not much more than that, though."

He thought he might have overstated the case. "Oh, we do manage to scrape together a few things to sell."

We walked about. His barn was a ragged little stable of a building; his implements and machines were modest. Yet with these he was making a living. And he was helping to feed New York.

I felt the magic of the productive earth. No, I had not idealized farms. To be in possession of a microscopic corner of something that had seen millions of years pass, and with the aid of sun and rain transform part of this corner of the earth into wheat and corn and melons and whatever else man required for sustenance—was not that the greatest of all wonder-working?

When I was on the train again I was more content than ever just to look out at the soil. One day it was the bright violet-red soil of Oklahoma. Nobody who has missed seeing it can believe there is soil like that. No more brilliant mere earth is to be found.

I had to speak to somebody—to the pleasantly calm man in gray double-breasted coat on the other side of the aisle.

He was but mildly interested. Yes, he saw that it was pretty red.

Immediately I wished I had not spoken to him. He seemed to belong to the group of conventionally appropriate but colorless human beings who have no enthusiasm for anything, and who frown upon anybody who has.

But while I was nurturing my regret, he came to life. We passed a Civilian Conservation Camp where the boys were combating soil erosion.

"If you're looking for something to see, there it is!" he said in disgust.

"They are doing great work in reclaiming the soil."

"Yes, I know; but just the idea of the damned thing."

"Why, I think the idea is almost better than what they actually do. For two or three years I saw thousands of these young fellows—sometimes girls, too—hoboing along the railroad tracks in gangs of a half-dozen or dozen. But since the camps were put in operation I have not seen one gang."

"But I don't go in for any of this political stuff."

"Well, I'm not in politics, I never expect to be, and I don't care three hoots for any political label that was ever invented. So I am at liberty to be interested in anything that appears to possess merit."

I tried to neutralize his prejudice. "While Governor Landon was still in office, he proposed sending me on a two days' trip up through Kansas just to see what the boys were doing with zigzagged water-holes, diversion ditches, and the like to slow down the run-off of water after heavy rains."

He smiled pityingly—for Governor Landon as well as for me—and shook his head in despair. "Why, you can't do anything about the weather. Trying to control rain! My God!"

"They don't try to control the rain. They only try to keep the rain, when it does come down, from washing all the plowed soil away."

He smiled more pityingly than ever, and dismissed the matter a trifle impatiently as if I or Governor Landon or some other unauthorized person had proposed command-

## Sustenance 45

ing the sun and the moon to stand still—or the thunderclouds: "Why, man, weather is weather, and that's all there is to it. When it's wet, it's wet; and when it's dry, it's dry. Nobody can change it. These farmers give me the bellyache. Always squawking about something—wanting somebody to make it wetter or dryer or hotter or cooler. Why don't they show a little management themselves? You can see for yourself how they live."

I thought of him a day or two later when I sat for an hour on a cold, rainy afternoon with a farmer and his wife in their front room. He had come down from Kansas. She had once long ago attended a normal school for a term or two, and pursued me with questions about Washington and Boston and Lexington and Concord. And had I actually visited the spots where Longfellow and Emerson lived? It was only after many answers and long waiting that I was able to squeeze in a question about their peach orchard, and the size of the crop this year.

They had, they explained, gone in heavily for late peaches If it were not raining, we still might find a few sticking around.

We went out to see—despite the cold rain. We surveyed the rows of well-pruned, healthy peach trees; we found peaches; we talked about how rain could rip red soil to pieces when it once got started.

On the way back to the house, I overheard the wife say, "I'm going to show him my cold-packed canned things," and the husband answer, "Oh, he wouldn't be interested in them, would he?" and the wife reply, "Yes, he would; I can tell; so you run ahead and get the key."

"Cyclone cellar, too," the man explained while he applied the key to the lock. "I guess you know we need something of the sort down this way sometimes."

We descended into a cement cellar—out in the back yard—so solid that it seemed to be hewn from a block of stone.

"I did my own cement work," the man said when he saw me observing. "It's a little rough, but there's plenty of it. She's tight, as you can see. No place for anything to creep in."

The woman's eyes were bright as she quite needlessly directed my attention to rows of shelves that were loaded with glass fruit-jars of berries, of vegetables, of peaches, of tasty-looking chicken.

"This is why we'll not be on relief before next year, anyhow," she said, smiling—"if we keep the cellar locked."

"But why do you can your chickens when you could let them run around on their feet until you are ready for them and then have them fresh?"

"Oh, that's easy," she answered, as if it were good to discover that people who traveled did not know everything. "The canned ones are almost as good—sometimes I think, the way I can them, just as good—and you save all the feed they'd eat. Besides you'd have to count on some of them being killed by automobiles out in front of the house—if you didn't kill them first."

She put up a shoe-box of peaches for me to take along, but exacted in return a book of views or some post-cards from parts of the country where history had already been made.

Somewhere in western Kansas I was awake just after sunrise. The land was as flat as a table-top, and there was scarcely a tree in sight—just immense fields, some showing the palest green rows of young wheat in the dew, some stocked with young cattle; and at infrequent intervals, houses and barns. At a house not far from the railroad a young-looking shepherd dog played in the sun with a piece of old strap, tossing it lightly into the air over his shoulder and then whirling to see if he could catch it; dropping low with paws outstretched to seize it, as though he were having great sport, and then, with some variation, doing it all over again. At another, a farmer was hitching his team to the low-wheeled wagon out by the barn. At another a farmer was driving into the field. And at a dozen others, a hundred others now, the farmers were already at work for the forenoon. There was something steadying about their undisturbed attitude as they rode behind their teams. The big city chatters, it pronounces, it jeers, it acclaims, it professes to find itself interesting—and often is—and because it controls the means of communication, its case is always heard; yet it is jittery, it is fickle, and it is troubled with moments when it wonders about the importance of what it does. But these west Kansas farmers go right on without any doubts about what they are attempting to do—working early, working late, making the best of droughts and poor crops, making the best of poor prices and hoping for better ones, making the best of solitude in the fields, making the best of whatever comes their way. There is no tinge of any high-and-mighty hocus-pocus in what they do. Their wheat, their beef are guaranteed to sustain life.

I was in a state of mind to reëxplore farming. I ate with farmers, I slept in farmers' houses, I talked with farmers about the state of the world: with a man and his wife who had been married a year and had a baby and a new barn, and meant to have a new house as soon as they could get the barn paid for; with the old man and his rheumatic wife who had said to the three children, "All right, we'll divide it up now, since there's plenty of it, and see what you can make of it while we rest a little"; with the farmer whose outbuildings had burned when the barn was struck by lightning, and whose cattle and horses and pigs were now sheltered under some strips of corrugated iron supported by cottonwood stakes; with a keen-eyed, restless farmer and his quiet-mannered wife who had sent eight children to college; with a woman whose husband had died and left her a thirty-thousand-dollar farm with a ten-thousand-dollar mortgage on it just before the bottom dropped out of land prices and left the mortgage bigger than the farm; with a farmer and his wife who had been school-teachers and had made their farm an attractive retreat against a low mountainside where there were springs, and a pond with bass in it, and trees and unnumbered song-birds; with a hillbilly farmer who said, "When it rains and I can sell everything we don't have to eat ourselves, we can just make ends meet, so you can see what it's like when it don't rain"; with a farmer who had been a stock-broker and was hugging the soil in an effort to restore his frayed nerves; with a farmer who preached on Sunday and advised boys and girls to go to college if they could; with farmers in western Nebraska where crops are thin and a pitchfork fight or two at threshing time helps to relieve the tension of long days; with farmers in eastern Nebraska who made pilgrimages to Lincoln to see the new state-house tower with the gigantic figure of the Sower aloft in the heavens commanding the plains in sweeping rhythm; with farmers in Iowa where the tall corn grows.

Here are people who are more than mere cogs in an economic machine. A farmer and his family who own the land upon which they live constitute a complete microcosmic civilization. Their farm is a device for living through which they exercise initiative, maintain the great fundamental sanity that comes to man by possessing and using his tools, experience the self-respect that grows from producing something essential, enjoy the sense of growth that comes from extending their self-feeling into their little world, and acquire a certain margin of spiritual freedom by meeting in the give-and-take of equals all such persons as buyers, salesmen, clergymen, office holders, teachers, agricultural crusaders, and the body of farm neighbors with whom they must coöperate in making the locality as livable as possible. In summer when crops are ready for harvesting, and money for hired help is not at hand, and the weather is treacherous, and the markets are shaky, a farm requires the agility of mind of a major general in the thick of battle.

I could not escape seeing the importance that the farmer attaches to his spiritual freedom. He dreams of a house that will be more than just a shelter, and of a farm that is more than a center of unrelieved production. He dreams of a hospitable world in which he and his wife and their children—especially their children—may live advantageously among other self-respecting men and women. It is but logical that the cornucopia, despite the fact that rural communities still have less adequate facilities for public education than the cities, pour forth into the lap of the rest of the country not only an abundance of food, but an abundance of mental drive. One finds it in all sorts of places—in the World Court, in the diplomatic service, in the Federal government, in the faculties of the oldest seaboard universities, in enterprises designed to rehabilitate country life, in art, in letters, in science. In one large Middle Western university that was having a series of lectures by three distinguished · men in three fields of science, all three of the visiting scientists that year, I was told, had come from one rural county west of the Mississippi River. So much has this energetic mind come to be prized in some parts of the country where boys of genteel background are dominant in college populations, that institutions go out in search of it as a means of invigorating their own intellectual life.

At one of the characteristic "cow colleges"—at Ames, Iowa—I saw in a week something of the facilities provided by a farm state for the creation of a more hospitable world on the farms themselves. On an immense campus of good-sized buildings—and a campanile from which late each afternoon floated cheerful music—four or five thousand students were busy, under the direction of a faculty that would do credit to any institution of higher learning, with courses that for the most part would elicit only expressions of disgust in an old-line college of arts. For they were busy not only with the usual courses for engineers, but with butter-making, poultry breeding, stock judging, soil conservation, the rotation of crops, the chemistry of soils, landscape architecture, farm housing, the sociology of rural life. A thousand of the students were girls occupied with all sorts of courses in household art and household management.

I was permitted to visit several of the "practice houses" where girls who are pursuing such courses must take turns in managing each part of the household. When they enter the house—for a period of weeks—they must make the interior from the loose furniture and decorations at their disposal. Each house, too, is provided with a baby borrowed from an orphanage, and every girl must take her turn, under expert direction, in living with the baby and looking out for him. The babies are so well cared for and so responsive to their environment that they are

## Sustenance 51

usually adopted, I was told, by somebody who happens along before they arrive at the age limit of two years.

But these students were interested also in poetry and the ways of the novelist, and in what a biographer looks for in a subject, and in city planning, city housing, labor relations, and international affairs. An Oxford University debating team that was in the United States came for a debate. Seventeen hundred students were out to hear the discussion, and more would have been there if the auditorium had been larger. The occasion was a happy one for everybody and resulted in many new understandings and in much new good-will. The next day one of the Oxford debaters—an attractive tall young Englishman whose bearing, whose urbane wit, whose inclination never to grow too serious bespoke a settled civilization not to be found in the Mississippi valley—told me that the incident in their visit which had impressed him more profoundly than anything else was at the late evening reception held for the debaters. Just before midnight one of the members of the Ames team for whom he had at once developed a great liking and a great respect said: "I am afraid I'll have to be running along. I tend some furnaces for my keep, and I must be up at five in the morning."

I saw, too, the entire college at a football game—an amazingly decent crowd to one who has seen athletic contests at most of the more sophisticated universities—and I understood quite well enough when the stands forgot the game, right in the heat of it, and watched a rabbit closely pursued by a small dog in a desperate zigzag, round-and-round life-and-death struggle across the gridiron. Here was the greater genuineness of a contest not arranged by coaches.

Of course I saw the fringe of young sophisticates that

develops wherever youths assemble—the much-made-up young ladies who came into the Memorial Union diningroom and started the hard day off with a long afterbreakfast smoke and a little game of bridge. But I saw another fringe, and one that seemed more characteristic A retired member of the faculty took me out into the edge of the country one evening when a light snow made the world very white to see a student who had published a poem on Robert Frost. He lived in a trailer that he himself had built on the wheels of an abandoned automobile.

When we arrived he was finishing his supper—a large dish of prunes. He had found, he said, without trying to advertise anything, that prunes were good inexpensive food. He was a student of electrical engineering from up in one of the Dakotas, and went into detail in showing us his convenient arrangement of electric lights and the best methods of wiring under three-ply. Yes, he liked Robert Frost. He had himself already faced the world—a world in depression—and knew what life could feel like.

There was a little community of these trailers—it was dark, but I seem to remember them among some trees not far from a little cemetery—all parked for the college year. In some of them, with study lamps showing through freshly laundered curtains, young married people held forth and attended college, when living in any less mobile fashion would have made college impossible.

And then I saw just how the more hospitable world was being established in farm areas. A teacher in a community high school introduced me to "ideal farms." Farmers and their wives, he explained, had not had the right kind of opportunity to see what a farm would look like if they could have it just as they wanted it. So, in the warmth and light of the school basement he and the children were building "ideal" miniature farms. They planned everything—the fields, the crops, the outbuildings, the house, the yard, the driveways, the interior decorations. "Well, sir, after the kids have had a year of that and then have spent a summer or two on the old home farm, you'd never know the place. Paint gets on the barn, hinges get on the gates, gravel or stone drives and cement walks get themselves made—and flower beds and better-looking window curtains, and all sorts of things." And yes, to be sure, there were others, hundreds of them now, who were doing the same thing—preaching the gospel of appropriateness and beauty more effectively, he thought, than Vachel Lindsay was ever able to do, for they were helping people to discover that there could be beauty in the things they lived with every day. He thought this might be the way to a healthier conception of beauty, too.

As I made my way northward toward the region of dairy farms, we ran into more snow. It came down with business-like steadiness as if it might be meaning to stay all winter. But the life of the farms went on. Fat pigs were at work rooting down through the snow into earth that was not yet deeply frozen; beefy-looking cattle stood with their heads low and their rumps toward the wind while they waited to be let in to shelters; and men in fields of standing corn husked with few lost motions and rhythmically tossed the ears into slowly moving wagons drawn by horses snug under blankets.

In the night the train pulled onto a siding along the single-track main line. Soon a milk train thundered by in the snow. Then a live-stock train rattled along more deliberately, leaving an odor in its wake. That was how it was! Trains everywhere were hurrying from small farms, large farms, with meat and bread and vegetables and fruit and butter and milk. They were rushing to cities that could not last without them—to cities quite near, to cities so remote that boards of education there have to import cows and their calves from time to time and take them around to ward schools to assure the children for a certainty that the ultimate source of milk is not a bottle; so remote that men who must learn about farms say while they pour cream over their cereal at breakfast, "I see by the *Times* that corn stayed up two points."

Who can say that the drama is not a great one?

# iv

# Southbound

IN Minnesota it snows in late February or early March just as if that were the opening of the snow season. For hours I had sat on a southbound train from Fargo and watched snow flying through the air. Down along the Mississippi toward Minneapolis the blizzard increased its fury. The wind drove the fine snow everywhere—in gusts, in sweeps, in vast moving areas of blinding, solid-looking white. Despite the special fittings of the double windows, the sub-zero cold squeezed in and made it more comfortable to sit over a little toward the aisle. Sometimes I was diverted by fellow passengers who were talking about Calgary, Banff, Medicine Hat, and Saskatoon as casually as if they had been speaking of Atlantic City or Binghamton. But I spent most of my time watching the snow. If you have spent weeks in the northern edge of the United States where only the sight of a farm-house and barn here and there prevents the calm whiteness of a snow-covered earth from driving you mad, you will understand how welcome a raging blizzard can be.

I was in the Twin Cities in time to catch one of the daytime limited trains for Chicago. From a car that was toasting and snug it was pleasanter than ever to look out into the storm. The high-level bridge across the Mississippi in St. Paul seemed like nothing more than an unreal shadowy projection of a bridge save where it emerged somewhat from the flying snow on our side of the river and was substantially attached to the earth.

Within the city limits the train crept along a bit cautiously. But as soon as we were away from the innumerable switches and signals of the yard districts, it plowed into the storm as if it meant to keep to schedule. The deepening snow muffled all noises, so that we seemed to be dashing out of Minnesota and across Wisconsin on hard rubber.

It was not quite so cold in Chicago. Always somewhere between the Twin Cities and Chicago you pass out of a cold that stings like fire, that seems to have come untempered from the arctic circle, into a cold that still hurts, yet is tempered enough to be tolerable. And in Chicago there was little snow—only a gust of a squall now and then that showed distinctly around the street lights for a brief minute or two and then was gone.

After I had claimed my reservation on a train that was to leave for the Carolinas and Florida a little before midnight, I went out for a walk in the chill air. I wanted another look at Chicago.

I always want another look at Chicago. To me, it is the one city that speaks for America. Milwaukee is a city that its residents may well be proud of—I thought of that as we came through this evening—but there is a cool, slightly corpulent well-being in Milwaukee that suggests a heavy influence from the Rhine. But Chicago is all Middle West. It has a direct attachment to the soil that makes New York

## Southbound

seem foreign, and a gusto that makes such cities as Philadelphia and Baltimore and Boston seem inert. Always when I walk over to Michigan Avenue and see how such a gigantic enterprise as Grant Park has been made from some unsightly lake shore and some lake bottom, I see Chicago as a great floundering spirit that is struggling to shake loose and rise up and get the mastery of something gross and piggish that prevents it from being quite what it wants to be.

And I never miss walking over—over to the colossal Michigan Avenue approach to the Park. For without exception I see something interesting there. Once when I walked over between trains I saw fourteen thousand school-teachers of Chicago assembled in this plaza—which they were calling Liberty Square—all in readiness to march through the Loop to the music of numerous high-school bands, and insist that they receive their pay—which they had not received for many months. They revealed a polite indignation, an expression of the independent spirit, that was more creditable to Chicago than all the commercialized ballyhoo of the Century of Progress. They carried floats: "If our schools are the hope of the country, what about Chicago?" "A Century of Progress for the world, but what in the world for us?" "Merry Christmas (a wreath of holly)! We have just received our December pay!" They paid sharp respects to the bankers who were not working very hard to help make school pay-days possible. I was refreshed. But whether or not there is activity, I can always gaze upon Mestrovic's two Indian figures that flank the approach. If the country must some day be blown to scrap-iron and dust by demons in the sky, here are two equestrian pieces in bronze that I hope they miss.

I walked over to them this evening. But what was this? Something rendered them and the entire park grotesque and inconsequential. To the north was an illuminated billboard a hundred and twenty feet high—I was told—proclaiming some make of automobile, and at the south end two others almost as large flashing the virtues of whiskies or cigarettes or breakfast foods—I have forgotten just what. In the intermittent snow squalls of the night they looked like monstrous contraptions designed to amuse idiots.

How was this? After the people of Chicago have dreamed out what may well be the most stupendous system of parks in the world, and have spent millions of their dollars in beautifying something that had been ugly, they must now stand by—perhaps because of some legal hocus-pocus—and see all that they have done nullified and debased by somebody who has said: "This is pretty soft. Now that they have it all fixed up into a place where they are sure to want to be, we'll just cash in on it. To hell with Mestrovic!"

I was ready to fight. Chicago was not my town; yet I felt as if some low-grade person had slipped in and tacked advertisements on the front of my house—or on the gravestones of some of my relatives. I stopped four or five different men who looked as if they might take issue with me. But they did not. They concurred. One of them was an architect. He almost hated to walk along there now at night. While we talked, I remembered that I was over there between trains. I jumped. I glanced at my watch. He walked along with me —all the way to the station.

There was time. I was in bed before I felt the lurch which announced that we were on our way.

It was late the next morning when I pushed up the blind and looked out. We were traveling in a different world. There was no blizzard. There was no frost. The hills were clothed in a half-green, living frowsiness that promised spring. Water-cress grew in field streams that meandered among walnut trees. A rangy man in an ancient-looking broad-brimmed felt hat plowed across a low ridge with a team of dark mules. I must get up and bask in the sun.

Before noon we were in Nashville. The sun was warmer still—where it could get down through the city's smoke. There stood the old state-house on the ledge of a hill like a Greek temple. Somewhere out in the country, too, stood Old Hickory's Hermitage. The last time I was there it was still holding out magnificently, with the aid of devoted Southerners, against the inroads of an industrial civilization. But it was strictly a museum piece in a region where mills were springing up every day, and where entire cities were being thrown together to house populations of workers.

Unmistakably we were coming into the South: the timetable said "Murfreesboro" next. That was where my school history with the green cover and red backstrip said the little river ran red with the blood of the Northerners and Southerners who met there. When we came to it, it was just the kind of stream to invite such a battle—narrow enough and rocky enough to enable the men to get at each other.

Murfreesboro was enough to keep me occupied for hours —until the contour of Lookout Mountain was distinct against a hazy sky. More school history was returning to life. Off yonder was where Hooker's army was encamped. Up ahead was where his men clambered through the thick forest and over the rocks of the shoulder of the mountain in the mist. And just beyond was where they and the enemy fought "the battle above the clouds." There was the record of the struggle—a group of monuments white in the sun.

History was everywhere. While we paused in Chattanooga for a fresh start on toward Atlanta, there was time to stroll about in the station and have a good look at the General, the primitive old locomotive that had figured so prominently in the campaigns of the region. And then almost before we were fully on our way, we were passing Missionary Ridge.

And there was Chickamauga! That was a battle. I can hear the roar of the batteries and the yells of the advancing men, and then the night-long moans of the dying in the woods as if it were but yesterday—from the same book. As we whirled by a road up from the battle-ground, a dozen or more children were coming out of the woods with fists full of new violets. That was better.

We were entering the heart of the South. Yonder against a worn-out red hillside that had been half washed away by years of rains stood an unpainted, run-down plantation house, with broken clumps of boxwood out in front. On every curve we swept past tumble-down shacks where pickaninnies by the half-dozen poured out to see the last cars of the train go by. At unimportant-looking stations, enough porters appeared on the platform to have carried all the luggage on the train. But they did not seem too much disappointed when nobody got off. In the doorway of a stable not far from a chimney where a house had burned, a white-haired old Negro sat patiently churning in a stoneware churn. These gaunt telltale chimneys stood everywhere. In two hours I counted twenty-seven.

Two men beside me talked. One of them called himself a realist. He said the South was sick, and was going to be for fifty more years, at least. Since he would never see it when it would be much better than now, why not get as much out of it for himself and his family as the law would allow? "For," he declared, "if you don't, the other fellow will—you can count on that." The other admitted that his colleagues in business thought he was "plumb crazy," but he contended, he said, that they were the crazy ones themselves. The South ought to find ways of paying wages. "Just think," he urged, "what a body of consumers would be created if all these niggers we've been seeing along the way had money in their pockets. Wouldn't they spend it?"

I was but mildly interested; I was too busy seeing the South in history—a region that had come into the greatest inheritance of tragedy yet bequeathed to anybody in the New World. The only approach to a parallel is in New England where the aliens have wrested control from the Puritans. But even this parallel is far-fetched and imperfect. Boston may be only a handful of Puritans trying to hold off the Irish, but the Irish are assimilable. They came to America full of dreams of the very thing that America is supposed to symbolize, and in a generation or two they are sailing away to other countries to act as ambassadors of the American ideal. But in the South, the alien race did not come voluntarily; they came with no such acquaintance with the fundamentals of the American dream, and from the first they were destined to be menials for people who could make them do whatever seemed desirable. So when the Civil War was over the South had on its hands enough unattached people of an alien race to constitute a small nation; a firm tradition that these aliens should render only the less important services of civilized life; and a wrecked economic system that greatly reduced the menial jobs to which these aliens were supposed to confine themselves.

Held off at arm's length and looked at, it is a nicer problem in sociology than most persons wish to think about. The imported people are multiplying. If they are held in semi-subjection, they will keep everybody in the South in a state of relative impoverishment. If they are fitted to render high educational and technological services—they have the capacity—they are certain, with their increase in numbers, to endanger the dominance of the white race. It is a dilemma of this character that the people of this generation in the South have inherited. And they are no more responsible for what has come down to them simply because they were born, than any other generation in any other place. And all this has come to pass where there is still to be found among men a genuine cordiality of spirit.

"You keep looking around as if you didn't live down this way," one of the two men said to me.

I told him that I grew up in Ohio and lived in Massachusetts.

"But I didn't think you quite looked like 'an honest-to-God damned Yank.'"

I assured him that I grew up in a part of Ohio where there was a good southern exposure. In addition, I was half Virginian.

"So am I—and the other half, too. And I am glad you told me. You know, we say around where I live that you should never ask a man if he's a Virginian. If he is, he'll say so of his own accord; and if he isn't, you shouldn't humiliate him."

He laughed as if I had not heard it all before, and as if the joke were quite undeniably on somebody other than ourselves.

"But just what part of Ohio did you say?"

"Ten miles from where General Philip Sheridan grew up, and twenty or so from where General William T. Sherman was born."

"For God's sake! Say, I don't know but what I'd keep that to myself if I were you—at least till we get past Atlanta."

We talked about Sherman and his March to the Sea. He reminded me of what Henry W. Grady said in referring to

Sherman twenty years later: "General Sherman . . . is considered an able man in our parts, though some people think he is a kind of careless man about fire."

Before I changed to the train that would carry me to Savannah, we talked long and pleasantly about the needs of the South. He told me— I had heard this before, too, in Virginia—of a white-haired friend of his who said that the greatest need of the South was "a strictly impartial history of the War between the States written from the Southern point of view."

The next morning, in deep marshy woodland that suggested alligators, deciduous trees veiled in the softest of hanging mosses were revealing signs of buds and leaves. And when I drove through Savannah to Chippewah Square, the air was balmy and the azaleas were blooming as if there had been no winter.

For two hours in the afternoon I walked through the city. Old ironwork made doorways inviting. The sun shone down with more warmth than was required. And many people of two races were on every hand to do whatever one wished done. In a little parkway along the river I sat on a sagging bench and listened to the conversation and laughter of the many Negroes who lounged in the warmth. One of them, an elderly man who was a bit stout, thought he would just take a nap. If the boat should come in, somebody was to shake him good and hard.

At dinner that evening I was the only person present who was not Southern-born. And of course I myself was not "an honest-to-God damned Yank." But I was enough of one to make the others self-conscious. They discussed the situation. They agreed to do something they were sure they had never done before. They would confess to me what they honestly thought about the South. But nothing was to be reported, nothing recorded. I was to hold their confessions sacred. The hostess, who was the daughter of a man who had possessed the pencil draft of the Confederate Constitution, agreed to make it easy for the others by confessing her heterodoxy, her radicalism, first. The dinner was delightfully long. The confessions were unlike any that priest ever hears.

Something in the total of all that was said kept me from wishing to sleep that night. I had heard something very honest, very intelligent, very dispassionate, very unselfish. It was good to know that there were people like that in the South—in any region on the face of the earth. I sat in a great, quiet bedchamber and read from one of the books that somebody had placed on the bedside table. Then I lay in comfortable darkness and tried to see more discerningly the fusion of tragedy and warmth of life that is the South.

At dawn I dozed off for a time, and dreamed that the train was standing immovable in a snow-bank in Minnesota. But when I awoke I was still in Savannah, and a mocking-bird was warming up with muted ventriloquial notes just outside my window, and two Negro women down below in the quiet street were talking about when they might expect enough strawberries on the market for everybody to have some.

## V

## Hunger

I HEARD voices, as if out of some half-forgotten past, and sat up, fully awakened to the life outside the window of the standing train. Nobody who had himself lived his youth in the hills could ever mistake those voices for any others. In their high pitch there was the true hill blend of plaintiveness and faint hopefulness. And in the rhythmic swing of the men along the dusty street, there was something of the humility of motion that comes from being always beneath a heavy load. They were wiry, stooped men in blue overalls and rough brogan shoes, and under coarse unseasonable broad-brimmed straw hats or sweaty black felt ones that had been keeping the hot sun out of their eyes all summer and autumn, their lank tanned faces bristled with a growth of beard. They had driven to town, to a row of slender iron posts supporting a continuous porch roof which reached out over the sidewalk in front of a grocery store, a feed store, and a post-office. Or they were starting home, after they had traded a few eggs for a pound or two of sugar, or some apples and black walnuts for a few yards of calico or muslin. Or perhaps one of them had slipped a gallon or two of moonshine to somebody who couldn't live without it. They rode in clattering remnants of automobiles, or—much more frequently—in scrawny-looking wagons that had higher wheels than surfaced roads required, behind mules that jogged along with ears sagging as though life were grim business. All passing neighbors they hailed with a flourishing gesture and a firm voice which implied that moral support is an important commodity.

I was in the region where Abraham Lincoln was born. These were Lincoln's kinfolk. But their great-grandparents, members of a generation that in some instances went as far as Illinois, as the Lincolns did, never quite squeezed all the way through the devious sieve made by the mountains between the Atlantic seaboard and the plains. So here they were, covering the hills, clinging to steep, barren-looking slopes far up the mountainsides, hanging on by the eyebrows wherever they could. Why? Because they were born there —the reason most people have for being where they are. They were little aware of any other world—and had not enough money to take them to it, even if they were sure it existed. They have never known what it is like to have enough of anything—except fresh air, and maybe time for thinking things over while working in solitude. For most things they are hungry, but especially for something which they believe the more fortunate of the earth must know. One of them startled me one day by quoting to me a sentence that I recognized as belonging in Maeterlinck's *The Treasure of the Humble:* "For the soul of man is a guest that has gone hungry these centuries back." Where had he come upon it? He had heard a preacher repeat it so many times that he had learned it by heart. He thought it was good. "For that's just the way it is." In southern and eastern Kentucky, northern and eastern Tennessee, northeast Georgia, western North Carolina, southwest Virginia and much of West Virginia, there are enough millions somewhat like him to constitute a small nation.

I got off the train at Elizabethtown. Flood waters—so I was told—had taken out a bridge right in the town between the station and the court-house square, and what seemed to be the Public Works Administration was putting in a new one. The lean men from the hills were everywhere—not only at work, but asking for work, waiting for work, and when work was not forthcoming, standing in clumps, standing in rows along the clean new board fence around the excavation, watching those who had been luckier.

After I had satisfied myself that there was one quiet room in the little hotel, I struck out to enjoy the warm autumn afternoon, and to explore the town. Soon I was out where I could see the streets ending in the open country. As I walked along under shade-trees that suggested the quiet of an old South, a man in overalls and work cap hurried across the street to me.

"Mister, you wouldn't like to buy some nice butter-beans, would you?"

He displayed some samples in one hand.

"I'm afraid I'm too far from home."

"Where is your home?" He asked the question very cheerfully, very honestly, as if it were always appropriate for one human being to be interested in another.

"In Boston."

His eyes came wide open. "Why, say!" And he looked me up and down. "I didn't know people like you lived over there."

A moment later, I learned from a chance remark that there was a hill town called Boston about ten miles over east somewhere, and that he had referred to it.

"Oh, I meant Boston, Massachusetts," I explained.

"Boston, Massachusetts! Why say, you're a long ways from home, aren't you? Just about how far is it from here anyhow—close onto a thousand miles?"

"Just about that."

"Well, well! What do you know about that? I studied about Boston once when I was in country school—the Boston Tea Party. But I never expected to talk with a man who had come from there. Whatever brought you way out here?"

I told him that I was to lecture in the evening at the Temple—before a meeting of all the teachers of central Kentucky.

"Well, what do you know about that? Why, I've got a boy on that program. But he's on this afternoon. He's a sophomore in our community high school out at—" and he mentioned a name that I remember as something like Happy Valley. "The school is providing the educators with a musical number at three o'clock—just about now, my guess is. But what are you going to lecture about?"

I told him.

"Why, say, I'd like to hear that. Any chance for a fellow that don't belong to get in?"

"Should you like to go?"

"I'd say I would."

## Hunger

"All right, then; here, you are to come as my guest. Just explain to the secretary that the speaker invited you."

He professed delight. But he would have to scoot along back home and do the feeding and all the other chores, and clean up a little, and grab a snack of supper, and get back to town. It would keep him humping.

Yet he walked on with me. He confessed that while he spent all his time trying to grow something and sell it, he was much interested in schools. "You see, I've got five of my own in school right now—sprinkled all the way along from the high school down to the first grade. And boy, maybe you think I don't have to sell a lot of butter-beans!"

He made a flinching gesture of apology. "As a matter of fact, I'm tickled to death to do it. If they have a little education—that's the way my wife and I figure it—maybe they'll stand a little better chance than we did. Anyhow, it's worth doing. There are so many things you can have around just to remember and think about if you know something."

The tempo of his speech made walking easy. On and on we went, out into the edge of the country and back, and then along one shaded street after another. He was marshaling all that he could remember from the wisdom of two or three famous teachers he had had in the little country school of his day. In great detail he showed me just why these teachers were famous. They had not given him so much, he supposed, compared with what great teachers in the big places must be able to give, but just the same, it had been something. It had kept him going.

In trips that almost completely circumscribed the mountain area, I was never without reminder that I was among people who hungered desperately for some assurance that they were not always to be as inconsequential as now.

Over at Mayfield, in the western tip of the state known as

Beyond the Rivers—the region isolated by the Mississippi, the Ohio, and the Tennessee and Cumberland—I found the record of one man, H. G. Wooldridge, who took more than ordinary precautions against permanent oblivion. He provided for such an array of monuments to himself as no one else would ever outdo in any cemetery—eighteen separate statues and shafts in all. The figures, most of them in limestone, face in the same direction, and at a distance their gray outlines in one compact group give the impression that the resurrection has at last begun. There are women and girls—sweethearts and relatives—men relatives, two representations of himself, one horse, two dogs, a fox, and a deer as well as a tomb and a shaft. Everything has been done with more than lifelike literalness. The men's cutaway coats are perfectly draped, the women's high collars and bows and mutton-leg sleeves have been done with all of a tombstone-maker's care for detail, and the horse and the dogs bear their own names as ineffaceably as stone can be made to bear them. He may not have achieved the kind of earthly immortality he craved, but he is not forgotten.

Just back east a few miles at Murray, where a well-equipped college in the outskirts of the town is slowly changing the spirit of the entire region, I heard the story of a mightier hill dreamer who was not quite so successful in creating his own personal record—not immediately. He, Nathan Stubblefield, who according to the story told to me had preceded any other known person with a speaking radio by at least a half-dozen years, had lived and died just across from what is now the college campus. He was known chiefly to his neighbors as a "queer bird," and when he invited some of them to come and place themselves in a magic square of a contraption that he had rigged up and hear voices, they thought he was crazy. And when some of them

## Hunger

participated in the experiment and heard voices, they could not help believing that there were underground wires, or some other connections besides the air, that brought the voices from the sending station. He gave demonstrations elsewhere—one between a boat on the Potomac River and land. He had the real thing. Somebody offered him money for it. He knew he ought to have more. He waited. Somebody in another part of the world came along with the same idea—plus the advantage of a name. Stubblefield was embittered—and forgotten. He spent more and more time in a seclusion that was broken only when he had to drive a mile to town for provisions. He rode in a rattling antiquated vehicle, very upright, with the lines clutched in one hand, and in the other, close in front of his eyes, a book which he read in supersensitive disregard of the world about him. Then he quit coming to town. Finally somebody chanced to investigate and found him dead. He had died without food, and rats had gnawed his face, Now the college was trying to make up a little for the great irony by purchasing the site—the college had already erected a marker—and establishing a Stubblefield broadcasting station.

I went less than a mile from the college campus and saw lank men working doggedly in the fields, and women with an attitude of "Well, I am trying to do something honest, anyway," carrying apples or pumpkins or firewood along narrow rutty roads to their stark kitchens, and children helping their fathers or mothers or playing together the least bit uncertainly—children who suddenly became young gods and goddesses when one talked to them with respect.

I saw them on Sunday morning, too. Everywhere through miles of hills that were sometimes fertile, sometimes desolate, men and women with brightened-up faces, and children in clothes a little better than the ones they wore customarily, were going into white churches in very rural-looking groves of hickory trees, coming out of churches, or lingering for a few cheerful words with neighbors who like themselves had been hard at it every day since last Sunday. For those who are troubled by the phenomenon, here is the explanation of the "Bible Belt." The church in these hills stands for something besides the grim work of plowing corn or cotton or tobacco and watching the sun burn the crop up. What difference to them does it make if often enough the church is dogmatic and "Fundamentalist"? It provides them with a rallying ground. It enables them to feel the warmth of being united under one banner. The liberal church that is self-consciously busy with its own liberality may appeal to sheer, undisturbed intelligence; but it is a cool affair compared with the church which these hungry ones require.

It is only by chance that their church is restricted and Fundamentalist. If chance had made it what the rest of the world calls liberal, these Kentuckians, Tennesseeans, and Virginians would cling to it just the same. They have so little of anything that they are frightened at the thought of letting the least thing go. They stand upon hilltop and mountaintop and call valiantly to their very orthodox heaven to send them more of something. And when their orthodox heaven does not send them more of anything, some of them turn moonshiners, or bootleggers, or feudists —or all three—but most of them go right on hungering, and calling upon heaven, and hoping—a little.

All the way over to Clarksville, Tennessee—over past Fort Donelson in its false impregnability on the high hills between the Tennessee and the Cumberland Rivers—the hill people sat in clumps together in front of little stores closed for the day, and on the steps of their houses, or trudged along quiet roads without seeming to be too intent on getting anywhere. There was nothing much in the hills for them to stir up. They were trying to be patient.

I have spent much time "lingering about" in Clarksville, high above the yellow river, and listening to the knots of men, black and white, who hang around the spreading tobacco warehouses and agree, not too dolefully, that "I guess they jes' ain't no work around any more." But this time the sunny sections of downtown, and the river with the high slender railroad bridge and trestle across water and wide sandy bottoms, were much obscured for me by the students in the little Austin Peay Normal School which had been established in the buildings of an abandoned denominational college by a former national Commissioner of Education. For these students were from the hills. They had the awkward but irresistible enthusiasm of the provincial. They were ready to try anything—anything that promised something better than what they had had. What did it matter if this boy had to grow ninety bushels of sweet potatoes—and sell them—merely to pay for one month's board and lodging in the little normal school? What did it matter if another boy had to work as a cook on a sand boat on the river so much of the time that it took him five years to finish two years of study? Or what did it matter if a frail girl who had spinal trouble could find nothing to do that would pay money except scour pots and pans in a cafeteria kitchen? What was the objection to doing that for two or three years when it enabled one to study? If anybody thought such things difficult or humiliating, then that person knew nothing about everyday life in the hills.

Then I pursued a journey across the mountainous northern regions of Tennessee—two or three hours on the train; a stop; a side trip; then to the train again. At the moment I seemed to be accumulating only isolated impressions. But swiftly the passing of time gave them a certain homogeneity.

I remember: Close to the railroad a low unpainted but weather-boarded house with a porch extending out from the slope of the house roof, and with slender rickety-looking posts reaching down to flat foundation stones. The dirt floor of the porch was two or three feet lower than the uncarpeted floor of the house. As the train whirled by, an elderly Negro in shirt sleeves had stooped over the tin wash-pan on the front step, and a little stiffly but with dignity and with a smile of content, was lifting the water to begin washing his face.

And this: To the northward as I traveled east, in front of a notched ridge of dark mountains, some steep foothills rose sharply, and far up the side of them, high above log houses, slender men were plowing the soil with wraith-like mules, or, still farther up, were dragging logs down for firewood. Children were everywhere—high against the dark of the woods, in the pale plowed field, down near the railroad—wistful, fearful, wondering children in clothes of overalling or shirting or calico, and invariably accompanied by an undersized dog or two. While we waited at a switch two little girls of nine or ten, in fresh new dresses, played tag in and out among rows of corn fodder that had been left standing in a small field sown to timothy. For miles as we went on, there were the men working on the sunny hillsides, and the children, and the dogs, and the log houses.

And I saw the coming of evening and night in the hills. A gnarled and crooked body of a man, with a loose white beard like Walt Whitman's, and with a heavy cane for a support, stood in the side yard of his weather-beaten little house and twisted his stiff neck slowly to follow the train as it crept past in the late afternoon sun. Boys and girls from a community high school a few miles back stopped their boisterousness for several seconds when one of them saw him and nudged some of the others. When they all got off at the next two stops I had the old-style red plush coach almost to myself. As the train creaked and rattled along, shadows filled the deep valleys and began to cover the hillsides. Women gathered their washings from the paling fence, or, occasionally at some better-looking house, from a clothes-line. Chickens were going to roost in the trees—sometimes not thirty feet from my window where the railroad hugged the hillside. High up where it was still bright, the men worked on. Then I saw some of them bringing their thin horses or mules down to clapboard-covered log stables. And then night was upon us and enveloped us.

The hills cried out. The hills would express themselves. Once when I had spent two or three days in this region four students at Lincoln Memorial University, Harrogate, dropped in to see me one after another. The first one wished to produce plays; another wished to go to a liberal school of theology and then come back and liberalize the native mind; another wished to enter politics; and the fourth was an avowed poet. "Any more of this?" I asked. "I know the college brand when I see it, and this is not it. This is good—or at least it is about to be." "I've got a whole load of it," he replied. "I'll bring some more down. But I'm going to keep on writing it, no matter what you think of it." His name was Jesse Stuart.

At Johnson City a college president took me to spend an afternoon among the mountain people—his own people. "You know what the magazines and newspapers say about us, especially since the trial over at Dayton. All right, see for yourself."

We drove for hours through narrow valleys, along mountainsides, through villages in hill fastnesses, over ridges that gave us sweeping views. "Look at those houses. Don't they look about as well as anybody could expect? And they're just like that inside, too. The people haven't much, but they use what they have and they wish they had more. They are a first-rate lot—really they are—if you don't try to be high-hat with them. Why, I come here and speak all over this region on Sunday evenings in their country school-houses and little churches, and I enjoy the experience just about as much as anything I do. And you would, too."

"But what I should like to know," I said, still thinking of his reference to Dayton, "is whether you ever discuss Evolution."

"As a matter of fact, I rarely discuss anything else. And they eat it up." Then he smiled off through the wind-shield. "But I call it Growth."

Over beyond the Smoky Mountains—and nobody has yet said enough about the beauty of these ranges veiled in soft blues—I spent a week-end with a small Quaker family. The husband is the head of the community school; the wife is a poet; and the young son is an inventor. Belatedly the wife's poems are beginning to appear in print. She writes with a subtlety as great as that of Emily Dickinson—though it is her own—and lives a life only less isolated. When she and her husband took me across the country to catch a train, we discussed the enforced seclusion of hill life. She told me how Robert Frost had come to a neighboring city to lecture; how they had gone to hear him; how she had had opportunity to speak a few words with him; and how on the way home as she and her husband talked about the unusual experience and savored it bit by bit, the thought that there were such people with such interests living in the world, and that she was shut away from seeing them and knowing them, filled her with such heartbreaking that she wept "bitterly and copiously—the first time my husband had ever seen me do it." And he confirmed her confession.

Up in southwestern Virginia as I walked along in the quiet that evening, I heard what seemed to be Negro spirituals in an old abandoned store or saloon. But when I peeped in I saw that whites were doing the singing. Listeners who looked as if they were hoping for something filled the hard benches that had been crowded in not only crosswise but along the walls of the room. There were fewer than a dozen women present, and not a white-headed man. One man was bald and growing gray, but the body of the congregation was made up of boys and men between seventeen and thirty, and they were of the working classes. They wore overalls and leather jackets and heavy shoes with rivets on the sides. Three or four of the young women helped the pianist with guitars and a banjo—as the spirit moved them they kept turning to some pegs on the wall and taking down fresh instruments—and the preacher, who was dressed like an Episcopalian but acted like a Methodist, stood and played a trap-drum that was half concealed behind the desk of the pulpit.

When two "brethren" passed the collection baskets for the evening offering, one of them paused a little unduly, a little deferentially, in front of where I sat on the end of a bench close against the rear wall by the door. I put in a quarter. When the two returned to the pulpit the preacher said, "Well, now, you know I always believe in finding out what we've got." He counted. "Eighty-three cents! Too bad it couldn't have been even money." Whereupon a big genial ruffian of a fellow up front arose and passed him two cents. The minister laughed. "I only wish it could have been a dollar. We always seem to be getting somewhere when it amounts to a dollar." I held up a quarter, and he sent one of the two "brethren" to get it. A man in overalls close beside me saw what I was offering, fumbled through the very meager supply of change in his pocket, and contributed another quarter. The preacher offered a special prayer for us. "We do get somewhere, I tell you, when it begins to come in in halves!"

He did not attempt to do much preaching. It was not necessary. It was easy enough to catch the drift of his intentions just by looking around. On the walls above the level of the seats the free space was covered with all sorts of Biblical pictures and such motto-posters as:

THE MIDNIGHT SPECIAL RUNNING WITH NO HEADLIGHT. IT'S A HELLBOUND EXCURSION. (A train was rushing headlong down a steep grade to a very black tunnel, and a bright red devil with arrow-head tail was ushering it in)

These people of the hills know what hell is. It is not necessary to get all the way into such widely advertised hells as the Harlan district. The endless steel trains of coal that come roaring, screeching from every thin notch suggest that they have come from inhuman regions. The experiences of my youth in one of the dirtiest of the soft-coal areas left me with impressions that still hurt. I like to believe, when I hear people talking lightly, that I appreciate the plight of the miner. But whenever I am about to enter such a region as the one stretching roughly from Cumberland Gap northward to the Upper Ohio Valley, I am terrified at how much of suffering I have forgotten. The natural hazards alone of the industry are as great as those of some battle-fronts. The work is heavy, and in low coal you must do it all, day after day, without ever being able to stand up straight. It obliges you to waive all claim to sunlight, and work in a dust-laden atmosphere that sooner or later covers the bottoms of the lungs with fine coal. And it calls upon you to risk explosions that burn men's lives out in a breath, and cave-ins that bury whole communities while they toil. As if these things were not sufficient to keep men humble, the coal operators with the least humanity in them have devised additional cruelties in the form of uncertain employment, disgraceful housing, racketeering company stores, and professional manipulators who keep different groups of workers arrayed against one another to their detriment.

If all the miners were to say on some zero morning in January, "Now we are not going to strike and picket the mines so that women and children will be left to freeze without coal, but we are going to insist that every able-bodied man in the country come and mine his own," and the male population of the country had to do it in conditions that now exist, we would be in the throes of an exhilarating economic revolution within a month. This entire coal region has become a social cauldron in which a million or two of fundamentally first-rate human beings fly in every direction, fly at one another's throats, in the despair of ever having anything better than they have now.

Nor did I find the western fringe of the region much better. Across two or three tiers of counties I saw petulant or resigned housewives scrubbing coal-begrimed houses, or gathering firewood, gathering runty apples, black walnuts, and persimmons, milking bony cows and carrying milk to hillside houses of deal-boards or logs—oftentimes papered with newspapers—or sitting on a rickety front porch caring for a baby that had to be content with a corrugated carton from the grocer's for a crib, until it seemed that the entire earth must be peopled with this unfortunate kind. I was ready to laugh the most raucous horse-laugh at those who speak with awesome solemnity about preserving the American high standard of living. Here was what could be done to life when the heartless conspired to induce human beings to be their worst.

And then one morning I stood before the children of these people—eighteen hundred of them—in a college auditorium. Even a believing mind found the fact difficult to accept. They were becomingly dressed; they were cheerful; they were confident. And they were alert. They looked up at me as if to say, "All right, now what are you going to tell us?" They saw the point before the speaker was quite all the way to it. They caught up the slightest trace of humor. They were ready to doubt. They were ready to inquire. They were ready to be in earnest. Where had I ever spoken to an audience more immediately and intelligently responsive? Could it be that these eighteen hundred were the offspring of those others who battled so desperately against total degradation?

I had been trying to hold off a cold that threatened me, and went immediately to the hotel and stayed there until toward the end of the day. Then in the twilight I ventured out. In the window of a fruit store I saw some extra large pears. I went in and bought one, crossed over to the quiet side of the street along the college campus where I supposed I should be unobserved, and walked leisurely in the growing darkness and ate at my pear. A college girl who was going briskly in the same direction paused as she passed, took a second look, and then as if she were much surprised, asked a bit breathlessly, "Why, aren't you the assembly lecturer?"

I confessed that I was—and that I was eating a pear.

"Why, I never dreamed that I was going to have a chance to talk to you. We were so thrilled—"

"I'd better walk along with you a few steps," I suggested, "and catch the full effect of all this."

As we walked on—she was going to supper in one of the college halls—she wished to know what I thought of the campus. I explained that I had been shut in all afternoon, but that I was to be there for three or four days.

"Then tomorrow, shouldn't you like to have me show you around? You know we do that here at Berea."

Such a pilgrimage over the campus, I assured her, would be pleasant.

"The main part of my day is taken," she explained. "You know, I guess, that we all work. But I'm free in the morning from seven-thirty to eight-thirty, and in the afternoon from four-forty to five-forty."

I preferred four-forty. She came to the little hotel—the Daniel Boone Tavern, operated by the college—and we saw the new music building and the fine auditorium in it, and the organ; the new building devoted to the fine arts; the newly enlarged library; the well-equipped new hospital— many of the mountain people are in poor physical condition when they come; numerous fireside industries; two little dwelling-houses on the same lot that bore the interesting name of "contrast houses"; and everywhere, students, students.

"And now," she said, when the hour was almost up, "I'll walk you back to the hotel, and then you'll be there."

She was an interesting, thoughtful college freshman whose manner and voice bespoke gentility.

"Should you mind telling me what region you are from?" I asked, before we came to the hotel steps.

"Oh—I am from down in the mining district. I expect you've heard enough of what that must be like."

I assured her that I had grown up in a mining district myself.

"Then I needn't trouble you with details."

"No. But your father, was he—"

"Yes, my father was a miner. He taught once for a time, but went back into the mines. But my father is no longer living."

Then while we stood on the steps of the hotel, with Greek columns rising high above our heads, and with the bells in the college tower playing a familiar romantic melody just as if we were in some over-contrived movie, she said with but a trembling hesitancy at one or two words: "What you said this morning about cleaning up politics struck right home to me. My father wanted to do a little of that down in our county. But last year two men walked up behind him one day and shot him to death."

So there could be no doubt. They were the children of the hills. Yet who would ever dream at the sight of them that they were? They had come into an atmosphere that was benevolent. With youth's bravura to support them, they had been able to put aside most of the old agonies. There was something to live for, after all. Blithely they were making furniture, weaving carpets, weaving tapestries, weaving women's suiting, making candies, decorating tea sugar, making brooms, reading proof, setting type, making beds in the college hospital, serving as waiters and waitresses in the college hotel, caring for lawns and gardens, washing windows, hanging paper, selling groceries, serving as firemen—in order that they might have something better than what they had grown up with. They set aside days for the celebration of education; they set aside days for the celebration of labor.

They were coming into possession. They were discovering that a man need have no sense of dependence, of humiliation, if only he has a half-chance.

They were contributing, too. They were glad to contribute. Young men at the hotel desk gave me the latest word on railroad trains, or on cabs that would render cross-country service. Waitresses remembered that I wished no toast at breakfast, but cared for two servings of cereal. A bell-boy wondered if I would be good enough to read some of his verse. He hoped he had not been influenced too much by Walter de la Mare. A group of students—some of them waiters—one evening gave a dining-room concert of remnants of English and Scottish popular ballads and other folk-songs that had been lodged in the hills for two or three centuries.

It was pouring down rain when I boarded an evening train for Cincinnati. While we rushed through the night with such speed that the trails of water on the outside of the wide window ran back almost horizontally across the pane, I sat in the seclusion of perfect incognito and saw these youngsters swarming out of the hills, taking possession of college, of hotel, of town, of farm, to find what they require —joyful, philandering, yet in desperate earnest. I saw them going back to their native hills to show their neighbors how to take the same number of square feet of lumber that had been used in an ugly, inconvenient, and uncomfortable house, and make an attractive one that any human being could live in with self-respect. Many of these who carried all this report of a somewhat good life back to the fastnesses would succumb to old habit; some would live a little more interestingly themselves without noticeably touching their environment; and some would change their entire little world into something incomparably better. Some, too, would content themselves with nothing short of an invasion of the most glittering centers. Imagination is in the depths of man, and is not to be awakened very completely in the first generation free of bondage. But I thought I saw how the hills, if they are not too completely debased by those who come from the outside, might be a source of supply for all of us after the more sophisticated parts of the country have settled into a mushy and sterile decadence, and the smoky industrial area in the heart of the continent has annihilated itself in perpetual warring.

## vi

## Parasite

PERHAPS I had received a special preparation for what I was to see during the next three or four days. I had attended the funeral of a very honest craftsman who had struggled through almost ninety years without surrendering to anything cheap. On my way afoot down to the little town from which I was to drive forty miles across the Ohio hills in the January bleakness to catch a train for Washington, I was alive with a great new admiration for the heroism with which a little man will go on facing all sorts of odds in order to produce something that at once satisfies his creative spirit and provides his fellow beings with handiwork essential to their comfort.

As I made a sharp turn in the road, a coal miner so black from his day's labor in a wet mine that he was only a limping unrecognizable smudge of a man appeared suddenly before me. As he came nearer he stared at me with eyes that seemed all whites, and then began to slip off his heavy cloth glove. "Why, hello, here . . ." and as he extended his bared hand, he called me by a name that I had not heard since country-school days. "Purty dirty," he said—of the hand—without shrinking in the least from the fact, "but I guess you've seen coal-black before." He was shriveled and stooped, like a man of seventy or seventy-five, and the day's accumulations of dust and moisture and grime in the depths of the hill were not enough to conceal the white of his hair below the line of his stiff canvas cap. But in the contour of his blackened face there was the faintest remnant of something I long ago saw every day.

We talked. He thought I looked well—not a day older than the last time he saw me, and that was not recently. He was feeling pretty well himself, as a matter of fact. Sometimes his back bothered him a little toward the end of the day—he had been pretty badly pinched, he explained, between a loaded car of coal and the rib of a side entry a dozen years ago now—and one of his feet had never quite recovered from the damage that a heavy lump of coal did to it the winter before last. But he was still equal to "three squares" a day when his wife could dig up the necessary beans and sow-belly. They were getting out a lot of coal over at the new mine where he worked now. And then abruptly there was nothing else much to be said on such short notice, save that I was mighty glad to see him and that he was pleased to see me looking so well.

Down in the little town a dozen other men of my own age who were coming home from work reminded me by cheerful salutation from across the street that I was in a region where I was known and where it was understood that I knew how men lived.

As I was whirled away in the late afternoon when the winter shadows were long, I saw several scores of people pouring out of a china factory that an old friend of mine and his son and associates had developed and worked at for thirty years. Two or three miles down the road we passed a great stoneware pottery built by brothers whose father had been a potter and had passed on to them the tradition of honest craftsmanship. A few miles farther on, we passed another pottery that sends its artistic product to every part of the world. The man who had developed that enterprise and its good name had likewise once been a worker in the early log pot-shops of the region. We passed, in all, a dozen potteries that I had seen rise up in a few decades—most of them in one. Then as the hills flattened out, there were farms. In the growing darkness men were busy putting cattle up in half-slushy, half-frozen barnyards, women were going from barns to houses with big buckets of milk, and children were closing up chicken houses for the night or chasing turkeys to cover when they persisted in putting too great a strain on motorists' high motives by roosting openly in trees that were within easy reach of traveled highways.

When I arrived at the station the ticket agent offered to put the bags inside his office, if I wished to feel free of them. He would see that they were up on the platform when the train arrived. "If they're not in sight the minute you get up there yourself, don't worry. They always wait, you see, till I tell 'em to go."

I walked out into the raw cold. The air promised snow. Two or three blocks away the tower of a court-house built in the President Grant era of architecture was trying to express the newer spirit through twinkling lines of incandescent lights that ran in every direction over it as if it were advertising a carnival. It provided something to walk to and I struck off in that direction.

A scarecrow of a man shaped much like a hastily made question-mark hobbled desperately up alongside. "Haven't a dime for a fella that needs one, have you?" he asked without preliminaries.

I slowed down and sized him up a bit as we walked along. "You really need it, do you?"

"Honest to God, Mister, if there ever was anybody that needed it, I'm the man. I was on relief for a good while, and then I got a job down here in this glass factory when it opened up. I thought I was all set for good. God, maybe I wasn't tickled to death. Then the third day I was there some mug walked in and told me I wasn't up to it. I s'pose maybe I'm not quite as good as I used to be, with this shoulder and this knee and all, but, Christ, I'm only fifty-four years old. That's not so old, is it? And now I can't get back on relief. They want to know why I didn't keep my job when I had one."

The earlier part of the day had awakened my memory. In his voice there was something that reminded me of another boy I had known in school-days—a lop-eared slender young devil who was something of a comedian.

"Were you born in this town?" I asked him.

"No." And he brightened up at the thought that he had ever had an experience common to other and better-dressed men. "No"—and in a sudden rush of returning self-respect he assumed the manner of the reminiscent raconteur—"I was born, as a matter of fact, in the county down south here—down among the coal mines. That's where I got this shoulder and this knee. You know lots of fellas down there 'get it' in one way or another. Well, I got mine one day when some roof decided to come down. They never could get all my ribs and the joints of my backbone quite put back where they had been. But hell, I was lucky; I oughtn't to complain. I was just under the edge of it. What if you had six tons come down on you ka-plop the way my boss had? God!"

We turned, as I indicated that I must be getting back to the station. He sized me up scrutinizingly, as if I might be wanting to get away from him. "But I guess people like you don't see much of such things as that."

He added convincing ghastly details. He mentioned the boss's name. It had all occurred beneath the very hill on which I had grown up. I was on the point of telling him, of saying, "I believe we know each other. Don't you remember the time—?" But I caught myself. It would hurt too much. So I wished him well, slipped a bit of money into his hand, told him I was sorry I could not do better, and while he stood amazed and almost tearful at receiving more than he had asked for, I hurried away to the station.

Almost as soon as I had climbed the stairs to the long covered platform, a piercing beam of light shot athwart a slight curve to the westward in the edge of the town; and before there was time for the agent to do more than rush up and say, "Here they are; he usually opens her up about here," the towering dark hump of a locomotive that suggested unlimited power by its ease of motion shuddered by, and a brightly lighted train of fifteen cars or more came to a stop.

"Right on here," the Pullman conductor suggested, "if you don't mind, and walk back through, so we can hustle along. I'll have your porter come up and get the bags."

I had to walk almost the entire length of the train. After the dull light of the street and the station platform, the brightness was dazzling. There were sleeping-cars in which the berths had not yet been made down for the night filled with cheerful people who seemed not to have a care in the world; a lounge-car filled with other cheerful people—mostly women—who were the least bit boisterous in their drinking; a dining-car filled with yet others who dined well; and then other and other standard sleeping-cars and bedroom-cars with affluent-looking luggage and passengers in every berth and open bedroom.

"These must have some superior philosophy," I wanted to admit, as the contrast between what I had been seeing and what I now saw clamored for an explanation. "These have managed the facts of life better." Then suddenly all that was there before me seemed as utterly unreal as something specially extravagant created for a picture-theater.

I cleaned up a bit, dug a book from one of the bags, and started at once toward the dining-car. "Yes, went up two points," a man was saying as I passed his space. He had lop-ears, like the school comedian's.

The steward squeezed me over to an unoccupied chair next to the window—and next to a sizzling hot steam-pipe. The other three at the table were two women and a man who were returning from California. After I had ordered, I picked the book up from the window ledge and began to turn to the place where I had left off. There was a moment of silence as if the three had discovered a strange breed right at the table with them; then one of the women asked, "Oh, what was that book I meant to read on my way back? I had forgotten all about it. I wonder where it is." Otherwise, nothing much was said. The women exchanged a few words of disappointment over Hollywood, and the man grunted once or twice. When he grunted the second time, one of the women admonished him: "Well, what did you read the newspapers for if you didn't want to know whether stock had gone up or down?"

After they left, the three new ones who took their places

had not yet decided what they would have beyond their cocktails when I was ready to go.

Already our porter was making down the berths I walked on to the smoking-room at the other end of the car. It was deserted. I dropped down into the corner of the long leather seat and went on with my reading. But something that the Englishman who had written the book said about China made me think of the school comedian, and see a whole region active in mining coal and making pottery and producing bread.

I heard voices approaching. "The trouble with this God-damned country," the chief voice was saying just as somebody pushed the green portiere aside, and men—five of them eventually—began to file in, "is that everybody who has anything left is being taxed to death for these re-liefers."

I slid over close against the wall, and soon the five of them were in complete possession, with cigars slightly elevated, as if there could be no possible doubt about anything that anybody in the group chose to declare.

"My God!" the chief speaker went on. Then he smoked avidly as if an idea were just beyond the end of his cigar. "We've got to stop paying relief, that's all."

"All right!" I said, and slapped my book shut with enough decision to make a bit of a report and startle them into seeing that somebody else was present: "Let's begin next Monday morning. I've just been down in a coal region that I know pretty well where a thousand miners have been squeezed out of work by the installation of improved mechanical equipment in the mines. Now what are you going to do with them next Monday morning?"

"Next Monday morning? Oh, my God! Give us a little time. Give us six months."

"But you can't have six months. These men and their families must have something to eat next week."

The other four smoked and looked toward the floor out in the center of the room, but their spokesman squinted at me, turned his cigar over in his mouth a time or two, and then demanded: "Say, are you a socialist?"

"Why? Does a man who believes that people ought not to starve have to be a socialist?"

"Well," and he squinted his eyes and the whole of his big face into deeper lines as if he were trying to think and to be amiable at the same time, "it always looks a little suspicious, doesn't it?"

Two of the others laughed at this superior reply.

"But what would you do next Monday morning?"

One of the others in the group began to squirm as if he were already impatient of alien ideas. "I'll tell you what I'd do; by God, I'd chloroform about half of them—for all they are worth to anybody They're a shiftless, low-grade lot—the whole damned caboodle of them—if you want to know what I think of them."

I smiled in his direction. "Maybe you're the man I'm looking for. I'm trying to pick up some specially bright new miners. How much experience can you offer?"

"Not much, by God."

"Righto!"

All the while, one man had sat well back on the rounded leather seat by the door and smoked with extreme deliberation as if he were of the judicial mind. "Do you know," he began, and looked about calmingly, as if there might in fact be a question at issue, "I suppose this may sound cold-blooded, but I sometimes wonder if a first-class war would be such a bad thing for the country. It would speed things up for quite a while, and of course it would relieve the over-

## Parasite 93

crowding—if you want to face facts. But I half suspect"—this to me—"that you are one of these theorists who never want to face the facts."

"I suspect that you are right—those facts!"

When I saw that he had not caught my meaning, I re-opened my book. After a moment, the thick-set, good-natured, red-faced man who had thus far done nothing but maintain an unvarying smile said, as if he hoped I were not yet too far in the book to hear his conciliatory words: "I suppose, after all, there is nothing to do but feed them. But it does seem as if we ought to begin pretty soon to have a gradual tapering off."

Soon they were talking in slightly lower voice about their errand in Washington. If Charley—whoever Charley was—had been able to see the right people, and the right people did not get too wise, their scheme ought to turn out to be a pretty good thing.

My berth was toward the other end of the car, and when I went to it with the thought of reading in bed, the porter and the Pullman conductor were having an argument with a man of thirty or thirty-two about his ticket. He sat on the edge of the freshly made-down berth with a good-sized flask beside him, and drank away a bit unsteadily from a paper water-cup as if he were trying to ignore everybody about him. Two young women sat on the edge of their berths across the aisle and drank with slightly more self-command from the same kind of cups. A stately gray-haired woman stood by the Pullman conductor.

"Well, let me see your ticket, then," the conductor was demanding. "This lady says this is her berth that you are in."

"I'm not in her berth—wouldn't think of such a thing. It's my berth—No. 12. That's what my ticket said, and—

and that's all there is to it. These young ladies here were right across the aisle from me in No. 11 and No. 9—have been ever since we started. Right there, No. 11 and No. 9. That's what it says, if I'm any good at reading. I asked them to go forward with me and have a drink or two—and we did. When we came back we decided to have another, and I got this of my own here out of the bag, and so we've been having it. Now what's wrong with that?"

"I'm sorry, sir," said the conductor, trying to be impressive, "but I must see your ticket stub."

"I'm sorry, sir," the drunk replied, very successfully mimicking him, "but I can't let you. Why, I paid for this berth—No. 12—and I'm on my way over to New York to relax a little, and that's all there is to it."

"But this car doesn't go to New York; it goes to Washington."

The drunk fished in his pockets and found the stub of his Pullman ticket. "There you are, sir!" he said triumphantly. "Doesn't that say No. 12?"

"Yes, but No. 12 in the second car up ahead."

He made a pass or two before his eyes, as if he were puzzled. Then all became clear: "How could that be? These two young ladies were right across the aisle from me when I got on, and here they are right across the aisle from me now. So who's right? Tell me! Who's right?"

"Let me see your ticket stubs," the conductor asked of the two girls.

They found them.

"Sure!" the conductor assented. "They are up in the other car, too."

Suddenly his face revealed greater bewilderment than ever. He picked up the flask, looked at it as if he now for the first time noticed something alien about it, looked at the bag that stood open on the white sheets of the berth, put the flask back in, stood up with all the formality he could command, bowed deeply—as deeply as was safe—to the stately old lady, and said like a man of the world, "I am very sorry; I beg your pardon." Then as if he had thought of something bright, he added, "But it was very good!" and followed the young ladies forward.

Some time late in the night I awoke without being aware of any special reason. I tried to picture the train somewhere in the middle of Pennsylvania. How comfortable I was! I tried to think only of that. I listened to the steady purring buzz of the air-conditioner in my berth. I listened to the deep roar of the train. Sometimes it is pleasant to do that —while the serpentine miniature world to which one has entrusted one's self for the night sweeps like some dim earth-fettered comet through dark hills, over mountain-ranges, and down into broad valleys. But a train roaring along through the night is no place for a man who has been taking final leave of anybody.

I thought the roar seemed muffled. I pushed the shade up without snapping on the light, so that I could see into the darkness outside. We were gliding along the Susquehanna River, and snow was descending without bluster in great substantial flakes. I let my forehead and nose rest against the cold glass of the window and watched. There is something very decent about snow.

A moment or two and we were taking the sharp curve onto the picturesque many-arched stone bridge above Harrisburg. Five minutes later we were creeping through the snowy maze of tracks just outside the station. Men worked—a small army of them—with shovels and brooms and picks and torches and oil, trying to keep ahead of the snow, trying to have every switch in working order so that it could be thrown. As I saw them out there from my berth, they appeared to work in absolute silence. All over the eastern United States men like these were out at three or four in the morning, had been out all night, keeping tracks cleared and switches working so that people could have a good sleep while they were getting to Washington or New York or Philadelphia or Boston. What if some of them should grow careless and some switch—the one ahead of us, for instance—should not close? It was good to see them working so painstakingly out there, drawn together in cooperation by a mighty need.

I was in Washington in time for breakfast. Congressmen and Senators moved jauntily or with dignity toward the hotel dining-room as if they wished to be seen but not stopped. Men in smarter clothes called to them in slightly doubtful hail-fellow-well-met voices, and said with an accompanying wave of the arm that they would come round for a minute before they left town.

I hoped to see two or three friends who lived in other hotels. The lobbies in these were alive with the same kind of men. They were very deeply in earnest. They were much concerned. They were hoping to get something. I went to the Senate office building to make a five-minute personal call on a friend who had recently been elected to the Senate. The same kind of men filled every chair in the outer offices of his suite. It would take all day, all week, for him to see them and hear them.

"Tell him," I said to the administrative woman who was his secretary, "that if he cares to be interrupted for five minutes by a man who is not looking for anything, there is one such out here."

"He will fall on your neck!" she assured me.

I did not mean to take more than my five minutes. But

he insisted. "Let them wait. It's the first time I've had a chance to draw a free breath for two months."

We talked about some old friends. He showed me how as a freshman Senator he was getting into things—into the real work of carrying on a democracy. He was working till midnight or two or three o'clock every night.

He put an idea into my head. I would drop in on some other Senators and Congressmen whom I knew. I was not unused to the political atmosphere; I had grown up in it. Until recently two of my college teachers had represented my native state in the Senate. Seven of my college friends had come to the Lower House. I was well enough acquainted with the ways of lobbyists—casually acquainted with them. But it would be interesting to go into the matter a bit more systematically.

I spent the day in making calls. Between calls I wandered along corridors and glanced in at other offices.

"I am seeing them in the lump for once," I told a fellow native of the hills.

"My God!" was his only commentary.

I begged him to answer a question: "How many of them are asking for anything that it is the legitimate function of a government devoted to the general welfare to give?"

"Well," he replied, and leaned back in his chair while a hesitant smile played over his mobile face, "you know I am optimistic. After you have left out the tourists and the high-school youngsters from your home state who just want to be able to say when they go back home that they dropped in to see their Senator while they were in Washington—and usually they don't ask for anything more important than your autograph—I should say about one in fifty! I only hope I haven't made the percentage outrageously high."

The next morning I went to see a Cabinet member whom

I knew. Could I come back in an hour and a half? He was very busy. Sitting all about in his outer offices were the reasons why. Some of them seemed to be good reasons, but most of them carried the unconcealable expression of the man who knows he is going to ask for something that he may not get, and perhaps ought not to have.

I enjoyed a profitable hour and a half. I wandered through the corridors of the great building where the work of the department was developed in detail. Thousands of men and women were working quietly, conscientiously, efficiently. They were bringing into form the information necessary to the intelligent passing of legislative measures. They were doing important scientific and economic research that would affect the lives of many millions of people directly, and the entire population of the country indirectly. They were educating the people in the ways of using this new knowledge to advantage. No one could see this work carried on without experiencing a new respect for the democratic ideal.

As I was leaving the building after I had spent fifteen or twenty minutes with the Cabinet member, a vigorous man of forty asked with genial abruptness: "Do you know him—the Secretary?"

"Slightly."

"Like him?"

"Yes, he's a great fellow."

He, too, was going to take a taxi—and to the same hotel. Yes, he thought it was a very nice hotel—homey, and all that.

Before the end of the day it was known that I knew Thus-and-so; that I got about over the country. Men who said they had seen me more or less in the hotel dropped down in some comfortable chair near mine in the lobby and wanted to know how I found things—out in the open spaces. For no sufficient reason I was invited to several dinners; I was made to know how easy it is to organize a man's reputation—especially when he is a writer—and put him out in front, if only he stands for the right things. I was apprised of the niceties of a new age—definitely, but in the casual manner that would not offend my intelligence if I already knew, or my self-respect if I were still ignorant. I had seen pressure groups at work for many a year, but I was assured that their technique had been refined—refined to the point where it was very difficult for anybody to see the difference between what they were after and the general welfare—if there were really any difference to be seen.

The day I went on homeward I sat for an hour in the hotel and read. Two men came and sat just behind me, oblivious of my presence. One of them was the promoter of some gadget that he had hoped to have the United States Army adopt.

"Well, so far as you can make out," his friend asked in great sympathy, "just where is the trouble?"

"Oh, as a matter of fact, I think it trickles all the way down from the Secretary."

"How much could you afford to sell it for—I mean a single one?"

"Oh, we could sell it at a fair profit for around ninety cents. So I figured that if we could get it adopted for say something like a dollar forty, we could make a pretty nice thing of it."

Upstairs—there was an unused connecting door in my room—a disgusted tearful man in the room adjoining was telling a friend that if he couldn't get some action on his scheme pretty soon, he would have to go back home and go to work. He had been waiting around for more than three months and hadn't been able to see anybody yet—anybody that counted.

I took the Friday afternoon "Lobby Limited" to New York. The two men and the woman who sat at the luncheon table with me in the dining-car were returning from a brief holiday in Florida, but they had just spent a couple of days in Washington, where the men had to see somebody about something. "You know I think it's an awfully clever idea," the man in the sky-blue shirt and double-breasted coat declared. "He says that all he needs now is the taste. You see, it's an established fact that dogs like scraps from the table better than any dog food that has ever been invented. Well, he has a marvelous food—simply marvelous—but the dogs still prefer the scraps—because of the taste. He has more than twenty—think of it, more than twenty—research men at work on the problem of the taste—Ph.D.'s from Harvard and Cornell and everywhere. If they can find the taste to put in the food that will make the dogs prefer it to the scraps, why his fortune is made. You see how it will be: every woman in the country will chuck everything from the table into the garbage-can and *buy* food for her doggie. It would help business, too."

I could have contributed a word to the conversation, for I had visited a laboratory—possibly the one they had in mind—where the best brains of the country were at work on the same problem. But when I glanced up as if I might speak, nobody's look included me, and I remained content to listen.

Florida, it seemed, was enjoying a return to prosperity. Miami alone was doing wonders. Monte Carlo? Why, Monte Carlo was nothing more than a Scotch Presbyterian bazaar compared with Miami. They were betting a half-million a day on the ponies and dogs alone. "The state racing commission thinks it will be a million next year. It would be fine if this spirit could spread to other states."

I learned something more about government, too. "Why do taxpayers have to plank down their money for somebody to pay to these Indians? Why shouldn't Indians have to take their chances, just the same as the rest of us?"

"Yes, and why not apply that to farmers?" the man who sat beside me wanted to know. "Paying them for plowing under their pigs! Plain stealing!"

The woman half-believed that I was listening—a male. She wanted to launch out and show her acquaintance with current affairs. "Don't you think farmers are a stupid lot, anyway? Joe, Hildegarde's head gardener, *fertilizes* his soil. If the farmers would all do that, there wouldn't be any need of all this A.A.A., or whatever they are calling it by this time, would there?"

When it seemed that nothing more was to be gleaned, I walked back through the train to the observation-car. Every chair was taken—even the one at the writing-desk. Men with wide-open eyes and relaxed cheeks inclined toward each other, made sweeping gestures with hands that held half-empty tall glasses, and spoke with great positiveness as if no word they might utter should be missed. In the singing roar of a train that was making seventy or eighty miles an hour, and the incessant sharp lurches of the rear car as the rest of the train made a whipcracker of it, I caught only occasional words—"General Motors"—"If we could only get him"—"New England Power"—"Tel and Tel"—"Nickel Plate." The man who sat right at my knees in a low-slung chair where I stood by the door was almost in tears. "God, think of that! If it had gone through, he would have cleaned up two million dollars!"

I walked forward through the train till I came to a smoking-room in one of the older-style parlor-cars. A man of early middle age who looked as if he lived much of the time out of doors sat smoking a pipe and reading a journal on architecture.

"You're the first man I've seen on this train," I began without fearing the consequences of interrupting him, "who seems to be interested in anything essential."

He took his pipe from his mouth and looked up as if he had not been at all taken unawares. "I thought I was the only one—till just now."

He moved over in suggestion that I sit down.

We talked. What I wanted to know was this: Suppose you could devise some giant perforated flapjack turner that would let all the solid productive people go down through and hold the soft parasites on top, and were to heave the fluff into the Atlantic Ocean, how many people would be left?

"In the region of New York, not enough to start the subway tomorrow morning!"

He laughed. "Oh, it wouldn't be quite so bad as that. As a matter of fact, we have more mills and legitimate commercial agencies in New York than we get credit for having. But I'm afraid if you carry your experiment through there'll be a lot of empty offices downtown and up around Murray Hill."

We talked all the way into New York. "Come and have a bite to eat with me, and we'll finish," he suggested. "I'm a bach. We can drop your luggage at your hotel, and go right on over to mine."

We still had much to talk about at ten o'clock. But I needed a quiet hour of reading in some book that possessed great reality—if I had one of that kind—and then a long night of sleep. I was coming down to the New York area some of these times—almost any time now—and find out what percentage were workers and what percentage parasites. Then I would go to some other cities, and eventually I would prepare a map showing the relative density of parasites to the square mile in the different parts of the country. That would constitute pleasant occupation for a long time.

Up in my room on the thirty-second floor, after I was all through with a hot tub and was ready for the quiet reading, I discovered that one of my bags—a small Irish kit bag—was not there. In its place was another, of the same size and color.

I called the porter and told him that one of the boys had been careless. He was very positive. There had been no carelessness. He did not permit any. The bags were the ones put out of the cab.

I called the Pullman Company's Lost and Found office. Some realist in this office answered the telephone. He suggested that it might have been a three-cornered trade—that the owner of the bag I had might not be the man who had mine at all. Anyhow, the chances were that he was on his way to Montreal or California by this time.

The hotel's house officer came up—an ex-Marine whom I at once liked.

"We'll go through it," he said simply. "We might find a clue."

We found it. By midnight I was on my way out to an address in the region of 204th Street.

They were kind Jewish people of sixty or sixty-five, very certain that the fault must have been theirs, very sorry that I had to make the long trip out at midnight. We chatted. Yes, he was in business, a nice little business of his own—

in music. There was one worker to be credited to the New York area. I had gone a long way out to find him, but there he was.

My enthusiasm was reduced a little on the way back. Our taxicab was stopped by a cordon of policemen and a vast throng. Some gangsters had insisted that they have a rake-off from a man's restaurant income, and he was resentful. He made trouble for himself and the police. And we had to wait a while.

The next morning my mind was restless and sketchy. I made a little schedule of some appointments that I had to keep, but my thought kept running back to what the architect and I had talked about. Some day I meant to carry out that experiment—perhaps not so extensively as I had at first planned, but extensively enough.

In the afternoon as I walked along Fifth Avenue near Forty-second before I crossed over to the station, I decided, just as the slenderest sort of little preliminary to a real test, to ask fifty people as I met them what their occupations were. In the interest of personal safety, I thought I had better accost only men.

"Pardon me," I said to the first one, "I am required to make a little study in personnel. Would you be good enough to coöperate by telling me your occupation?"

"Counselor on public relations," he answered, scarcely stopping. The next was a stock-broker; the next a real-estate broker; another was a perfumer; another kept kennels; another was a liquor rectifier; another dealt in balloon advertising; another was interested in utilities holding companies; another was an expert on tomorrow's market; another was a Protestant minister; another was an estate economist—"tell 'em where to put their money so their kids will inherit the highest possible percentage of it"; another said he wasn't much of anything anymore; another was a dog caterer.

"Oh," I said to this last man, "perhaps you are just the person I am looking for." His eyes opened at the prospect of business. "How much do you charge for the delivery daily of the diet of a Great Dane?"

"Oh! Oh! A Great Dane! He eats more than a man! He eats more than two men! He is a terrible eater!"

Then he got down to business. "He weighs a hundred fifty—maybe a hundred seventy-five?"

"Something like that," I assented.

"Well, maybe I could do it for thirteen-fifty a week. After the first week I could know."

When I told him I was only thinking of some coal miners out in Ohio, he shrugged his shoulders and looked puzzled.

As I came up to the station, two swarthy men stood talking together in front of Thompson's restaurant. Perhaps I would have time for one more answer. I had not tried any of their kind.

"What we do?" one of them said in broken English as the other turned and walked away a few steps. "Why? You want to go into business with us?"

I said I was not thinking of that, and started on. He jerked his head in my direction while I was still in hearing, and said to his pal, with a smile that was more pity than contempt: "He is funny; he must be from somewhere else."

In the observation-car on the way home, two men who held tickets for Providence and talked about the easy money they believed could be made pretty soon now, drank so many times to the health of two women who had chanced to sit at the luncheon table with them, that they almost changed their plans for the entire week-end. But when the women got off at Westerly, the two men insisted that I come over and join them. Couldn't they see that I was up to some nice little game, myself? It was written all over me. And what especially did I think of the state of the nation? So much depended on that. When I told them—perhaps with too much guile—that we seemed to be in need of some thinking—a little thinking—one of them said—the one who was in the rubbery state: "But the trouble with the G— G— God-damned country is that we people who use our heads are so hopelessly in the minority—the submerged five per cent, you might say. Isn't that so?"

## vii

## Heat

"BUT couldn't you have that other train stop at Emporia and let me off?" I asked the General Passenger Agent in Chicago. "That would allow me to start several hours later."

He gave his head the slightest little twitch of a doubtful shake. "There are only two people in the world that that train ever stops in Emporia for: William Allen White—you know, the author—and—"

"I'll be glad to be the third one," I argued, as amiably as I knew how.

He looked up into my face. He considered.

"I travel several thousand miles every year on your line."

I thought I felt him wavering. Then he made a little movement as if he had decided. "All right, I'll take a chance." And with a firm hand he wrote out the authorization for the conductor. "I can't say that I'd exactly like to get down there ahead of time myself right now."

"Hot, eh?"

"According to the evening paper, 104° and still going up. Of course, that report may have been inaccurate—you know, cooked up and sent out by the Chamber of Commerce in some other town. There's been a lot of dirt done Emporia in that way Take this saying, for instance, that it's always hot in Emporia. It simply is not true. There's nearly always a long stretch of about a week around Christmas or New Year's Day when the thermometer hardly ever gets above eighty."

Two nights later, Emporia was living up to its high repute. The stocky little fan in my room was all that it was advertised to be. But what could a fan do when the air outdoors was just as hot as anywhere else, and the walls of the building were an oven, and the mattress on my bed was an electric pad? In the end, I abandoned all thought of sleeping and tried to amuse myself by listening to the two o'clock conversation of the men employed in the filling stations and garages that hemmed the hotel in on three sides, while they sat out front to rest for a time and to imagine that they were cooling off.

The next forenoon before I left town I spent an hour with William Allen White. When I saw a new sign, Gazette Building, Air Conditioned, or something to that effect just ahead down the street, I was cheered at the thought of one cool hour. But the new building, I discovered, was only for tender-skinned doctors and the like. William Allen White was in the old uncooled building next door. He sat at his typewriter back in the depths of the place hammering out an editorial—with beads of sweat all over his cherubic face and in the edges of his whitening hair. In the intervening second or two before he looked up and noticed me as I approached him, I thought I must now be seeing him very much as he had worked when he had pounded out his famous editorial on "What's the Matter with Kansas?" or that other editorial, which should bring him an even ampler immortality, on his daughter Mary after she had been killed by the low-hanging branch of a tree while she was out horseback riding.

When I came down from his office a thermometer in a shaded doorway registered 106°. Over at the railroad station, when I walked out on the long platform that is surrounded by so much open space that it always seems to say, "Now you are to have room; now you are on the prairie," a breeze as hot as if it were right off the top of a stove caught me full in the face. As soon as the train stretched its dark length before us in the burning sun, I fled to the cool interior of a sleeping-car. The great quiet that chanced to prevail for a moment somehow also suggested vast distances in a region where everything is done on a grand scale.

At Newton I walked on the shaded side of the platform while the train changed engines. A man who had just covered the western half of the state was in a talkative mood. "Everything is burning up!" he declared. "I don't see how anything can be saved now—and in another week or so, nothing can."

When we were once again on our way southward, it was easy to see what he had meant. Women as well as men were working desperately in wheat-fields that stretched away to the horizon in every direction. Wheat had escaped the worst effects of the drought. And most of it had been harvested. But some of it had not. The women and men were hauling grain from threshing-machines that piled the bleached straw high in great shapeless mountains of pale buff, or collecting the heaps of filled bags dropped by combines whose sputtering tractors spouted short jets of blue smoke and flame as they crept swiftly over parching fields of yellow. Where there was pasture land, cattle already beginning to look a bit underconditioned wandered from one "tank" to another in the low corners of fields, snortingly shook their heads in disgust and bewilderment at finding no water, and then with the most hopeful steer of the herd leading the file, started in to do it all over again. In a great corn-field that we passed, many of the blades had already "fired" until they were as colorless as wrapping paper. In an area planted to alfalfa, a train just ahead of us had started a fire which was sweeping across the fields with dull flames and hot-looking smoke like a fire in prairie grass.

At a stop just before we crossed over into Oklahoma I swung off to walk the platform while the train loaded mail and express. The heat from the pavement caught me round the ankles as if I were on top of a kiln.

"Pretty hot!" I said, still interested in heat as something to be observed and talked about, to a man who smiled when he saw me wilting.

"I'll say it's hot!" He mopped his face and fat neck. "Soon be too hot to sweat; then we'll just sizzle, just fry. I've lost five pounds already this week."

"And I have to go on down into Oklahoma."

Immediately he became fraternal. "Now see here, brother, I wouldn't worry one minute about that. I come from down there, and as a matter of fact our state is usually cooler. May seem a funny thing to you, since we're down nearer the equator. But my guess is that you'll find it quite a little more comfortable down there. And you know we always have cool nights."

He was right. When I arrived in Oklahoma City that

afternoon at five the thermometer at the north entrance of the hotel registered only 104°.

Oklahoma City is always surprising. You are never quite prepared to see what you find there, no matter how many times you have been there before. The hotel that I prefer is in itself a surprise. It does not belong there. It belongs in New York—not only because it seems to have been built in New York, but because it affords a roominess and a composure that hotel guests in New York are always praying for and never finding. When I went up to my favorite room on the twenty-third floor and the bell-boy threw the door open, the room too was somehow not just as I had remembered it. It was better. Somebody who knew how to make a room restful had supervised the decoration and furnishing more in detail than I had noticed on other visits. And when the boy threw open the heavy steel-sash windows with a mighty heave that let a hot gale sweep into the room and through it, and I walked over to have a look, first to the east and then to the south, I was surprised again, for the whole city seemed unlike its former self. In fact, it was. It always is.

Tulsa, its rival for state supremacy, is incomparably more attractive. But Tulsa gives an impression of stability, of a certain Fifth Avenue sense of well-being. Hasn't Tulsa two thousand—or is it three thousand?—offices devoted to oil?

Well, Oklahoma City has the oil itself. Off to the south are thousands of new houses where workers live; close to the hotel and on to the north for a few blocks are skyscrapers —including a slightly reduced Empire State Building—that seem to have been whisked away from some Atlantic Seaboard congested area where space was an acute problem and transplanted by some blindfolded god or goddess in a region where space is the last thing on earth that anybody should need to think about; and on to the northwest are areas of spacious residences that exude abundance. But oil bespatters all these diversified parts into a unity. The countless steel derricks that stretch away to the high horizon on the southeast reach also right through the southern residential section to the heart of the city in such bewildering numbers that one cannot help wondering how the surface of the earth provides room for them all. And if the derricks themselves thin out before they get north across the city, the profits from them only increase. Oil is flowing—still; the city must be made bigger—especially bigger than Tulsa. What if all sorts of incongruous juxtapositions of things do result? What if I do stand at the window of this metropolitan tower on a hot afternoon and hear roosters that crow lazily somewhere as if I were at the window of a farm-house? Changes are rapid. Much is to be done. And every time I look from my high hotel window, somebody seems to have done some of it. If it is not a handsome new railroad station or two, it is at least a few hundred more oil derricks.

Up there where I was, far above hot pavements, the air actually became cooler by midnight. With a large reversible fan purring directly above my bed, and with a tempestuous breeze whipping through my room and rattling anything that was loose, I found it possible to sleep. But I was awake at daybreak. High temperature was stimulating, especially when the east was directly in front of my eyes. While thousands of blinking lights in the interminable forest of oil wells paled slowly, I could see the light of an approaching sun grow clearer. The coloring was framed in my window: from the top down, very deep blue, blue green, dull glowing, a strip of lead, a sliver of brightness, and then, just at the bottom close over the window-sill, the distant dark high rim of the earth far beyond the glimmering oil field. A moment later a ray of sun caught me full in the face and in the one eye that was not buried in the pillow. It was a terrifying red sun that suggested pure heat

For days I made Oklahoma City my headquarters. Regularly I went out into other parts of the state in the morning when odorous asphalt was bubbling and melting, and came back in the evening in time to spend at least the second half of the night in my somewhat cool tower. At Edmond I stood in the sick garden of a friend and ate undersized peaches as sweet as honey—attested by the bees—that were falling prematurely from a tree withering in the drought. At Bartlesville the thermometer registered 108°. It was at Bartlesville, while I waited in the railroad station one evening for a train which was late, that a stout Osage squaw and her daughter, each sporting some gorgeous, filmy-looking covering indicative of their nation, walked in and coolly reserved two drawing-rooms for a trip to Washington, D.C. As they went out, the daughter, who was graceful and beautiful in her tribal covering, caught her high-heeled shoe on the door-sill. No damage was done, and they climbed into their long-wheel-base automobile and drove away.

Then one hot day I had to break camp for a longer journey through the western end of the state. I traveled over rolling plains that were burning up, past range after range of unforgettable, mountain-like sand dunes that looked even hotter than the prairie, over low red mesas and around smaller, truncated cones which reproduced in miniature all the variegated coloring of the Grand Canyon, through ravine-like hollows with trees in them that looked cool from a distance, but hot and dried-up when one came close to them, and in the evening stopped in the melting little city of Clinton—an interesting combination of railroad center and wild-west street scene in a movie. It is better than that. For the crowds of self-respecting people who fill the streets after supper give the impression of a very solid reality. They have faced something. And they glance at you casually without undue self-consciousness as if they had sturdiness of will and honest sensibility in the right balance to face something again.

I fell in with them, went everywhere they went, lost myself among them I went to the street carnival that was in town—where I soon wearied; to the chief movie theater —where it was too hot to stay; to pop-corn stands and soda-fountains and candy shops, and, finally, to one café specially advertised with paper icebergs as being air-conditioned. The refrigerating plant did not seem to be working.

"What's the matter with your cooling system?" I asked the cowboy-looking girl in New York clothes who stood behind the desk.

"Gone haywire," she replied a bit languidly as if she had answered the question several times already. "Too much of a strain."

She looked me over. "Say, I can't quite figure you out. Do you mind telling me what your line is?"

"Oh—," I replied, trying to find some easy explanation, "notions, I suppose you might say."

"Gee, boy, the next time you make this town I wish you'd bring me a nice little air-conditioner that you can carry around with you—you know, in your handbag, or maybe in your hat, so as you can just go cool anywhere."

"A kind of filmy bridal-veil of frosty cloud around you—"

"Sure! And a little of the frost sticking to you. When so many people still need work, why hasn't somebody thought of that?"

I passed a gaming joint, and dropped in. A little wild-

## Heat 115

west shooting might take my mind off the heat. But the place was filled with honest-looking, humorous men, most of them in work-clothes, who played with a cordial, chaffing respectfulness not to be encountered at a bridge party. The policy of the house was set forth on a large placard:

> Positively no swearing.
> No drunks allowed.
> If you can't pay, don't play.
> Dealer gets last hand.

Over an adjoining lunch-counter I saw a placard that I had seen in a little restaurant in Kansas:

> Don't use too much sugar, and stir like hell. We don't mind the noise.

The mere name of the town's chief hotel—the Calmez —had somehow suggested heat. There were some cool-looking, romantic murals in the lobby, but they only aroused my suspicion. And when I had unlocked the one room left in the house that evening—on the leeward side of the building, close over some spreading hot roof—I knew that my suspicions had not been groundless. It was hotter than any farm kitchen—and there was only one window. I went back to test it out a little at half-past eleven, but it was unbearable. To put in time, I walked westward along a tinsel-looking street that was bedecked with pennants and streamers announcing the carnival, the special sale of this or that, the candidacy of politicians. When I came to quiet, I sat for an hour on some church steps that rose high above the level of the sidewalk. Along the horizon in the southwest there was lightning. But it was infrequent and feeble.

I went back to my room a little before one. The heavy,

loose-jointed fan filled the room with its rumbling and squeaking, but it was not getting much fresh air in from the outside. I lay sleepless and sweating throughout the night, and listened to the fan. The next morning I was as limp as if I had spent the time in a tub of hot water.

At noon the temperature was higher than ever. I looked forward hungrily to the trip back to Oklahoma City in an air-conditioned train. But the thermostat in our car was up to 81°.

"Can't you get her any cooler?" I asked the conductor when he came through.

"Sure!" he answered, ready to defend his road. "We can make her as cool as you like. But the passengers have been complaining. It's so hot outside that 70° or 72° is too much of a shock—when they get on and get off, both."

Despite my need of sleep I was awake with a strange, throbbing wakefulness as if I were dosing myself with quinine in the early stages of a fever. I heard every word that passengers uttered in their conversation about the danger of high prices. I looked out at the window and saw every detail of a landscape that was burning up.

The train swung into the edge of the wide valley of the Canadian River, which makes its way southeastward across this part of the state without troubling too much about keeping in the same channel from year to year or getting all of itself under bridges that have been built out of special deference to it. The dry soil of the valley as far ahead as the eye could see was so vibrant with heat waves that it seemed on the point of bursting into flame. Whirlwinds—miniature tornadoes that sometimes carried their funnel or spout of dust aloft fifty or a hundred feet—were continually originating, moving slowly with intermittent spurts of new motion across baked fields of shriveling corn or stunted young cotton, and then with a puff or two, dying out as abruptly as they had begun. Once the train was held at a crossing tower for a few minutes. Right alongside in the field came an army of black men, women, and children, with enormous straw hats drawn down close over their shoulders, hoeing the dusty soil round the famishing cotton desperately as if some irresistible demon of heat had got into their sluggish blood.

I had to go south to Ardmore for the night, down near the Texas border. I had never seen Ardmore. It might be the most perfect oil town ever built. But it was farther south —nearer the equator—and I could not relish the thought. The heat was getting into my own blood.

As I walked into my room at the hotel at nine-thirty, I jumped at the sudden, heavy chiming of a clock somewhere near. Why did clocks have to strike at night?

I went to one of the windows and looked out. Scarcely more than two blocks away was a great illuminated dial as large as a full moon. It stared at me.

I called up the desk. I must have another room—back from things where clocks could not get at me. I had once covered Ohio, Michigan, and Indiana when some big courthouse clock had banged away every night just outside my window. Wasn't it easy enough to see that clocks had got my goat? Besides, tonight I was half-crazed by heat and sleeplessness.

The clerk sought to comfort me by telling me that the clock did not strike. Anyhow, there was not a vacant room in the secluded side of the hotel—or in any other part of it, for that matter. He had reserved this one for me because it was a large corner room with wide windows.

The clock did not strike! Of course it struck. He had become accustomed to it—and immune. Hadn't I heard it at nine-thirty just as I came into the room—in a little dido of a tune just as if it were warming up for something important? A strange clock if it struck the half-hours and omitted the hours! It would be pleasanter to sit on the curb out somewhere in the night air than to lie there in a sweltering room waiting hour after hour for a clock to strike. But I knew of something that I could do that would be better than that: I could take a late train, ride in a cool berth till half the night was gone, and then change somewhere and ride back in another in time for the next day. It would be a little expensive, but it would put me out of reach of the ungodly clock.

I sat down on the floor by the window to wait. Once when I glanced toward the bright dial it suddenly swelled out to ten times its normal size. A moment later it was not half as large as the face of my watch. A hot shiver swept over me, and a flash of something rushed from my chest to my neck and cheeks and temples as if my heart had suddenly decided to hurry. I felt my pulse. Ninety-two! Well, what of it? Weren't we having hot weather?

But I could not dismiss the thought from my mind. I am not certain that I wanted to do so. I recalled Rudyard Kipling, and pondered what heat did to men in India. I remembered the long lists of deaths from heat that I had been seeing in the newspapers every day now for a week. I had read only that morning in Clinton about a man crazed by the heat and the loss of his crops who had seized an axe and slain his family and himself.

It was quarter to ten.

I would be very calm for fifteen minutes and content myself with watching the long minute-hand creep with imperceptible little jerks right up to the hour. That would slow down my circulation.

But all I did was to hold the tempo of my burning mind in check unnaturally and pile up an irresistible uneasiness. By the time the hand was at four minutes to ten, some terrible doom seemed to hang on the approaching hour, whether the clock struck or not. Let it strike! It would relieve the suspense. I would do what I had thought of doing: take that late train—if there was one—and ride until I could just take another that would somehow bring me round to Durant, only forty or fifty miles from Ardmore, by ten o'clock the next morning.

The hand was at the hour. It would have to get just past before it started the whirring that measured the number of strokes. It moved past! In silence it just floated along as if it were carried by white clouds in a summer sky.

I felt as if I had no bones in my body. And when at last I moved, and then got up to go to the office to ask somebody about this hallucination of clocks striking that had taken possession of me, I felt as if I had no muscles either, and as if I required none. Only when I stepped into the elevator and heard a half-dozen high-pressure salesmen God-damning the government did I experience a certain return to life.

"Say," the clerk began when I walked up to the desk, "you must have thought I was lying to you about that clock. I just now learned that somebody had been fussing around with the bells in this church right out the street here a little ways, and I guess that must have been what you heard."

Durant the next day consisted of two or three impressions. The most vivid one was that of a gang of young Federal student relief-workers, stripped to the waist, the sweat streaming down over their faces and over their sun-browned muscular bodies, as they waded about in the soft cement which they were shaping into an outdoor theater. Next to that in clearness was the feel of the gust of heat that swept the station platform when I walked out on it to take a train that was to carry me to Muskogee, and send me from there over among the rough northeastern hills to Tahlequah, the seat of the Cherokees.

"Well," I reflected as I slowly ate iced watermelon in the cool dining-car, "at least there is nothing new to dread; nothing could be hotter than Durant."

But Tahlequah was. I did not know that human beings could carry on the ordinary pursuits of life in a place as hot as Tahlequah was late that afternoon. The thermometer stood no higher than it had stood in Bartlesville or Emporia. But in both these places there had been a breeze. Even a hot breeze causes a little evaporation. And here in Tahlequah, tucked so cosily among the rough hills, there was not even a hot breeze. I could not see a leaf stirring.

The chief street hugs the base of the hill on one side of a small flat area on which the court-house stands. I assumed that it was the court-house; I investigated only far enough to receive assurance that there was no clock anywhere about it that struck. The little hotel where I was to stay fronted this open area on a side street and faced the afternoon sun. The woman at the desk when I registered thought the room might be endurable by ten o'clock. But I was skeptical.

Since no place was cool, I walked along the chief street to see the town. Everywhere there were ice-cream parlors, soda-fountains, and luncheonettes. All of them were busy, and in nearly all of them radios or phonographs barked or syncopated. One de luxe establishment proclaimed that it was cool. I hurried in. It was not. But since no other place seemed to be, I stayed and ate fruit sherbets and drank cold limeade. The radio contributed an endless melodic number in which there was a frequently recurring refrain in deep bass voice that somehow caused me to see stolid Osage Indians that I had talked with over in the northern part of the state, and to hear what I thought must have been the surly low bellow of buffaloes maddened by heat and thirst.

I sat for an hour and sweltered, content to do nothing more than let my eyes record whatever chanced to come before them: lusty, good-natured, bantering students from the college out at the edge of town; workingmen heavy with the odor of sweat who glanced about half-timidly, half-defiantly, as if they were not in such places every day; and bevies of short, attractive Cherokee girls who said in their bright looks, "Yes, to be sure, we know the world is burning up; but life is interesting and must not be missed."

When I went out, whole families of Indians lounged at full length on the fading grass under the young trees on the court-house lawn. I remembered that I had seen some of them there when I first arrived. There were stalwart, over-sized men, short women, and many sizes and shapes of swarthy children—all as immobile as logs. They knew how to keep cool.

The Cherokees seem to have mastered many of the arts of living. They settled in this region after they had been driven from every other habitation farther east by whites who were zealous in having everybody become like themselves or perish. Here the Cherokees asked only that they be left in peace to live from the soil and bring up their children according to the great traditions of their nation.

And now, ironically, it is their racial strength of character that threatens their racial existence. White men have discovered that Cherokee women are most acceptable wives. Many of the women are beautiful with a subtle beauty that springs not so much from shapeliness of body or aesthetic features of face as from qualities of spirit accumulated in ten thousand years—or fifty thousand—that shine through in the face. At the dinner table that evening, where I went more to watch and to forget the heat than to partake of food, an old Cherokee woman of eighty or so sat opposite me. She was one of the most civilized persons I have ever seen. She was unobtrusively cheerful. She was self-possessed—in everything she said and did. She expressed her ideas—and it was clear enough that they were her own—with an intelligence that lighted up the whole of her wrinkled, closely checked face. And she listened as if she were quite certain that nothing which anybody was going to say would catch her unawares and disturb her unnecessarily.

In the evening I sat out in front of the little hotel for two hours. Something slightly cooler than the day temperature drifted in from the oak-covered hills. I decided to try my room. There was no fan to stir the motionless hot air. I threw myself on the bed to see if it were possible to live through a night of such heat.

In ten minutes I knew in some vague, terrifying way that I was confronting an issue: heat and my life had become wholly incompatible.

I lifted my hand and let my thumb and forefinger rest on the sides of my throat. My blood seemed not to be circulating, but boiling—churning wildly through my veins at two beats to the second.

I felt dizzy when I went to the telephone to call up the college president for whom I was to speak the next morning and tell him that it would be impossible for me to fill the engagement. He was surprised that I was already in town. I must come right out to his house on the campus. The temperature out there would be several degrees lower. A guest-room awaited me. He would be down for me in five minutes.

## *Heat*

When he came he took a second look at me and offered the simple admonition: "You had better go easy."

In the guest-room there was at least a faint circulation of cooler air, and spaciousness, and books in the bright circle of light on the bedside table—books placed there by somebody who knew books. And outside my window among the trees there was perfect quiet. By one o'clock I felt a growing calm. By two o'clock I slept.

But it seemed that I had just gone to sleep when I was awakened by a startling image of the hills I had grown up in a thousand miles away the better part of a half-century before. I was aware of a strangely unreal but very familiar music of birds singing. And the room seemed full of light.

I turned my head a little toward the window. Day had already come and a dozen Kentucky cardinals in tree-tops and high shrubbery were taking advantage of the slight morning drop in temperature. Soon they were reinforced by two mocking-birds. I did not sleep again. The friendly, confident voices of the cardinals filled my memory with so many interesting matters that I had no desire to waste time by drifting back to unconsciousness. It was pleasant not to sleep, yet not to move, not to make effort—to do as the Indians had done.

Three hours later students were hustling in every direction along campus paths. In yet another hour I was up and standing before hundreds of them in an auditorium that the night had not cooled. But they were so successful in disregarding the heat that for an hour I was almost successful in disregarding it myself.

Later I stood before one of the two Indian murals in the hallway of the "old" building of the college. Buffaloes strained every muscle and every nerve in their desperate efforts to escape from Indians who were riding up alongside, gaining inch by inch, with spears already uplifted, or who were close enough to drive spears home with mighty thrusts as the confusion of flying hoofs became ever the least bit more intense. There it was—the desperation of the hunted that I had come to feel in the heat. In my great effort to be free of something that was everywhere and enveloped me, I felt an undeniable ebbing away of all the energy of mind and body that I had taken for granted since I could remember. Students moved up and down the stairway, ceased their philandering and became a little silent when they saw me looking at the painting, or spoke with great friendliness as if they had discovered in me some special ally of theirs. They were hopeful with a solid energy that I had lost.

That afternoon a young professor took me out to a summer camp on a rocky cliff a few hundred feet sheer above a good-sized river—the Illinois, strangely. We sat in an open lookout where an occasional breeze fanned us warmly, and watched hot cattle deep in the valley directly beneath us trying to keep cool by wading back and forth through the river where the water was not quite deep enough to make them swim, and listened from time to time to the shouts and hoots of boys enjoying the river where some dry-looking trees leaned far out above the water, while we talked about the poetry of Edwin Arlington Robinson. Directly in front of me, a little farther up the valley in the burning cornfields, the same impotent miniature dust tornadoes that I had seen in unending procession two days before whirled into being one after the other, and then died away.

In the evening I rode back to Muskogee in a shuddering gasoline train of two cars that had been standing out in the sun all day. As we made our way through deep hollows and around rough hills toward the more open country, farmers stood with their wives before their houses in brief after-supper respite and surveyed the destruction that the drought was bringing inescapably. In twenty-four hours there had been a change in the looks of the corn.

Both the atmosphere and my mind seemed to be abnormally clear. For I not only saw everything, but everything made a sharp impression. I could still today sketch accurately a half-breed in his best clothes who walked along a mere wagon track of a road through scrub oak and undergrowth by the railroad right-of-way, and the sour look he gave me when he saw that I watched him from the little train as it slowly climbed a grade; and, a few hundred yards farther along, a dark-skinned girl of sixteen or seventeen, with her shiny face half concealed by some overhanging branches, who watched down the road expectantly. As we rounded a high hill an old man talked to his daughter and wife and pointed off toward the southwest at something higher than the horizon. I followed the direction of his extended arm, and far beyond the flattening hills I saw clouds standing high with their tips still lighted by the setting sun. Since we were moving toward them, I watched them as they swiftly changed their contour and their color. Once I thought I saw a quiver of light deep in the dark recesses of one of them. A few minutes later when the sun had gone completely, the lightning was clearly visible. It was fascinating, as the hot train and the refreshing clouds pressed on toward each other, to watch the swift changes that were everywhere taking place. Moment by moment the thunder-heads stood higher in the sky. Soon in the growing darkness the whole southwest was aquiver with light.

By the time the train was in Muskogee and I had checked some luggage, a storm was imminent. I wondered if I might have time to walk uptown and back.

"How long do you think it will be before it breaks?" I inquired of a seasoned old man on the station platform.

"Well, you can be sure of one thing, it'll be long enough," he answered a bit hopelessly.

"But there's plenty of lightning—and thunder, and clouds."

"Don't mean nothin' at all." He looked me over as if I must be pretty soft. "They just come along once in a while to hector people."

Then he became scientific. "You see, this is how it is: the sun has been borin' into the face of the earth until it's so God-damned hot that when the clouds do bring some real water along, it all goes back up in the form of steam before it can get all the way down. You just watch—and see for yourself."

We sat together on a bench in the open. Some enormous drops began to plump down all about us and on us. He caught me glancing at him.

"You mustn't pay any attention to that. 'Tain't nothin'. Them's just a few big ones that got all the way down through because of their weight. But it won't rain. It can't."

In fifteen minutes the thunder had become a little less business-like, and the lightning had degenerated into occasional pale shiverings in the sky. The old man was triumphant. "Didn't I tell you? Why, God, it *can't* rain!"

For a week I zigzagged in long swings up through the Mississippi Valley toward Minnesota. Kansas was burning hopelessly. So was Missouri. When I got off the train one morning in St. Louis a red-veined thermometer in the Union Station already stood at 98°. Iowa, too, seemed beyond hope. And so finally did Illinois. I moved in a ghastly, suffocating nightmare in which the things that ordinarily constitute the texture of my life had not the slightest feeling of substance in them. Why should I try to think about next year's work, or familiar places, or family and acquaintances? Why should I engage in deliberate thought about anything? It was enough to manage somewhat automatically the passing hour, the passing minute.

Then one evening I took a train for Minneapolis. Minneapolis was reported as "somewhat cooler." Perhaps I could hold out for another twelve hours.

Our sleeping-car was not air-conditioned. So I sweltered in a berth where a sheet stretched across wide open windows kept out the cinders and most of the air, but let in all the noises as we crashed through small towns past jangling crossing-bells, and all the odors of stock-pens as we swept alongside miles of freight trains that carried protesting live stock of every description out of the drought area. But at some indefinite hour in the night, I felt a refreshing breeze struggling with the sheet, and despite the noises and sickening smells, I dozed.

In Minneapolis at eight-thirty the next morning the thermometer outside the hotel stood at 68°. I knew what I meant to do with the day of free time just ahead. The food displayed in the coffee shop looked tasteless. The theater across the street that proclaimed with much glitter "a drama that unleashes a thousand emotions" promised nothing. I meant to sleep. I meant to cool off.

## viii

## Evergreen

WHENEVER I travel out of Boston to the north, I always find myself wishing that the Puritan stock had prevailed throughout New England. Not that I have prejudice against the disconcerting newer peoples who have come into the region, or against the Boston which they have created. Boston is still one of the two most interesting cities in the United States. Nor have I any sympathy with the foolishly restrictive habits of life that rightly or wrongly have come to be associated with Puritans. But it would be enlightening to have the Puritans in possession of the region as they once were, so that we could have a specimen, an unmistakable demonstration, of what a people of one blood and speech, and of more or less the same notion of a satisfying life, could do when left to themselves.

Of course, I know that such a New England could be only a dream. For one element in the Puritan philosophy rendered suicide inevitable. The Puritan was top-heavy in his belief—the evidence is strong—that God's sons in New England should make the most of their opportunity to acquire earthly possessions. When the magic of the industrial idea held the imagination of the world, and the mill-owners of New England saw how their profits could be made yet greater by utilizing the Italians and Irish and other needy Europeans who would come over and work for lower wages than the mill-owners' thrifty Yankee neighbors demanded, the region as a Puritan stronghold was doomed. For not only did the prolific new peoples operate the mills, and take over many of the farms abandoned by men and women who had moved on into the new West, and establish themselves in all sorts of small businesses with the renewed energy of a transplanted people; they discovered that they were rapidly coming into possession of enough votes to overthrow the political supremacy of the class that had welcomed them as employees. They could substitute for the Puritan's hard-looking way of life a way that they knew more about and that to them seemed easier.

I was busy with some such cycle of reflection one day as I watched out at the train window when I was leaving Boston for Portland and beyond. I had just been seeing parts of Boston that reflected little of the Puritan's notion of the good life; and now along the tracks were stocky, cheerful laborers who worked with swift un-Anglo-Saxon motions. Farther on in a suburban town other alien-looking men were enlarging the area of a cemetery. They were filling in low land with frowsy waste earth, tin cans, glass bottles, boxes and crates, and covering all this with a layer of soil that would grow grass. What fun people must think it would be, what a sweeping acknowledgment of man's godlike stature, to be carted off and buried in a dump-heap!

And then, before I had recovered from a sickening indignation, we were in the open country, and a white house with an attached barn as trim as the house itself stood above a sloping walled-in meadow that was as clean to the edges as a lawn; and back of the house was a hill pasture dotted with granite boulders that were too huge to be moved; and along the sides of the meadow and pasture, and rising high on the hill beyond was woodland of pine that was lustrous dark green in the wind and sun.

We circled a hill on which a white church-tower rose so high above the trees that it made the sky seem nearer the earth than it was. Then we were among the clean meadows and white houses and barns again, and always in sight of stone walls—stone walls that separated meadow from woodland, pasture from orchard, roadway and lane from paddock. Houses built on granite foundations, where they belonged, and boulder walls everywhere gave a tonic look of permanency to the landscape. That one's race ever should have had the toughness of fiber to establish themselves in these hills in any fashion is a heavy entry to their credit. But that they should have had the endurance to do it so permanently is little short of miraculous. Once I computed what the stone walls on three New Hampshire farms would cost at prevailing prices for wall building—to say nothing of the cost of digging and prying the boulders out of the fields and getting them to where they were needed—and the walls would have cost from two to three times what the farms with all late improvements added were worth at the highest market prices.

Could anything be better designed to rehabilitate the spirit than to visualize this region as it was in the latter eighteenth century? The hills were alive with men and women who were rolling boulders—living on simple fare that was hard to get, yet rolling boulders, building walls, through long days, through long seasons, through long lives. In one village where everywhere the walls still stand solidly, down hillsides, across hollows, up through new woodland once an apple orchard, I saw in a churchyard the gravestones of two of these of the boulder-rolling period who had lived to be (the man) an even hundred and (the wife) an even ninety. And he had taken time out to help fight the Revolutionary War.

But one does not travel far to the northward without being aware that the Puritan possessed something besides toughness of fiber. For only in certain parts of the South is there a comparable expression of the proportioned and the beautiful.

After two or three decades of piecemeal trips over New England I have dreamed often of a continuous pilgrimage along a wide U-shaped line of beautiful old houses that I have seen—from somewhere in Maine down through lower New Hampshire into Massachusetts, and then up through the Connecticut valley past the region of Walpole into Vermont and on toward Lake Champlain. One might well start at Wiscasset. For where is there another small community that has a higher percentage of wholly acceptable houses—proportioned exteriors, inviting doorways, and interiors designed to give one a new respect for life? The trouble, though, is that other communities do have a share of such houses. I am never able to make the long trip as I have planned it, because I am constantly tempted aside. Sooner or later I cease to be on a journey and am dwelling in an atmosphere. Everywhere in these communities were builders who knew what to build and how to build it. And the persons who engaged them had the intelligence to understand builders and allow them to use their knowledge and their skills.

Their meeting-houses, too, were just as rightly built. These likewise pull one aside from a direct journey. The white spires rising miles away above the dark green of the landscape are irresistible in their invitation to come nearer. The Puritan's God, according to account, was terrifying enough to frighten anybody, but the Puritan made Him as acceptable as possible by housing Him in a beautiful church.

The journey, or rather the atmosphere in which one travels, becomes a kind of complete spiritual record of the Puritan at his best. Here on the southern rim of Maine is the college that Hawthorne and Longfellow attended more than a century ago. Here is Longfellow's land of "My Lost Youth." Here farther south still is the region of secondary schools of durable name that were founded by discerning Puritans before the country had come to see that institutions of much the same kind must be provided universally. Here, too, is the land of Whittier—a better poet than he usually gets credit for being—and of his "Snowbound," which youths in an age sputtering with snow-plows find difficult of comprehension. Here all the way over into the region of Mount Monadnock, about which Thoreau wrote, though not so well as Edwin Arlington Robinson, is evidence on every hand that the provincial New Englander did not give the whole of his time to the rolling of boulders, or even to the building of good-looking houses.

Here is a record of work performed that affects one in the profoundest, the subtlest of ways. Where can the listener hear so much that the sea has to tell as when he hears the waves pounding along a chill Maine coast that men have persistently clung to while they have believed in something important? Or where—in America or in any other country —can one have just the fantastically real experience that one can have by standing on the highest hilltop in the MacDowell Colony in New Hampshire? Just off to the west there, as a kind of fixed point in both time and geography, Mount Monadnock; to the northward forty or fifty miles past the bulk of the low-lying Crotched Mountain, in a haze of blue untouched by the smoke of factory chimney, foot-hills and modest sun-lit peaks; to the eastward, close in front of one, Pack Monadnock and Temple Mountain in an intimate ruggedness of green much like Scotland—yet unlike Scotland; deep in the narrow valley of the Contoocook at one's feet, and closely surrounded by high wooded areas dotted with white houses and barns, the village of Peterborough, well-kept, self-respecting; and floating up out of the valley the music of the chimes of All Saints' Church. Yet everywhere about one, and merging with this idyllic repose sought out each year by artistic-minded men and women in pursuit of evanescent shadowings, is a solid life. Men work in hay-fields, gather early apples in a hundred orchards, care for Guernsey cows that range over the granite hills, haul in wood that later is to be sawed in lengths for the long winter.

Nothing has yet come into the region to deaden the spirit with an overlaying of sophistication. The severe man on the hillside farm along the back road may have an informally managed dark mustache that makes him look like some benevolent character in one of Conrad's tales of the sea, and he may waste few words that the day requires, but he takes time to tell you that his barn had forty-six active swallows' nests in it this year. For he likes swallows, and he thinks that perhaps his barn holds the championship. The clerk in the post-office, when business lulls and nobody is waiting, does not mind saying that in his humble opinion the reason why so many of the supposed ideas from California are only crackpot schemes of somebody's is that Hollywood is out there. "They get them from the movies." The deaf old man who grows good roasting-ears and pretends that there is a secret about how he does it sees no reason why he should not say "Howdy-do" to the bright young office-girl fresh from the city who walks alone in all the quiet roads she can find just for the thrill of it. "Ain't we all humans together?"

It is not surprising that there should have been poets in this New England. It is not surprising that Edward MacDowell should have found here an atmosphere where his restlessly sensitive genius could feel at home; or that over across the way a little, St. Gaudens should have worked; or that over still a little farther westward, Kipling should have managed to make out for a time. Nor should it be surprising that poets and playwrights and novelists and painters and composers in such numbers that it would be unfair to mention only a few, still filter into every part of the region from the Maine coast to Vermont and give themselves to work. Even the arts requiring an audience immediately present have found here a world in which to survive. If you use the Stearns Barn Theater of the Peterborough Players as a center, there are enough other theaters of more or less like kind within traveling distance in New Hampshire to enable you to go to plays night by night all summer long without duplication. Is it not appropriate that those who strive for a living simplicity in the theater should produce plays in a barn where the marks of somebody's honest ax are on every beam and rafter?

It is not just the view. It is not just the quiet. It is not the temperature. These in some combination may be found in other regions. It is the sum of all things taken together, including the record left by human beings who struggled with high persistence. Never was life here a soft experience for anybody. Never was it filled with the great leisure that is sometimes imagined necessary to develop the arts among men. It was a hard life, but one in which the people were free—were obliged—to create their own better world right out of the one they were working in—if they were to have any. Through a series of almanacs that reaches from the beginning of the twentieth century back to 1729 I have often leafed slowly to read the marginal jottings—amounts in pounds, shillings, and pence borrowed or paid back or made a matter of record for some other reason in the period of the Revolutionary War; the seasons' chief events as recently as the latter part of the nineteenth century. Nothing in the entries suggests a skittish metropolitan activity. "Twenty below zero." "Nellie came." "Haircut" (November, January, April). "Rebecca died." "Sun set on Monadnock." "Ida married." "Visited Ida." "Mother died." "Snow storm—with a big lot of snow on the ground." "To Greenville." "House sold." "Auction."

There was time; there was much snow; there was solitude. People could take their choice: they could subside into pettiness and go mad—and some of them did—or they could occupy their minds with transcendent things, and enjoy the profoundest of all sanities by making something useful. Men who never thought of pretending that they were cabinet-makers nevertheless did know how to make twisted-leg tables, high-boys, upstanding chairs, and clocks that have more than an antique value. They and their wives were the original "creators" in America—the designers of what life required. There is a certain great rightness today in coming upon automobiles bearing license plates from Massachusetts, Connecticut, New York, and the District of Columbia parked solidly for a half-mile on both sides of a New Hampshire road, and a crowd of two hundred substantial people with eager faces uplifted as if they were now at last to learn the way to some great salvation, hanging on the words of an auctioneer who stands high in an old sleigh and offers for sale the home-made candlestick used by some unknown country woman in the making of her hooked rugs.

All the way over into lower Vermont and up toward the Canadian boundary this atmosphere that is stimulating to honest effort persists. As one crosses the valley of the Connecticut out of New Hampshire certain elements, it is true, are lost, and certain others added. In some respects the Vermonter is less like his Puritan neighbors to the south who turned industrialists than like the farmers of the Middle West. In some respects he is not like his neighbors over in New Hampshire who remained farmers. He wonders if they do not put on airs, and they accuse him of being behind the times—very far. And in some respects he is not like anybody else in the country. A New Hampshire wag evidently felt this when he erected a sign by the railroad and public highway just at the boundary: "You are now leaving the United States. Entering Vermont."

Yet in Vermont the active-minded do not feel any loss of an invigorating air. In a state where the citizens decline outside aid in the beautifying of their region, where, in order to receive a fair share of the price of milk, the farmers organize with a refreshing militancy suggestive of the days of 1776, and where both women and men make war on the billboards that disfigure the landscape, there are certain to be other interesting sincerities and rebellions well suited to help a living mind retain hope.

But northern New England in summer is not enough. It is necessary to see it in winter also if you are to understand what the Puritan spirit has been able to do for itself when going it alone. Of course you should see it also in the first approaches of autumn when the meadows are white in the early morning, and the swamp maples are deep scarlet, and chilly-looking great blue herons fly southward over marshes of bronze, and the morning noise of the crows across the meadow comes to one's ears with a crisp new ease, and the buzz-saw up the road shrieks and sings in ascending and descending pitch as it nips off one stick of wood after another. But whether you see it in autumn or not, you must see it in the dead of winter.

I saw it thus in its full winter occupation when I once made a swinging trip all the way down from Bangor, Maine, to Amherst, Massachusetts, and then up again into the north of Vermont. In central Maine the wind had come after the last snow and taken much of the gray from the pine woodlands. Along the Maine coast the sea bumped and thundered against unshakable rocky points just below white houses from which the palest of blue wood smoke rose steadily.

A friend took me across from Bowdoin College to Gardiner in the biting cold. Something in the looks of Gardiner in winter says: "Well, you see we are holding out." I saw the cluster of small Christmas-tree pines that had been stuck down in the earth round the new memorial to Edwin Arlington Robinson to keep it from looking quite so stark until some young trees should grow. I saw some of the members of his family, who cherish his memory while they work and study and live. I sat in the warmth of a house that was bulging with literary reminiscence and talked for an hour through a long speaking-tube with Laura E. Richards, who in her middle eighties assured me that she was right in the midst of things. And I walked the streets of the city and felt anew the debt of gratitude that somebody owes to John Hays Gardiner for his austere friendliness to all sorts of faltering young persons and to at least one disheartened middle-aged poet who hailed from the same town.

All the way across into central Massachusetts a nice balance between white and dark green, between the solitude of the fields and the presence of fellow beings guaranteed by smoke rising from the chimneys of houses, prevented the scene from being desolate. In the Northwest the threat of madness to the sensitive which the sight of the unending snow induces springs largely from the fact that there appear to be no people—so far are the houses apart. But here there were plenty of houses. Here the people themselves were to be seen—dodging into the village store, piling new snow onto the mountainous ridges of snow already along every path, feeding hungry-looking chickens on protected areas that the sun, aided by shovels, had cleared of snow—somewhat.

Amherst was white, too, but the students who filled the town created the impression that they were not quite so much at home in snow as the ones I had seen in New Hampshire and Maine. In the frostiness I wandered out along the street past the house where Emily Dickinson had lived. Everything was so quiet that she might at the moment have risked slipping back across under the trees to Sister Sue's house with a new poem. But perhaps the snow was too deep.

Before we had long been on the way northward, signs of new snow appeared. The first intimation came when a train from Montreal shuddered in close alongside us at a station, with all the cool parts of the front of the engine plastered with snow and ice. While both trains stood there side by side, and we could see a car filled with people within arm's length of us but could hear nothing, some flakes drifted down between my window and the French-looking man and his squirming young daughter at the window opposite. By the time the train was fully away, the flakes were larger and more numerous. Mountains in the distance were obscured; then the nearer foot-hills; then the hills just across the fields.

Soon the evergreens were gray. Soon they were white. Soon they were bending under the weight of the white until their branches sloped steeply downward like the sides of close-standing tepees. In the luxury of a comfortable chair in a warm train I sat all afternoon and looked at an unending fairyland. Vermont was being buried—anew.

Children on skis going home from school had to stop and wave at us with mild disdain. Who wanted to bother riding a train on such a day as this? Old men in comforters and big durable-looking mittens came out of houses and took an exploratory look at the snow as if they expected much more to come before the end. At one farm-house Robert Frost's Runaway stood comfortably in the barn with his inquiring face thrust out where the upper half of a door stood open.

The train fought valiantly, but the snow was beginning to tell. And the mail to be unloaded and loaded seemed to increase in volume as we went farther into the snow. Oh, well, we could swing off at the stations and know how the snow felt. In one college town just before twilight the chimes in a tower high on a hill were filling the muted air with Scotch and English and American folk-tunes.

Once when the train crept along at a snail's pace and then came to a full stop to let a laboring freight train get out of the way, we were within a few feet of the front of a neighborhood general store. Somebody who looked as if he might be the proprietor came to the door. Already he had lighted the one big suspended lamp that the front of the store required. Four or five men who sat around the stove paused in whatever they were discussing and peered out at us just as the train lurched into a start and obscured the view. Once, an hour later, when the engine was finding the going heavy through snow that was now drifting, and I tried to look out into the darkness to see just what the world was like, I looked right into the bright living-room of a farmhouse that evidently had stood there, almost on the right-of-way, when the railroad was built, and saw a family sitting in after-supper comfort before a great fireplace. There they were, the Puritans of northern New England—undisturbed.

# ix

# Smoke

IT is the smoke of battle. It hangs close to the earth in a great dark semicircle up through western Pennsylvania, northeastern Ohio, southern Michigan, and northeastern Illinois. All sorts of supplementary lines extend over into eastern Pennsylvania, down into North Carolina, and from the region of Chicago by way of St. Louis down to Nashville and Birmingham. But this half-moon between western Pennsylvania and the southern tip of Lake Michigan is where the epic battle is most persistent and most intense.

## I Travel by Train

You may not see what it means when you are on a first trip through the region—or on a second or a tenth. You may still see things as individual incidents: a fight between laborers to control some industry in Johnstown, Pennsylvania; a fight—a more genteel-looking fight, though more savage—between capitalists to control some other industry in Youngstown, Ohio, or Cleveland; a closed eight-acre building for sale in Akron; some very business-like picket lines in front of a factory in Detroit; some policemen charging into a crowd of workers in Chicago. Or if you can look with enough detachment, you may see a certain monstrous poetry in it all—in the dark, serpentine trains a mile long creeping into vast areas of aluminum-looking stacks that sometimes shine like silver when the sun occasionally gets down through the smoke; and automobiles, steel rails, power shovels, and tractors pouring forth out into the brighter parts of the world by the hundreds, the thousands, the millions. But if you make enough trips, you will some day make one that will suddenly fuse with all the others you have made, so that you see what the region means when it is put together, and where it belongs among contemporary influences.

Some such moment of illumination came to me on a trip that brought me into Pittsburgh early one wet smoky morning when I was on my way over south toward the West Virginia boundary. Only a few of the great mills showed signs of life. In the murky, acid-laden twilight—although it was eight-thirty o'clock—it was difficult to feel sure which of the mills seemed the more infernal, the ones that spouted unearthly looking flame into the heavy skies, or the ones that stood idle and rusty and coldly impersonal behind their securely locked barbed-wire barricades. Just how did the human beings crowded into cramped houses that rose like the stairsteps of a rookery on the steep hillsides look upon the great American dream?

A kindly, middle-aged, executive-looking man sat beside me in the little red-plush accommodation train and read the morning paper. He noticed that I was intent on what I saw outside.

"Pretty gloomy, isn't it?" I said.

He was resentful. His kindliness vanished as if it had never been. "Just why do you want to run down the town?"

I assured him that I was doing nothing of the kind; that I was only wondering what the effect was on people who were obliged to live like that.

"They're getting just what's coming to them—trying to bring in these God-damned unions and all that sort of nonsense."

"But I thought it was the depression."

He did not deign to answer.

Later in the day after I had been heartened by the sight of several hundred college students whose faces still expressed very little of life's hatreds, I took a long walk in the rain on the railroad tracks that followed the Monongahela up southward. Ahead I saw a coal tipple, and stopped a miner who was coming from work to ask him about it and about the height of the seam of coal. He looked me over in a flash, took his pipe from his mouth, answered my questions, and abruptly walked on. Soon after, I decided that I had gone far enough in the rain and turned back. He was saying a word to a half-dozen men whom he had met. As they came on and I was about to meet them I could see that they were all eyes. I stopped and tried to ask them a question. "We're not talking," one of them said, and they all walked on in silence. I hurried a little. I caught up with the lone miner. He did not try to shake me, but he did try not to talk. As we walked along, he between the rails and I in the path along the ends of the ties, a very brilliant Kentucky cardinal alighted on a young black locust close by the right-of-way and sang as if the day were bright. "My favorite bird," I said. He took another glance at me, but one that I thought expressed less resistance. "You ought to see the two we've got in our side yard—the old man and the old woman both. God! how he can sing—and fight, too. They've been there all winter. I stick a nail in the end of an ear of corn and hang it up in a cherry tree for them to work at. And my wife puts out suet for them."

"Live in your own house?"

Yes, he did. He did not know just how long he'd be able to hold on to it, but he still had it. He went into the matter. He went into family history. All the way back to town he talked willingly, almost furiously.

When I left him he smiled as though some joke were on him. "When you stopped me up there awhile ago I thought you might be some stooge from the company."

I saw! There it was—the whole of the smoky semicircle to Gary and South Chicago. It was a battle zone, with wire fences, and search-lights, and private policemen, and machine-guns, and spies nosing around in what should be people's most private affairs, and employers who declare that they are ready to trust their employees just as far as they would trust a rattlesnake, and workingmen who have the same kind of hatred for the company they must work for. When business shows an upturn, and for a time more men are employed, there is brave talk about some new spirit of coöperation. But with a falling-off of work, the old spirit begins to show through again. In the heart of the country in peace time, it is war.

Every outrage to the human spirit that any war is sure to

bring, this one has already brought. But the greatest of them all is an enforced blindness. It has sealed men's eyes to the fundamental matter at issue. For the issue is not wages, or an open or a closed shop, or the details of working conditions—though the contestants profess to believe that it is some of these things—but the rightful ends of human life. Unless this fact is recognized and somebody goes to work to solve the problem on this basis, the war will go on until one side or the other is annihilated—or both—and the social structure of the entire country is strained dangerously or wrecked.

Here something has infringed upon the instinctive aspirations of a normal human being. Like a great parasitic growth it has superimposed itself upon the diverse and commendable life that was there, paralyzed much of it, and insisted that henceforth concentration of effort was not to be in behalf of any idealistic dream of friendliness among men who were neither masters nor servants but only concerned with the general welfare; it was to be in behalf of an industrial production that would bring all the legitimate joys of life with it as by-products. Here man has ceased to be a being with a variety of interests that attach him in useful ways to his fellows of every sort, and to the earth. He is an operative (bearing a numeral), a striker, a strike-breaker, a name on a black-list, a reliefer, a non-employable, a flop. What is a man compared with acres or square miles of machinery that has cost money? Who is thinking about even the details of the rightful ends of human existence when a factory—to take a minor instance—will be idle three days of each week and then run on a twenty-four-hour basis for the other three so that a housewife who has three or four workers to cook for must be up at all hours of the day and night for those three busy days, when the entire family might contribute its same share to production by working in the daytime, sleeping at night as most animals prefer to do, and otherwise enjoying a somewhat normal existence?

On one trip through this region—more than three weeks in all—as I listened and talked with men in dining-cars, lounge-cars, or hotel lobbies when they discussed the industrial war, I did not hear one person speak of the ordinary aspirations of human beings as though these might have anything to do with the case. When I raised the question with one agreeable white-haired man in the dining-car who talked in calm tones, he said quite casually: "Oh, well, you've got to remember that in the industrial world a human being is only so many energy units, and they can be replaced."

Here is the issue. There is something hellish in any scheme of life that treats a human being as only so many standardized energy units that are to be used or allowed to go to waste according to whether somebody announces that twenty thousand will work that morning or that twenty thousand will not. What has become of all our declarations about the right to labor and to live in self-respect, when a vast population of hundreds of thousands of able-bodied men may be told that on Wednesday it will be beautiful for everybody to engage in productive enterprise, but that on Thursday it will be forbidden to anybody to do so, no matter how much he might enjoy the experience, no matter how essential the experience is to him if he and his family are not to face starvation?

The simple truth is that these hundreds of thousands are no longer free men—free in the sense that a farmer on his own land is free, or a small shopkeeper, or a man who works for his neighbor or in a small factory that he has grown up with in a town of diverse interests where he has a chance to bargain with the men who require his services. "Just what the hell are you free to do if you live here?" a dark-haired, ambitious-looking worker begged me to tell him. "Just how free—to do what? Are you free to go into the telephone business in this town? Are you free to go on the air if you want to say something? Are you free to run a daily newspaper? Are you free to own a police department the way the company does? Are you free to hire anybody—to do what? Are you free to live where you want to live and send your kids to school in the town where you want to send them—or where the company tells you? Are you free to have a job and work at it? Well, maybe—next year. I haven't had any yet this year."

But most of them that I encountered are not even so free as this man. For they, like their employers, are so much concerned with the immediate necessities of the battle that, even if they are better philosophers than people who have been touched by life less tragically, they are in no state of mind to consider all the subtler dislocations that result when human energy is utilized in wholesale fashion in a highly depersonalized system of profits. Who has time to reflect on why the war is being fought when everybody from the industrial president to the humblest industrial worker is fearful that the stupendous battle, already quite out of hand, may go against him before the next rising of the sun?

But the smoke of battle obscures not merely the cause of the war; it obscures the logic of what is taking place at the moment. This is not just an accidental war between two groups who somehow fell into a disagreement about wages and hours. It has a history—a history that should be clear enough to anybody with eyes who has been circulating through the region during the past twenty or thirty years. The rapid development of so many new industrial establishments called for more man-power than could be found locally. In order to have the vast armies of men required by mass production, it was necessary to lure men away from what they had been doing. Anybody with a memory recalls the crowded trains that brought workers by thousands from over wide areas of the country; anybody with a memory recalls the clamoring of men who sought the high wages offered by factories already manned. Unbelievable numbers of people from throughout the Middle West were sucked into these centers. "Let villages become cities," it was decreed; "let wasteland become cities." And it was done. Men who had become multimillionaires overnight proclaimed that at last we had discovered a road to prosperity that was endless. And so it seemed. Then there came a time when the number of men required to supply all reasonable demands did not grow; relatively at least, it slumped. The magic half-moon did not seem quite so magical. And in the course of the years that made the industrial region itself look a little unstable, the very means of mass production that it had perfected and exemplified until it had been held up to the world as a model of the efficient way of life, was enabling the regions that these men had come from to get along without their labor. So if vast populations in all these industrial cities that had grown like hothouse plants now had nothing to do where they were, they could get nothing to do where they came from, either.

If the general sequence is kept in mind, nothing that is now taking place in the region seems illogical. Here is the final word in a concentrated industrial civilization. Industrialists had at last perfected a technique—they boasted of the fact, or declared it with oracular warning to anybody who got in their way—that rendered men helpless by rendering many of them unnecessary. No longer were the ordinary means of bargaining for a livelihood applicable. Just how much of a chance has a lone workingman, when he goes to the offices of a billion-dollar corporation consecrated to the production of profits for stockholders, to bargain on even terms when the corporation can have more men than it knows what to do with without so much as asking for them?

Nobody ever heard of a sit-down strike in the factory of a personal employer who himself was devoted to the craft that his business utilized, and who knew his men personally and himself heard their grievances. A sit-down strike in a community that has evolved according to normal individual needs is unthinkable. But in this great industrial warzone, where life has been so completely depersonalized, the methods of mastering production during the past two or three decades have made such a monstrosity as the sit-down strike not only imaginable, not only logical, but inevitable.

Most men cannot live without some attachment to something that they can feel is their own. There ought, in truth, in any man's life to be many such attachments. His roots in life ought to be so diverse that no one unfavorable wind could completely wreck him. Yet in these great concentrations of population devoted to one industry—or one branch or one process of one industry—a man cannot feel sure that he has even one attachment. But here is his one chance. He is led into an inescapable partnership. Yet how great can his assurance for the future be when his only attachment to food, clothing, and all the other barest necessities of existence for himself and his family is through an impersonal organization that does not know him, that cannot feel the slightest personal interest in his aspirations—because it is not a person—and that has the power to sever arbitrarily even this one attachment to existence when he goes round to work tomorrow morning? He is going to have something —at least a job—that nobody can take away from him or render profitless.

"Why, say, don't we have anything at stake?" a quiet, experienced machinist with a high-pitched little voice asked one Friday evening in a city of less than a hundred thousand that I chanced to be in when the report was circulating that three thousand were to be dropped the next week. "Why, I've been working for them for twenty-one years—so long I wouldn't know how to do anything else even if I could find it."

He reflected. "So they have to protect their investment, do they? Well, say, suppose they'd just give all their time to that. Suppose we'd say, 'All right, if your capital is so much more useful to you than we are, why don't you spend all your time with it? Just don't bother with workers at all.' Wouldn't dividends go up?"

But worse still—worst of all—the smoke of the battle blinds too many eyes to certain possible outcomes of the struggle. I have heard this blindness expressed a thousand times, but never better than by a frank representative of the employers with whom I spent a pleasant two or three hours on the train. He asked me if I favored a sales tax. I told him that I did. He said that he did, too. In fact, that was the only kind of tax he did favor. When I protested that his plan would be rather hard on the consumers, he shrugged his heavy shoulders, smiled, and said, "Oh, well, why not be honest about it? They have to pay in the end anyhow." He expressed his theory. He was a realist. "We have only so much wealth in the world. It evidently was the way God Almighty intended it. And we have some people who can enjoy art and literature and religion and all those finer things. So we have to choose between having a relatively small number enjoy a high standard of living while there are a good many others in poverty, and having the living standard of all of us pulled downward—maybe almost to European levels. Personally, I prefer to keep the first."

"But how are you going to keep it?"

He glanced at me as if he had suddenly discovered that I was a pest, and then looked out at the window for a moment before he answered. We were approaching Toledo. Then he faced me as if he wished to be very impressive. "We are going to sit on the lid so tight that she can never blow off—that's how!"

It ought to be easy enough to see that it was never done in the history of the world. It ought to be easy enough to see that if the high standard of living is going to be maintained for the "relatively few" at the expense of all the others, these others who have had little or nothing will sooner or later rise up and say, "All right, you've had it awhile; now it's our turn." It ought to be easy enough to see that where men have been made into masses, the side with the greater number of votes—and in extremity, with the greater number of fists—will come out on top. But the hatreds of battle have become so acute that not even such an inevitable sequence as this can be seen with any clarity, if at all.

And when total blindness has not resulted, a pronounced or a subtle distortion has. This industrial phenomenon, it must be remembered, is not a natural development of anything peculiar to the inhabitants of this region. It is something that the distribution of raw materials and markets over the United States made it easy to develop just here. The people of Pennsylvania and Ohio and Michigan and Indiana and Illinois are among the most substantial in the United States. From the earliest days they have been busy with all sorts of enterprises that have contributed to the interest of life. But the industrial battle-front inescapably pulls thought away from what they have done and from what many of them persist in doing. It pulls thought away from everything except itself.

I sat one morning by the water-front in Toledo and let my eyes enjoy what was before them. Bridges were opening for long, low freighters that were coming in from the lake just yonder, or going out. Other craft were chugging about in the broad river. I saw Toledo as I had never seen it before. Toledo was a port! Toledo was poetic! A lake, a broad river, high bridges, the deep voice of steamers in the quiet of the morning. How far, I wondered, was it down to where the river broadened out into the lake? I wished I had a map. Could I get hold of one without going back uptown? A man came along who looked as if he lived there, as if he might own a part of the town.

"No place near here where I could get hold of a map of Toledo, is there?"

He looked me over calmly, coolly. "You're not one of these damned college professors or newspaper reporters trying to horn in where it's none of your business, are you?" He was half serious.

The magic of the morning was gone. I wandered aimlessly about and saw everything with great literalness for an hour—through a region where streets were frowsy and weather-boarding was falling off houses that were alive with Negro children and Negro women and Negro men. How did they all happen to be just here in this part of the country and this part of the town? And why weren't the men working? And why were the houses falling to pieces? I tried going back to the river the next morning, but it was now just a part of the battle-front.

It is so all through the war zone. Detroit has many attractions—though it is not so interesting a city to the visitor as it was when it pointed out Belle Isle rather than an automobile plant as a proof of its attractiveness. But who gives its attractions so much as a first thought when the conversation in the dining-car, the lounge-car, and the hotel lobby is on how to break up the C.I.O., how to handle relief now with so many thousands more dropped from this or that plant; when the conversation in the coach-smoker and in the drug-store next door to union headquarters is how to keep the lines unbroken, how to have the dues coming in so that there will be something to work with; when the impression left by downtown is not downtown itself, but fringes of pawnshops and second-hand stores with all sorts of cheap men's suits hanging on wires out in front and offered at bargains? Flint engaged a distinguished city planner to think ahead for the municipality, and he did. Flint has had the services of educators likewise competent. But what the world reads about Flint is a crisp report that somebody there has said that so many thousand families will have to be moved out of the city, just as if they were live stock that had to be got out of a drought-stricken area. Such a city as Kalamazoo has enough admirable civic institutions and community enterprises to put to shame a suburban city of two or three times its size. But whoever hears of all this educational and artistic and dramatic and musical activity in a single city when the overshadowing activity of the region in general is war?

Not an institution established to promote human welfare has escaped. Political government is but a fixed center about which the forces can concentrate for intensified battle. The church is disorganized and confused and hesitant and subservient. From the general warping, education has suffered less than any of the other institutions, perhaps because until recently, at least, teachers have been recruited from diversified groups and for that reason—and others—have resisted the sharp alignment. But in many of the chief cities of the region teachers in the publicly controlled institutions have confessed to me in greater and greater numbers that it is becoming increasingly difficult to maintain an honest attitude and feel safe. In the privately controlled institutions, where contributions from the well-to-do are depended on for support, the outlook for spiritual independence and a courageous catholicity of view cannot be bright when the well-to-do are rapidly coming to belong to a single class—the industrial-financial class. A president in a privately endowed college summed the matter up when he said to me, "You know, when I engage a commencement speaker I have to remember that he is going to speak to my board of trustees as well as to the graduating class."

The press, too, has suffered. If you have been in other parts of the country where struggle is not quite so intense, and where hatreds are somewhat distributed among many differing groups, you need only to read the head-lines in most of the newspapers in this region in order to know that you are in a war zone. Plenty of newspapers are open enough in their partisanship. Plenty of others induce in you the feeling that you are reading somebody's strong effort to keep away from the partisanship he feels—to keep away from anything that possesses the hardness of reality. One newspaper man of much experience declared that there was an accepted formula. "I'm not saying that we're all exactly alike, any more than the papers in any other section of the country. But if you carry a lot of scare heads about unimportant matters that have emotional appeal—like Wally and the Duke, for instance—churn up a hell of a lot of indignation against something in China or somewhere else so far away that it's never going to come back on you, get in plenty of prize-fights, plenty of Hollywood, plenty of Emily Post, plenty of funnies, and then frost it all over with some nicely flavored patriotic hokum, you've about as near a sure thing as you're going to find where you've got to be careful."

But the most tragic distortion has come to art—to the conception of art. The highly concentrated machine civilization inescapably deprives all men except a few at the top of the pyramid of any important expression of their personal selves in what they do. It kills off art at its source as rapidly as it can be done. Then it clutters up the landscape with monotonous, unlivable-looking streets, ugly houses, endless rows of hideous billboards in pleasant meadowland and in front of wooded hilltop, so that nobody can see anything near at hand that is satisfying to any sense of fitness. And then, unable to get away from the terrifying fact that the beauty of life has been destroyed, it proclaims crusades in behalf of the aesthetic, and spends millions of dollars on art museums and art collections so that the people may go and see and remember—sadly—that the spirits of men were once so free that they expressed themselves in these poetic ways. And Mr. Henry Ford receives credit for being a great benefactor to his age by saving a few things in their somewhat natural environment from the irresistible uglification that he has spent a lifetime helping to create. After taking all the beauty out of the texture of life, the promoters of the ugliness of industrialization try to make up for the deficiency by pasting some artificial beauty on the outside. "It is," Eric Gill once said, "as though we had contrived to turn out fodder for cattle which had no qualities but that of nourishment, and then, feeling the need for the sensation of greenness, we trained a special kind of workman to produce green for our delight."

Thus the region of smoke has come to be the greatest irony that the mighty of the earth have ever seen grow out of one of their creations. For after proclaiming and perfecting techniques that would in truth enable men to live together in abundance, they discover that what they have done prevents men from living together at all—save in a state of war. Men have been driven to feel not only insignificant but superfluous. They have been brought to suffer the great torture of not knowing whether their own best ability, conscientiously offered, will enable them to exist. They have been forced, when they do have opportunity to work, to surrender personal ways of doing things and the personal tools of life so essential to emotional balance, and have been made to work in nerve-breaking mental straitjackets. They have been detached from ordinary individual responsibility for their conduct and obliged by circumstances to act in masses—where man is never at his best and is usually at his worst. They have been incited to a blinding hate when they ought to be moved by good-will. Here is a more terrifying demoralization than any that has ever before enslaved intelligent men.

It is not a question of who started the war, or whether he did it intentionally or not. It is not a question of who wins the war. It is a question of becoming intellectually honest and doing some elemental thinking that will render the continuance of the war impossible. For only a madman could believe that a region alive with strikers and strikebreakers and pickets and hunger-marchers and armed private policemen and legions of spies, and menaced by a hundred thousand men out of work today and a half million tomorrow, and tens of thousands of families left to be fed at public expense or starve, is the ultimate of man's ability to think.

# X

# Dust

DEALERS in novelties say that dust-storms are no longer news. But if ever you are in one for days and try to make your way around in it among the people who are struggling on with the business of living, you will remember it—and especially the people—as if you had witnessed some silent dramatic event in the heavens that occurs but once in a thousand years.

I had received no warning of the one I have in mind. I was to drive thirty miles across north Texas country to catch a Sunday-noon train. Two college girls who were going home for the day and who knew that I had to make the trip offered to take me along. One of them had been in a basketball tournament the night before, and as soon as we were on the way she curled up in the back seat and slept. The driver confessed that she herself had been awake all night, but for a different reason. Her fiancé had been rushed to the hospital for an emergency operation. She had been unable to sleep—at all. And now that she knew he was going to live, she did not want to sleep. It was so good to be alive that she had to stay awake and enjoy the experience. She had invented the necessity of this trip just to participate in the great brightness of the day and the easy rhythm of gliding over low rolling hills that afforded long vistas. In a world where so many people give the wrong reasons for everything they do, her profound joy and unaffected frankness were so startling and so beautiful that I sat in a kind of enraptured amazement and listened all the way.

When the dark, long train, bound from Ft. Worth to Denver, appeared in the distance, it looked like some Valkyrie of the industrial age winding among the tops of the rocky low hills before it descended to the end of the town and the station.

The conductor gave me a seat in a sleeping-car. For a time I was content to sit and reflect—and look out upon a gray landscape that was already showing signs of spring. Automobiles like shiny beetles scooted in all directions over distant flat hills and down through long sweeping dips where there were trees and countless specks of grazing cattle.

Then I put in much time eating little—and reading—in an old-fashioned dining-car that was in a constant state of tension as the train followed curves and counter-curves in its effort to keep on the ridges—or between them. After luncheon I walked a few station platforms while the train loaded much mail and baggage.

An hour later when I looked up from the book I was reading, a thin haze paled the sun. Soon after, the pages before my eyes were suddenly darkened. When I glanced up this time the sun had disappeared. In its stead, there not far ahead of us, a heavy bank of cloud stood up in the sky. Already a stiff wind was blowing.

"Rain!" I said quite declaratively to the porter after he had snapped on the lights for me.

He smiled as if I had been trying to work off some stale joke on him. "No, not rain."

Suddenly we were in it. Tens of thousands of acres of dry red soil had been plowed for cotton, and the wind was sweeping it up, driving it, whirling it in every direction. There were waves of it like the waves of a heavy rain-storm —but much darker. There were areas of quiescence, where the waves were thin; there were other areas where you could not see three hundred feet from the train. Once I watched a clump of trees some distance ahead through a "thin" area. Swiftly we were coming nearer. Their bare tops were spotted with heavy, dark-looking bunches of mistletoe. As the train took the curve toward them, they began to grow indistinct, and when we passed where they should have been they were not to be seen at all. Gusts of fresh dust, originating in the plowed land on every side of us, whipped and swirled about the train as if the train were the cause of them. How long the storm had been busy before we ran into it I do not know; but already along depressions in the highway that paralleled the railroad, it had piled drifts of dust a foot and a half or two feet deep.

We swept into an area of at least a few thousand acres where the fields were in pasture. There was but a thin veil of dust above it. The dust had not yet become general. Then we ran into a greater area than the original one where the wind was sucking the red soil from the fields and whirling it everywhere—whirling it so high that the individual clouds of it lost all identity in the impenetrable darkness that was filling the skies.

I left the train within an hour—at the little town of Vernon. The car in which I had been riding was doubly tight and air-conditioned. Yet when I was ready to close the bag that had stood open on the seat beside me since I began my reading, I could write my name on the sides of the bag or on any article in sight within it.

After I had arranged at the hotel for a few comfortable hours of rest if I should desire them, I walked to the limits of the town to watch the storm in its growing full force. For in the early phase of a storm, even so small an area as a city of some thousands that does not originate dust itself provides the haven of a slightly thinner area. It was possible to see a half-mile. Stark warehouses, and box-cars on sidings, and bare telephone poles stood in so many different degrees of obscurity that I seemed to walk in a world created by an impressionistic artist who had a strong preference for the matter-of-fact.

But the people were sharply, abnormally real. They called across from one front yard to another in quickened neighborliness. They stood at front gates where they had come out to say good-bye to relatives who had driven in from the country, and looked about and made sweeping gestures with long arms and shook their heads dubiously. They shared some great awareness. They spoke with the emotional directness that one hears in the early days of a war.

While I ate supper I could see clouds of dust steadily

drifting through the streets. "Seems to be coming," I remarked to the waitress who brought me my dessert and saw me watching something outside.

"Lord, this is nothing—yet. Last year you couldn't see that building across there a part of the time. And we had forty days of it. I've still got about a half-acre in the bottom of my lungs. If it comes like that again I'm just going to curl up in a corner and croak at the beginning of it and save hospital bills."

By eight o'clock something that was not the darkness of night clothed everything in a gray obscurity. Street lights, if they were not too far away, seemed bright enough in themselves, but no rays of light extended from them out into the darkness. And I had to take a bus for thirty or forty miles across into southwestern Oklahoma.

"Will you be able to see?" I asked the driver before I climbed in.

"I'll try to. But heck, she's getting everything churned up good and proper."

The headlights of the bus penetrated only a short distance, so that we seemed constantly to be driving into a gray, intangible wall. Pairs of pale spots came out of the wall and grew bright as they passed us. Once a car shot like a bullet from the gray directly in front of us. But there was time.

"Good thing there are not too many aviators like that coming along," the driver remarked. "Oh, well, I've got good brakes."

He needed them—several times. But eventually we arrived in Altus.

When I went up to the room that the hotel had reserved for me, I found that the windows were not only closed but carefully locked. Yet little paths of red dust a half-inch deep curved gracefully from the corner of each sash across the inside sill.

I opened one of the windows a little to see what would happen. I could see no dust coming in. The worst, I decided, must be over. I opened the other. I still could see no dust. But the fresher air was agreeable. I would sleep.

After what seemed hours I was awakened by a prolonged ringing of the telephone in the next room. A man whose business was oil was receiving a long-distance call at five in the morning. The deal seemed important. Yes, he would dress and get out and away at once. But for a half-hour he coughed and sneezed and cleared his throat. When at last I heard him going, I went back to sleep. Much later I thought I must have slept a long time, and I had a vague impression that I had heard windows rattling most of the time. But it was still dark.

When I reached over to turn on the light I had a sudden taste of earth that was not unlike the taste of clay I had known since youth. I sneezed. Then I noticed a strange furry feeling in my ears.

It was eight-thirty.

I walked in bare feet to the southeast window and looked out. In the east there was not so much as a place for the sun. The reddish-gray wall was everywhere, though apparently thinner, more nearly translucent, when one looked straight up toward a sky that might be clear. Off to the south there seemed to be a stream of water in a mist, with reddish flatland just beyond. In the stiff wind, the clouds of thick dust and thinner dust followed one another slowly. At a moment when visibility was fairly high I saw that my stream was a low, white stucco building, and that the flatland was the long red roof of another just beyond.

I happened to put my hand to my head. My hair was as

gritty as if I had been turning somersaults in a sandpile. I lifted a bare foot. The bottom of it was covered with clean-looking dust. I touched a protected window-sill. It was so thick with dust that I could have made a topographical map on it. I walked over to the dresser where a bell-boy had put a pitcher of ice-water when I arrived. Red dust had been sliding down the inner sides of the pitcher until there was a stretch of land entirely around the body of water.

Downstairs when I had finished my breakfast I said to the stout woman who gave me my change, "I see you have a little dust."

"A little?" And she gave a subdued snort, as if I had done her town an injustice. "I guess you had better walk out and see what it's like."

I walked several miles—out to the edge of town and then on into the country. The same impressionist who preferred matter-of-fact subjects had been at work here. And the fascination of the indefinite was increased by the suggestion of something luminous in the dust. It made me feel that a little farther ahead I must inevitably walk out into clear day. The dust must be flowing away. As I walked on, I thought that the farm-houses were becoming the least bit more distinct than they had been; that the bodies of the trees were more substantial; that the roads went farther before they were swallowed up. But when I turned to walk back townward, I was aware of the same illusion.

Toward noon the dust overhead seemed thinner. Once when I looked up I thought it must be like this to live at the bottom of the sea. It seemed lighter somewhere up there. Once I saw the sun. But it was blue—as blue as the sky. Soon after, it was a much deeper blue.

"Just how does your red dust make the sun blue?" I asked a man who looked as if he ought to know.

"It acts as a screen," he replied simply, "and cuts the red rays out."

Despite the physical unpleasantness, I enjoyed wandering about. More and more I was aware of the people who were everywhere at the bottom of this dark semi-opaque sea. Something in their manner showed that they were increasingly conscious of a presence. They seemed to move along with little resistance and no friction. They were sticking closer together. Over in the court-house where men seeking relief employment filled the corridors and the basement, the men in charge seemed to be making an unusual effort not to be abrupt. And up at a junior college two or three hundred boys and girls revealed a determined cheerful concentration that was exceptional even for the youthful and the earnest.

In the afternoon I had to go fifty or sixty miles across the country. The face of the earth was somber with a substantial darkness that was unlike night. The friends who were taking me entertained me with fascinating Indian lore of the region. Suddenly, while they spoke, something unbelievably gigantic right over us loomed black and more substantial than the dark dust. Then we could see the details. We were close against a ridge of the Wichita Mountains. In themselves these mountains are strange enough, rising as they do like monster rock piles on level green plains. But in the dust when one comes upon them without forewarning, they are unforgettably grotesque. Yes, I thought when I had recovered a little, it must be like this at the bottom of the sea—with mountains stretching up in dark water toward pale light.

The next morning after I had spent much time shaking the dust from towels and clearing my eyes and ears and throat, I slipped down to the little coffee shop for breakfast.

Across the U of the counter a red-faced young truck driver was smiling wide as he ate his fried eggs. His face invited conversation.

"What makes you so blue this morning?" the sole waitress asked him.

He smiled all the more as he tried to look serious. "Well, you know I went to sleep with my mouth open last night, and when I waked up this morning I found I had swallered my farm."

The man next to me saw that I was interested, and leaned over as if he possessed inside information. "Hear about that fellow out west of town yesterday?"

I admitted that I had not.

"Why, he was driving along, not going very fast because of the dust, and saw a big ten-gallon hat just at the edge of the road and thought he had better climb out and get it. But when he picked it up there was a man under it—just his head still above the dust.

" 'Why, say,' he said to him, 'is there anything I can do for you? I never saw anybody drifted in quite as deep as you are, just a-walking along.'

" 'Just a-walking along?' the fellow says. 'God, I'm on a horse.' "

Up on the hill at the college for teachers that morning, some girl students put on a musical skit entitled *The Dust Storm King,* written by a versatile woman who knew her subject. The setting for the performance was perfect, for dust pressed in close everywhere, and left only such protected caverns as college auditoriums, or houses window-stripped with adhesive tape, free—that is, relatively free—for breathing purposes.

Something in the way young life refused to be smothered by the dust attracted me. Late in the afternoon I tramped back toward the college. Half-way between downtown and the campus were some public-school buildings on a hill that made it easy for me to keep my direction.

As I approached the main college building, I heard musical instruments. They seemed to be on the top floor. I climbed up and up until I came to a room close against the roof. A competent-looking young member of the faculty was busy with a student orchestra of thirty-five or forty pieces. I dropped into a chair near the door and listened and watched. The building commanded a great expanse of western Oklahoma. But this afternoon all visibility was lost a little beyond the college campus. In this strangely unnatural shadowland, energetic boys and girls from ranches and small towns gave themselves to music.

The conductor asked them to turn to a sequence of selections from Gilbert and Sullivan. When they were all in readiness—when the most deliberate violinist had at last got her chin adjusted—he said, "Just a minute. I wonder how many of you ever saw a Gilbert and Sullivan opera."

One girl with a sense of humor spoke up: "Why don't you ask us how many of us ever saw an opera of any kind?"

This question was not put, but the first one was. There was just one person in the orchestra who had ever seen anything of Gilbert and Sullivan's produced. Yet they caught the spirit of what they were undertaking, and played as if they might have been brought up on *The Mikado* and *The Pirates of Penzance*. It was a sight to be remembered: an orchestra of youths who had grown up in greater intimacy with farm machinery than with musical instruments leaning into Gilbert and Sullivan with a gusto.

Down on the first floor I talked with a woman who declared that she herself had found the people of the region so perpetually interesting that she would not think of living anywhere else. I sketched the orchestra as I had seen it in a brightly lighted room completely encompassed by dust—the students playing as if they found a certain novelty in violins, cellos, percussion and wind instruments, the alert lithe girl at the piano ready always to run a little ahead for the benefit of everybody and show how it was all to sound when put together.

"It must have been . . ." and she mentioned a name that I have forgotten. "If it was, she is probably the best pianist we have in college. Comes from out here fifteen miles or so on a ranch. For a time she came every day an hour or so before classes in the morning and practised; then she stayed for another hour after the college day was over and practised again. Some time ago she quit coming. I was troubled. I wondered if she had had to give up college, as so many of them have had to do. Then one morning she reappeared. I expressed my misgivings—and my delight. 'Oh,' she said, 'my father sold his wheat, and I stayed out to help him load it.' "

She had to tell me how interesting it was to watch the transformation of these youngsters who came in out of the dust. One day a girl in worn dress and old tennis-shoes appeared at the college and wished to enroll for a part of a term. She had bolled cotton—gleaned the cotton that opens out after the regular picking season—and saved the five dollars required for registration. And here she was, ready to enter college—but with no money to live on. Sometimes she had only a nickel a day for food—a pint of milk or a hamburger. For three years she worked in the cotton-fields and came each February for nine weeks in college.

This teacher created a secretaryship for her—and an opportunity for her to break down her feeling of inferiority. When she had a little money, the teacher went with her to buy her first coat—a twenty-four-dollar coat at half-price. She began to speak to people, to accept invitations to go to the college auditorium for concerts. Life ceased to hurt and became exciting. And today the position she holds makes her biography seem like a Horatio Alger story—but better.

Yes, this teacher liked the people who came in out of the dust. She would hesitate to say what percentage of the boys who had come to college in her time had walked on carpets before they came; she might have the percentage too high. But they did come. In the old days they drove in behind mule teams; then they came on trains; now they arrive in automobiles, new, old, or borrowed. They are country boys with long-distance eyes and healthy wills. They help her to live some of the poetry essential to her temperament.

In one of the other Dust Bowl colleges the dust was so heavy that all activities were suspended. In another, when I spoke to a student about the drama of dust if one could only forget the staggering cattle, the pneumonia, and the general destruction when it stayed too long, he said with something of the provincial's sense of the tall story, "But you know we've decided to discontinue them."

He spoke for his region. He told me about the "chisels" that cut narrow trenches—scarcely as wide as a hand—eighteen or twenty inches deep, two or three feet apart across fields for the water to collect in when the weather is wet, and for the dust to roll into before it gets started when the weather is dry; about the increasing number of deep wells from which Dust Bowl farmers were now irrigating their wheat; about the success of concerted effort to put more of the dry land back into grass; about all sorts of refinements of this or that method designed to make life a little less precarious. No, they were not going to move out—any more than the people of any other region. Did anybody believe they were going to let a mere occasional assault of nature deprive them of the prerogatives that are supposed to belong to human beings in general?

# xi
## *Waste*

WHAT I am thinking about is something I saw while I traveled in 1937, but the germ of the idea was planted in my mind while I was on a trip in the early spring of 1932—right in the trough of the depression that we all are now so anxious to forget, but must not. I had come into St. Louis on a night train, and since I am longer than a sleeping-car berth, I felt the need of a walk that would enable me to extend myself.

I struck off northward from the region of the Statler and Lennox Hotels into the vast area that is inhabited by whites and blacks and all shades of browns. For days I had been going from one intellectual center to another in which charming women, young and old, had talked brightly about books and authors and themselves, and men with many academic degrees had delivered learned theses on the economic situation—with all the foot-notes included—at so many dinner tables that I was more than ready to get out and see human beings in the raw.

Everywhere there were men. They sat close together on the outside steps of their frowsy tenement houses; they were lined up on the curb with their knees high, their feet resting in the shallow gutter—the Negroes like crows on a limb; they were standing in quiet, friendly groups on street corners where they could get the full effect of a warmth from the skies that cost nothing. Whites and blacks seemed not to avoid each other, yet I was sometimes aware that I passed from one racial zone to another.

I began to count as I walked along. In two hours I had gone all the way to the river up at the northeast corner of the city—not by the most direct route—and I had seen more than a thousand men sitting around, waiting for a chance to work, for a chance to earn something to eat. And hundreds of these buildings—it seemed to be half of them as I walked along, though it was probably not—were tenantless, and boys had already begun to smash the windows. The former occupants had not gone to any other city, but they were not here.

When I could see that the river was just there ahead, I walked over a block or two to a towering grain-elevator where the railroad tracks followed the river bank. I wanted to spend some time with the river—I always do. Then I noticed the grain-elevator a little more in detail. Over the entrance it said, "Capacity 1,500,000 bushels," or something like that.

I started back toward the downtown region. Before I had gone three blocks, I saw a queue of men a little ahead on the other side of the street. I stopped a man who wandered along as if he had no very clear destination in mind, and asked him what all those men were doing in a queue in such an outlying region as this.

"There's a little woman over there who gives them free soup once a day. She and her husband conduct a mission—you can see a cross and a red heart right over their heads on the window—and she's trying to keep some of them from starving."

The whole matter seemed to be distasteful to him. "Why, are you interested in such things as that?"

When he decided that I was, he confessed to me that he had been walking along there trying to decide whether to go over and get in the queue himself.

He was an upholsterer, he told me. He and his wife had saved money and bought a house. They had managed and skimped until they had paid for it—"every red cent." Then the depression came. He had now had nothing to do for two years. People were just letting their furniture wear out. The only way he and his wife could live was by mortgaging their house. Then they had to take a second mortgage on it. And now they were going to lose it—next week probably—and little enough good had it all done them, for now they might starve anyhow.

I crossed over and got in the queue myself. The men were cheerful at the prospect of food. They chaffed; they declared that they were going to have to tighten up their belts another hole if she didn't "open her up" pretty soon. Then a man came along the queue begging the men to accept what looked like subversive propaganda of some kind. Some of the men refused to take any—or said they already had some. I accepted the slender pamphlet. It declared on the front page that Jesus saves. It invited everybody to come to the meetings in the evening and learn how great tribulations can be made endurable.

At last somebody came to the door—which really stood open—and gave a signal. The men poured into the little room, filled the benches at the long oilcloth-covered table, and instantly were busy with their cabbage soup and slices of bread without butter.

I asked one of the young converts who was acting as a waiter if I might see the woman in charge. She came from a kitchen that smelled not of cabbage soup but of frying beef—a spare little woman who kept pressing her palm against her forehead while she told me how she managed to carry on. "Lots of people," she said, "send me a little check every now and then. Several of the professors out at Washington University send me something regularly—out of their salaries. And think of it—it's just wonderful—I have had three big gifts of twenty-five dollars each this month."

She noticed that I watched her pressing her forehead. "I have a frightful headache this morning. We have meetings every night"—she called my attention to the little auditorium next door—"and then, of course, I have to keep everything going in the kitchen. And there are so many special cases. A man came here this morning and asked: 'Would you keep me and my family from starving to death?' 'I certainly would,' I told him. My husband went with him —just over here on the next street—and found the whole family of them, husband, wife, five children—and another on the way—huddled together in a little abandoned storeroom. They are all so badly gone that they've got to have something more than cabbage soup—which is just the best we can do for the three hundred or so who come here off and on. So I sent my husband out for enough beefsteak for the mother, at least. I've got a whole big bucket of things ready to send over to them as soon as the meat is done."

She pressed her forehead. "Why don't you try a little

aspirin," I suggested, "until you can catch up with your sleep?"

"Oh," she asked apologetically, "was I pressing my forehead again? Well, maybe you won't quite understand, but we trust in the Lord to cure our headaches."

"You'd better help Him out a little with some aspirin," I urged.

She laughed at my skepticism as if she had not minded in the least. "I may have to—but not just yet."

How did I happen to come in? I assured her that I was just a wandering author who found most human beings interesting. I put a very modest bit of money in her hand and told her that it was great that she was able to keep so many of them alive.

"Now see there!" she exclaimed, as she looked at the money before she found a pocket for it. "The Lord does provide. That will just pay for the beefsteak!"

Then she went on in an effort not to express pride in what she was doing: "But if you want to see a lot of them, go down to Father Dempsey's place." She told me where. "He feeds thousands of them in one way or another. Some of mine go down there for supper after they have been here at noon, and manage in that way to make out. Of course, it's not much; they don't get any variety at all. But it will keep them from starving."

I went down to Father Dempsey's. It was a kind of down-and-outers' hotel established by a priest who had insisted that Jesus meant what he said. An old building—it looked like an abandoned high school—had been converted into this haven where men could stay even if they had little or no money.

The man at the desk was generous enough to show me all over the place. "We'll begin at the beginning," he said in a rather matter-of-fact voice, "down in the basement where they come in. You see, many of the fellows have had tough lines so long they've become nothing much more than ordinary bums so far as their physical habits are concerned; so in order to protect everybody else we begin by putting them through this delouser—you know, just the same as in the war. While they are going through, we put their clothes through—if they are any good. If they are not, we try to get them some that are." Then we went on up through the building. Great areas had been cut up by means of thin partitions so that every man might have a little privacy. At several doors he knocked and then showed me what the rooms were like, and how the men often tried to make them appear livable.

With time for deliberate observation we looked into the lounge lobby and reading quarters. Men in all stages of nervous breakdown filled every available chair and seat in sight. The ones still somewhat in command of themselves were reading—or trying to read. Some listened to the phonograph or radio and stared off into the distance wildly, intently, as if they were not far from insanity. A slender, nervous-looking light-haired young fellow and a stoutish ruddy-faced man whose hair was completely white sat in strange contrast side by side and let the tears trickle down over their cheeks from weary bloodshot eyes without any effort to check them or to conceal them.

"Pretty tough!" I said when we finally walked back toward his desk.

He glanced at me as if he had discovered that I was very inexperienced. "Have you been down along the river to any of the Hoovervilles?"

I told him that I had not; that I already had some notion of what one of them must be like.

But the next day I went down to see one of them—with a friend. "This one," he said, "ought to do as well as any."

Sixteen hundred people had taken possession of the bank of the Mississippi between the fluctuating water-level and the railroad tracks close above, and had built for themselves tiny boxlike huts out of scraps of boards, corrugated packing cases, the tin of large containers, tarred paper, and plastering laths. Down over the water's edge they had slender little privies that they had to keep moving up and down the bank as the water rose and fell. They had established for themselves a post-office and information desk that was presided over by a swarthy young architect who had had nothing to do for two years.

I spoke of the evidence of good behavior everywhere.

"Oh, yes," he assured me. "They are really a very decent lot. We are right out in the edge of things here, where you might expect we'd need plenty of patroling, but as a matter of fact, about the only time we ever call a policeman is when somebody jumps off the high bridge up there."

"They jump off, do they?"

"You bet they do. They get tired of waiting for the depression to be over. One jumped off last night. And one jumped off just a little while ago. That's what they're doing up there now—trying to recover the body."

There was a great silent amplitude in the Mississippi.

But most of the inhabitants were trying to hold on, were trying to remain decent and save a little of the best of themselves. Women had put up clean remnants of white curtains, had arched bits of drapery neatly, had found ways of using this or that blue tassel or other oddment of finery that they had salvaged when they were evicted from more respectable quarters. One man who had been a house painter had painted his shack a pleasant pale green, and had put up a sign of his own making which announced to the world that he was prepared to do all kinds of high-grade work. But neither he nor anyone else along the street of clay seemed to be able to find any more paint. One family of children had come upon a depression puppy, and they insisted that he eat as long as they did. But it required only one look to see that nobody in the household was eating overmuch. A very intelligent gentlemanly old man—whose face bore the puzzled expression of a terrier that has been whipped when in fact he has not chased the cat—a sensitive, poetic man, had fenced his ten-foot yard neatly with pointed old plastering laths and was spading the ground and pulverizing it preparatory to the planting of lily bulbs. When he had sized me up slyly and had evidently decided that I was not regarding him with ridicule, he told me all about his project. The summer before he had carried water up from the river every day and watered every foot of his yard, so that he had flowers nearly all summer. "But," he added with pride in his work, "I've got to begin all over again this year. So many people along here wanted starts, that I've given away most of the bulbs I meant to plant myself."

Three young Negroes had made for themselves musical instruments, and were going about playing for all parts of the street. They had a wooden whistle, an old washboard which one of them played with improvised thimbles on his fingers and thumb, and a kind of xylophone made by nailing tomato cans tightly on the top of a box that served as a sounding board and then bending the edges of the open ends of the cans until a musical scale resulted. The man who performed on this—with drumsticks of his own make—also performed on a cymbal made from the bell-like bronze shade of a lamp.

Somebody had devised a church, too, that was large

enough to seat eighteen. I asked a dark-eyed, pleasantly impish young lady of eleven who had joined us somewhere along the way, and seemed much concerned with having us receive a good impression of her town, what denomination the church was. She shrugged her shoulders ever so slightly, looked away as if she did not know the answer, and then with her head as much as her hand directed our attention to the evangelical-looking pulpit that bore the simple decoration of the cross.

These two days were the beginning of my better understanding of poverty. I had felt poverty's pinch as a child—and after. I had grown up in a mining community where all about me were undernourished children and mothers whose clothing was so scant and so tattered that they were ashamed to venture away from their own door-steps—all because nobody who worked in the mines had more than a total of half-time employment, and no guarantee of that. Poverty was painful; poverty was humiliating. But between 1932 and the period in 1937 that I have in mind now, I came to know how infinitely more than this poverty is. In the beginning of those evil years, men and women could attach all their misfortunes to the depression and then find hope in assuming that when the depression came to an end their misfortunes likewise would. But by 1937 they were seeing that for them the depression was to have no end. No matter how great an effort they might now make, they were to belong to the impoverished class as long as they lived. At first they had been fearful—fearful about tomorrow. The immediate future was something too difficult to face. Then they had experienced a great hatred. Who had been responsible for this, anyhow? Certainly they had not. And then, in the end, they were overwhelmed and numbed by a terrifying futility.

# Waste

So by 1937, I had come to complete sight: Poverty, despite all the sugary words of comfortable people about the blessings hidden in adversity, is the most devastating evil that an intelligent, sensitive mind can suffer. Those who do not like to think about anything unpleasant would dissent from this view. They would excuse themselves by insisting that poverty develops strength of character. But have you ever heard anyone suggest that poverty be made universal so that everybody become strong?

The truth, quite on the contrary, is that poverty stultifies a human being as inevitably as a continued injection of poison into the blood. By a slow numbing it renders men and women incapable of any sharp awareness of their own best qualities of character; it robs them of their sense of high enterprise; it undermines their confidence and prevents them from extending the essential part of themselves, their self-feeling, into the life of the world about them. It unbalances them in the wrong direction, by crowding their lives full of inescapable considerations of the scant, the petty, the under-dog point of view.

That is what poverty does. In ninety-nine cases out of a hundred some such spiritual deterioration follows any sharp, extended poverty. But when the poverty begins to look as if it had become permanent the deterioration is hastened. The possibility of yet some eleventh-hour way out, which will keep a man from despair for a long time, has vanished. A man who feels that his riches stultify him can get rid of them in a day. A man who is caught by a poverty that to him looks permanent must keep his cause of stultification, for nobody is ready to take it over. He walks abroad in the morning and offers to sell his way out. It may be that his only possible contribution is physical strength; but whatever it is, nobody chooses to buy. On his way he sees grocery stores bulging with every good thing to eat, clothing stores bulging with every good thing to wear. Yet he must content himself and his family with food that the well-to-do would not think of letting their dogs eat, and he must walk among his fellow mortals in coat and trousers picked up at a second-hand shop or pawnshop, and shoes bought at a church bazaar or dug from an ash-can. Something like that is all that he sees ahead for himself. Doesn't he feel that the world is a fine place filled with thoughtful people, and that he himself is a miraculous being only a little below the stature of a god?

And those who are not so poor as that, yet who know that something too formidable for them to grapple with unaided will in like manner enslave them as long as they live—are they much better off?

"I'll tell you—I'll tell you exactly what it is," said a woman of high intelligence and discriminating speech who had been reduced from a modest, earned subsistence to this upper level of poverty by the knavery of some shrewd investment brokers; "it is getting up every morning and feeling that somebody you know is dying at the moment. I suppose it must be because you are conscious of your own slow death. You declare you'll outface it. I've done that a thousand times. But no matter what you do, nothing in the world can look the same. I must be careful not to use quite so much of anything for breakfast as I really need. And what is the very cheapest thing I can get for dinner? I spend time trying to figure that out. And then I never buy one thing without wondering if I ought not to have spent a little more time and tried to find something cheaper. I buy the cheapest dresses; and when they are out of style I make them over—as long as the material will hold together. I like books—current books—but I can't even rent the ones

I'd like to own. I like flowers. But I tell you, the colors of the dahlias and phlox fade when you can't get out of your head the fear that next week you may not have enough to hold soul and body together. I walk in the woods and try to feel some of the life all about me that I used to feel, and it only makes me sad. Nothing, I tell you, can be the same—not even myself. I try to be, but I know all the while that nearly all my neighbors—even the ones who do not mean to—attach so much importance to economic status, as though it were an index of intelligence, that they discover through my threadbare state a deficiency in me that they had not until just now ever dreamed was there. And they are right. For something has passed from me. I am no longer myself. I cannot even want to be myself as much as I used to."

On a long swinging trip up the Ohio valley and back again to the Mississippi, I became poverty-conscious. In the edges of the South I saw share-croppers and other tenant farmers by hundreds, by thousands, whose families looked like nothing so much as weather-tattered scarecrows—and they were living a life that was productive for everybody but themselves and their class. I stood in a station while a toothless old woman who looked as if she had never had a square meal in her life was saying to an old man of the same sort: "But I says, 'The Lord gives,' so I s'pose the Lord takes away, too." And when I got on the train I sat for an hour with a business man from New York—a most engaging and friendly person—and heard him tell with great satisfaction how he was able to make good profits in a venture in the Piedmont district of South Carolina because he had to pay only a dollar a day to his workers for a ten-hour day—so great was the oversupply of workers. And in a number of cities, restaurant managers told me that so many children and grown-ups fed daily from restaurant garbage-cans, that they required "the boys" to sort the garbage when they put it out in the alley, so that the hungry would not have to dig through all the potato peelings and other wet stuff in order to get at the breadcrusts and halves of bananas.

As I traveled through the southern half of Ohio and on into West Virginia I saw deserted mining towns where the coal had been worked out, or where strip-mining with power shovels had supplanted men altogether; steep hillsides where the abandoned were trying to produce corn, beans, and potatoes in soil that was largely sandstone or flintstone; river and creek bottoms lined with people who had got possession of a hovel—or an abandoned box-car—and were living in it and growing as much as they could make a half-acre produce. I saw children who had started out with the eagerness of all new life, and with the best of biological equipment, gradually fading through undernourishment and general want until they were taking on the character of their harum-scarum surroundings, and proving incontrovertibly that most people are not poor because they are "like that," but "like that" because they are poor. There seemed to be no increase in life anywhere, but everywhere a decline. I experienced a strange enervation, as if the total of human energy had been so diminished that I was running short myself. When the train swung sharply round a hill where a dilapidated old brick house of much dignity stood among some leaning cedars, I wanted to rush up the hill through the dying orchard and past the cedars, throw the door open and cry: "In God's name, is there any life here, or is the last of it going?"

And West Virginia was more disheartening still. For generations the West Virginian has lived a life of the greatest heroism in his effort to realize for his children the vast dream that he brought with him from beyond the mountains. But he has been too successfully robbed of everything that should be his natural heritage. Somebody from somewhere else has come in and got possession of his coal, and has hauled it to other regions for the production of profits there. Somebody has come in and taken his timber. Somebody has come in and taken his oil and gas. He has been forced to be content with a daily wage paid to him by one of these somebodies from somewhere else. Often enough the wage has been inhumanly low, and the mining-town life in which he has been compelled to bring up his family has been disgraceful beyond description. He harbors a well-grounded feeling that, through somebody's trick, life has irreparably defrauded him. Is it surprising that he is in a state of mind that the inflammatory might touch off?

Not one word of fundamental blame can be attached to such people. They start out in childhood as bravely as any other new biological and mental life. But they are not many years old before the pressure begins to show. Between Parkersburg and Clarksburg, as the train climbed a steep grade so slowly that it was going but little faster than a man could walk, we were about to overtake a young woman who was carrying a two-year-old child briskly along a path in the meadow just above the railroad tracks. The child, a light-haired, blue-eyed girl that might well enough have been the original of one of Sir Joshua Reynolds's studies, looked back over her mother's shoulder and watched the train so that we saw her full in the face all the while we were coming up. She was filled with wonder and delight and confidence. But as we passed, and the mother's face came into view—she could not have been more than eighteen or nineteen, and, with shoulders back the least bit to balance the weight of the child, moved with the litheness of a schoolgirl—it revealed the hardness, the suspicious glance, the shadow, which told that she already felt the contest going against her. The next day I watched a girl out of the same hill region while she played the violin—brilliantly. The straight, sandstone-colored hair, the face that bore the marks of some uphill fight, the nervous body, and keen mind, somehow constituted a person who seemed ready in a moment, because of her sense of inferior opportunity, to fly into battle.

I caught something of poverty's sweep. I saw poverty with a certain wholeness. I saw it like a section of a map in second color spreading a smothering blanket over millions of people and chloroforming their thought and wills. During workdays they labored at something that—as things are now organized—was guaranteed to be insufficient. And then on idle days and Sundays they could do nothing but wait, wait, and hopelessly try to put in the time until somebody who owned the land they tilled, or the mills they operated, and the rattletrap houses they lived in should find it financially profitable to give them the least bit of a better chance.

Yet all the way back from the Alleghenies to the Mississippi I encountered people who baited me into seeing how far the impoverished are from being justified in hope.

"It wouldn't hurt to have a little new housing down there, would it?" I asked of the agreeable man across the aisle in the Pullman who had traded newspapers with me a few minutes before.

"Ah-h," he said, with something that was more like displeasure than disbelief in his voice, "they like it. They wouldn't feel at home if they had anything better."

"Possibly not, now that they are inured to this. But how about their children?"

He looked at me strangely as if he had suddenly discovered a bearded Russian commissar sitting there across from him. "Do you mean to say that you think things like that can be changed?"

I must have bristled up ever so slightly, for I echoed his language: "Do you mean to tell me that with farms already overproducing, and with limitless supplies of bricks and cement in the earth to be had for the making, there should be any decent family in the United States without abundant food and comfortable shelter?"

He laughed. He looked at me pityingly. "In my town we have an up-and-coming club of four hundred and fifty men—practical men, if you know what a practical man is—"

"Usually a man who never sees anything until at least ten years after it has happened. But go ahead."

"Well, I was just going to say that if you were to come and tell them all this that you've been telling me, they would simply laugh at you."

"I am sure they would."

He was puzzled. "Why, man, you can't change such things as that. Don't you know that some things have money in them and others don't? Why, that ought to be as simple as a, b, c. They just happen to be doing the things that don't have money in them. There's no money in coal mining—or not much, anyway. It simply isn't there. There's no money in this tenant farming—and a hell of a lot of other things. My God, isn't that plain enough? It simply isn't there."

"But why isn't it there? If a man works twice the usual number of hours a day producing food that the rest of us have to have, or risks his life in a coal mine where the casualties are about as great as on a fairly quiet sector of a battle-front, why shouldn't he be paid in proportion to what he contributes—contributes to the rest of us? I noticed that you had bacon and eggs and toast and honey for breakfast this morning. Did they come out of the top of some pleasant skyscraper somewhere?"

He shook his head as if I were a small boy who couldn't understand long division. "Why, all this goes along with our development. Aren't you in favor of progress—or are you? These people are the least fit—so they don't survive, that's all. They've had their chance."

"Who decides that they are the least fit? And what sort of chance do their children have? Here—here's what I tore from the newspaper I traded to you. One of the members of the Rockefeller family left his estate to be held in trust till 1950 and then distributed among his great-grandchildren. There are more than two dozen of them now, according to the newspaper, and there may be twice that many by 1950. Even if there should be, every one of them will automatically become a millionaire. Now when some children are started off in that fashion, and others from the first day of their lives are undernourished, physically and otherwise, in hovels like those we saw back there, isn't it a bit dogmatic to assume without further experimentation that those in the hovels are inferior by nature?"

He was outraged. He threw up his hands in an impatient expression of disgust. "Oh, my God! My God! We'll feed 'em. We'll pay the taxes and feed 'em. What more can you ask?"

"At least a little," I answered. Then for an hour each one of us looked very steadfastly out at the landscape on his own side of the car.

And no sooner had I arrived at my destination than I had a related point of view thrust upon me. I was to spend a week-end in a college where the guest-rooms were in the main building. I busied myself on Saturday evening with the page proofs of a little book on Edwin Arlington Robinson. In the middle of the evening as I wandered through long corridors to rest my eyes for a few minutes I came upon the president of the college and his wife and two other guests. One of these was a physician in his sixties, and a patron, I believe, of the college. We all sat together for a time in one of the parlors. The physician professed to know something about me—at least he knew that I was a writing man of some sort—and immediately asked what I was working on at the moment. I told him something of the little book on Robinson.

"Don't know the first thing about him," he confessed, as if he were not too much ashamed.

I had stopped my proof-reading just where Robinson was in despair because of his long struggle with poverty, and then unexpectedly found himself saved by the bequest of Professor John Hays Gardiner. I thought the quietly dramatic incident might be impressive, and related it.

"He suffered from some weakness," the physician declared diagnostically, "or he never would have let himself get into such a predicament. Why didn't he get out and work?"

"As a matter of fact, he did. But if he used up his energy at something else, what was to become of the poetry he wanted to write?"

"No matter what. He should have worked and saved money, and made himself the leisure in which to write—at anything—as a garage man, if necessary. I worked *my* way through college, and it was good for me."

"But afterward, you did not work as a garage man in order that you might practise medicine for nothing."

He looked at me as if I were beginning to hit below the belt. "It's a question of demand—natural demand. There's a demand for medicine. People are ready to pay for it."

I had visions of miles of medical propaganda that I had seen, and of countless cards issued by local medical associations which announced that beginning next month if you didn't care to pay the following scale of fees you could send for the undertaker—or words to that effect. But I only remarked: "We are just in a cave-man stage of democracy unless we give every human being opportunity to kick free and be the most of himself possible, and compensate him for whatever of general usefulness he can best contribute."

"Utopian!" he declared with a finality that both of us were ready to accept.

# xii

# Creole

THIS is a confession—of something I meant to do, and of why I failed to do it. I meant to write about the deep South—the old South that was left when human slavery was gone. It had always fascinated me. I was constantly trying to find ways of routing journeys so that they would take me through the region and give me new glimpses of something already familiar or something still to be explored.

And now after alternations of summer sunshine and soft, slushy snow in north Texas, I was to have days of free time in New Orleans. I would have something better than hurried trips through the Vieux Carré. I would make my way upstate and see ante-bellum plantation houses. I would go all the way up the river to Natchez and wander about among old houses of such beauty that they seem to have sprung from some poetic existence no longer possible to the American mind. But especially would I explore New Orleans to my heart's content. I would breathe the Creole atmosphere.

It was a wet, heavy morning when I arrived. Yes, the hotelkeeper could let me have a room, provided I did not want to keep it on into the week-end, for everything in his house had long been reserved for Mardi Gras.

This was as it should be; this had the true New Orleans note. And when I went up to my room, it also was in the right tradition, for it was as large as all four of the rooms I had most recently occupied in succession, the ceiling was far away like the sky, and instead of crashing metropolitan roars bursting in at the windows, there only trickled in some friendly clattering noises from the narrow street just below.

But down in the lobby after breakfast, I did not seem to be in New Orleans. The great briskness of life seemed somehow inappropriate. Quickly I was comforted, though, when I saw a book-shop right in the lobby that sold books on "old New Orleans." I was comforted still more when the young woman in charge told me that she was a relative of George W. Cable's. Though I doubted—as did she—whether he could find a publisher for *Old Creole Days* if he were seeking one today, it was good to have his material on record. Then just as quickly I oscillated back to a troubled feeling when I encountered the overbrisk guide by the door who wished to show me about. I could see New Orleans in three hours—if only I entrusted myself to him. No, I did not want any guide. I was ready to pay him to keep away. Didn't I know well enough what I wanted to see?

The skies cleared a little, and in the dripping sunshine I walked over to Canal Street. All the people in the city seemed to be on the sidewalks. Yet I did not see a single face out of the old New Orleans. They were cheerful, energetic faces, looking ahead. At once I liked them. They were not what I had been expecting to see; they were more interesting.

I crossed Canal Street, and wandered contentedly into Royal. Two men just ahead of me were talking about Kingfish Huey Long. In the part of the United States where I live, I am sure I never heard one word about Huey Long that was to his credit. And here were two men in broad daylight who spoke deliberately, earnestly about him as if he had been one of the saviors of mankind. For me there was a great stimulating liveliness in their considered speech. I kept within hearing of them for a minute or two until they turned in at a shop.

Then I loafed along other streets—along Bienville, where, I remembered, E. H. Sothern once told me he was born; along Chartres; along Toulouse; along Bourbon; along St. Louis. But nothing in the entire quarter interested me as I had thought it would. I felt no magic in such names as the Old Absinthe House, the Caloboza, the Spanish Arsenal, the Gate of the Lions, the Old Davis Dance Hall. The "old" houses seemed dreadfully secondhand. The antiques were self-conscious. How could there be so much unemployment everywhere in the United States when all these shops had to be supplied with antiques?

Nor did any restaurant advertise the kind of luncheon I wanted. Why should I go into a dark, cavernous-looking place decorated with swords and other too-ancient-looking souvenirs and eat a meal of foods suited to a starving pirate, when I wished only a lettuce salad and some corn-sticks and coffee. So I tramped all the way back to the hotel—and then crossed the street and ate in a busy, cheerful cafeteria.

For a time I was by myself at the table. Then a blue-eyed waitress who might have been from East Boston unloaded a man's tray for him opposite me.

He nodded quite cordially. Was I a stranger? He thought I must be. Yes, he himself had always lived in New Orleans. He hoped I was finding the city an interesting place.

Yes, I was. "But tell me about this man Huey Long. Up where I live, you never hear anything to his credit. Is there anything?"

"Plenty!" he said, drawing the word out for emphasis. "More to be said for him than against him. At least I've about decided so."

"All right, go ahead and present his case for him. You see, I've never heard what the defense had to say."

He was not hesitant. "Well, we've got about as fine a system of surfaced roads as you'll find in the South—and you've got to give the credit to Huey. Until he came along nobody knew just what we had here in the state, for there were no roads so that you could get around to see. Maybe he did build the ones in front of his friends' houses first—I don't know. But he built the others, too. And all these free bridges—they were Huey's idea, too. And instead of a crumbling old fortress for a state-house we've now got about as fine a one as anybody. And didn't he put our state university on the map?"

"But don't all those things cost money?"

"Sure! But we've got it. We're paying off the bonds. We can. And we've got the roads and the bridges, and all the rest. Why, the tourists who are swarming in here to see what we've got will pay for everything if they keep on coming at the rate of the past two or three years."

He grew enthusiastic. There were other things to be said in Huey's favor. "Didn't Huey wage war on the telephone company when it was soaking us, and save us a lot of money? And didn't he make the oil interests come across with a little of their share of the taxes? Got free textbooks for the kids of the state, too, so that a lot of the ones that'd been too poor to go to school could go. Why, that's what I call a damned good record for one lifetime—especially when it's a short one."

We talked for an hour. Then he thought he had better get back to the office before they found out that they could get along without him.

I strolled back to the Vieux Carré. The cathedral anyhow would be worth time. I had always liked the etching of it that hung above the bookcases at home.

But by the time I arrived, the cathedral, too, was the least bit less impressive than I had thought it was going to be. I believed I liked the etching better. Maybe, after all, art was an improvement on—other art.

I stepped inside. The sudden great quiet brought me strange assurance. I stood motionless. I wanted to stand thus for a long time.

Then some hard-eyed beadle of a person drew near and said in a raucous voice, "Right this way to see all the points of interest!" He brought a dozen sight-seers together over on the other side and then walked back toward me. "All the points of interest! All the points of interest! All the points of interest!"

I wanted to tell him to go to hell with his points of interest. Was there nothing else to be found in a church? But instead I turned on my heel without a word and walked out into the intermittent sunshine and across to Jackson Square. The grass was green and the flowers were in full bloom, just as if there were no antiques in the world.

Beyond the long shed of the wharves almost directly in front of me, the spars of some kind of ship rose just to sight.

"What is it?" I asked a policeman, and nodded.

"Warship—the new 'Brooklyn.' You can go aboard if you want to."

I went aboard; I chatted with some sailors, and from one boyish new recruit received special attentions when he learned that I was from his home town; I enjoyed the hospitality of some courteous officers.

When I came ashore I walked forward on the wharf to study the thin bow of the ship. A half-dozen loafers sat on some crates near where I stopped. While I watched a gull with a broken wing swimming about in the heavy-looking water of the Mississippi trying to get food that did not require flying, they discussed international affairs.

"This Mauslini, he's a purty big shot, all right."

"Yes, but Hitler's goin' to lick hell out of him some of these days—unless all the papers are giving us bull."

The destiny of nations was a game. They laughed. "Just like bein' any other kind of champeen. Mauslini thinks he's good. Then Hitler comes along and shows him just how good. Then some of these days somebody will come along and show Hitler, too. And maybe not so many Goddamned days, either!" They guessed that the Kingfish if he had come along a little further would have been the one to turn the trick. The Kingfish was bright.

At dinner that evening in the house of an old friend, my hostess regretted that she could not help me to a surer estimate of the Kingfish's qualities. "You know, there's a difference of opinion about even the monument or tomb that they say they're going to build for him up at Baton Rouge. Some say it's to commemorate him, and some say it's just to hold him down."

But two guests at dinner offered to help. They were driving back to Natchez the next afternoon. Didn't I wish to go along and see the beautiful old houses?

Yes, I still did.

The next morning, though, the rain was pouring. For two hours after breakfast I tramped restlessly about in the hotel. A man who looked as if he might be from somewhere else sat in a deep chair in the lobby and read *Every Man a King*. I amused myself by watching his face as I marched back and forth, and tried to imagine just what he was reading about when I saw the expression on his face undergoing changes. He did not notice my watching. He was so dead in earnest that he was oblivious of everything around him.

While I marched I decided not to go to Natchez. Instead I climbed into a taxi, went to a newspaper building and asked to be directed to the editorial rooms. After I had waited a moment a man came from somewhere into the quiet of the office and asked me what he could do for me. I told him that I was looking for somebody who was ready to loaf for a half-hour, at least. I wanted to get the low-down on Huey Long.

"I know the very man you are looking for," he said cheerfully. "This way!"

And soon I was sitting face to face with an energetic gray-haired man who had been in the newspaper game all his life just because he liked it.

In a room noisy with typewriters he sat back in his desk chair and answered questions and talked. No, the paper had not gone along with Huey in his career—exactly; but Huey was an amazing person. He helped me to see the struggling, eloquent young advocate, the dapper young governor, the vindictive, cruel fighter of the later years. He pictured and half-impersonated Huey in his hotel room when his enemies were so hot in the battle against him that an emergency had to be met—lying in bed with a telephone on either side, calling his friends in every part of the state, calling them by the dozens without the use of a note-book or telephone directory. Huey knew all the tricks of warfare and he had the brilliant ability to carry them off successfully more times than not.

"But the total effect of his life, now that he has been dead a few years—?"

"Well, he speeded us up. You can't say less than that for him. We are doing all sorts of things in the state now that we probably wouldn't have thought of trying if he hadn't happened along."

Hadn't I seen some of their roads and bridges? Huey probably paid too much for them, but they were worth seeing. He thought I had better spend a day or two at Baton Rouge. I ought not to miss the new state university and the new state-house.

The next morning I was on the way. I did not waste even the time I spent on the train. While the long aisle of the coaches was curving and straightening and counter-curving as we sped through wet country, I startled approachable-looking people by asking them point-blank to tell me what they thought of Huey Long. Nobody declined to answer. Nobody was neutral. Huey was the most dangerous man the state—perhaps the nation—ever produced. Huey was the greatest governor the state ever had. Huey was just an ordinary thug. Huey would have been the next president of the United States—and a good one.

One man confessed that he was a prejudiced witness. "I work for the Standard Oil Company." He laughed. "But you've got to hand it to him."

Another man was an artist in his outlook. Huey had the great redeeming quality of interest. He was no worse than his enemies, and not half so stupid.

He smiled reflectively as he talked, and half of the time looked out at the window or up along the rows of heads above the seats of the coach. He liked to remember Huey's earlier life. It made what he called a hell of a good story. Huey was alive. Huey was ready to look out for himself—and did. Wasn't it something for a man to get out and hoe his own row—through law school, through years of thin practice, and later through the heavy barrage laid down by financial interests who suspected—and rightly—that he was their enemy? Wasn't it natural for him to champion the underdog? Hadn't he been one long enough to appreciate how it feels? And were his ideas so crazy? Did I know of any instances where Huey backed the wrong side when the future welfare of the people was at stake? Weren't we all going to have to come to something like Huey's notion of spreading the wealth— "You know 'spreading the wealth' is what he called it originally"—if the machine were to go on running, if the wealth were to remain wealth for anybody? Weren't the rich themselves beginning to talk about the need of prosperity for the wide base of the social pyramid? Just who, then, had been so crazy?

All the while he talked we were skimming along through flat wet country thick with bare-looking little houses not much larger than chicken houses. They were very much in one style—a story-and-a-half front with a set-in porch taking a good large notch out of the first floor, and a tiny, one-story shed of a kitchen behind. I had said little, because I was interested in listening and looking.

"This is the Huey he wanted to be," he said as he fished in his pocket and found a worn clipping from one of Huey's speeches in the United States Senate:

"Nonetheless my voice will be the same as it has been. Patronage will not change it. Fear will not change it. Persecution will not change it. It cannot be changed while people suffer. The only way it can be changed is to make the lives of these people decent and respectable. No one will ever hear political opposition out of me when that is done."

"So," he said as he watched me finish the words, "you must be beginning to see that I'm for him."

Baton Rouge was alive and inviting. The new state university was as great a delight to the eye as I had been told it would be—even if the football stadium did bulk rather too large.

But it was the new state-house that I was most anxious to see. Everybody spoke of it as if it were Huey Long's chief work—and monument. I had been prepared to expect something impressive and appropriate. I had seen the tower of the Nebraska state-house at Lincoln, and knew how effective a tower in the open can be. Nebraska, though, has not given enough thought to its state-house approaches. Out there I was disappointed in the close view. But in Baton Rouge somebody had given the approaches much thought. I came suddenly to the end of the street, and there diagonally across immensely large formal gardens of great beauty, through Spanish moss clinging to a few trees in the corner of the gardens close in front of me, the gray tower rose four or five hundred feet toward a blue sky that was flecked with white clouds. It was a strangely useful-looking tower, too, with columnar lines of windows that added to the effect of height and lightness.

With a certain hesitation I walked toward it—through blooming azaleas and roses and camellias that were alive with mocking-birds. I was out of the world of ordinary realities. But eventually—it seemed a very long, very agreeable time—I was aware of the slamming of automobile doors, and the ordinary conversations of men, and the presence, directly in front of me, not of the white tower, but of the broad, slowly rising steps of the entrance, the two gigantic groups symbolizing the Patriots and the Pioneers upon the buttresses of the steps, and the entrance doorway rising so high that it seemed almost presumption for anything so small as a man to enter through it.

Did I wish to have some one take me about and explain all the marbles and bronzes and panels and plaques and murals? No, I did not, though I felt that the somewhat heavy opulence of decoration would require time from anyone who would have his impressions clear. But, yes, I did wish to go to the top of the tower.

It was like being suspended in a very steady plane not too far above the earth. The Mississippi off to the right stretched away southward in such lazy-looking calm and sense of dominance that one saw it first. But there was the city spreading in the sunlight before us, and beyond it the new state university, and directly beneath us the formal state-house grounds.

"He's buried right there," some woman over on my right was explaining to another who stood beside her, "where you see that small area in the very middle of the grounds."

There was a more or less continuous procession from automobiles across to the little area. Some of the men uncovered as they came up to it, as if they were entering the tomb of Napoleon.

When I went back down, I spent an hour or two among the bronzes and murals before I took the train back to New Orleans. On the way out in the morning I had been impressed by everything I saw—rows of palmettos just outside New Orleans, hundreds of men at work on some Federal project, plantation workers busy in wet fields, cabbage in rows, berry bushes white with bloom, houses on stilts above ground that was marshy from recent rains, children of various shades playing along wet roads. But I have only one memory of the trip back—two strapping Negro men walking along a track that paralleled ours, each carrying a heavy railroad tie with an ax sunk deep into it, the handle sticking down close along the tie, and behind them a short distance a Negro girl of fourteen or fifteen, lithe as a young tigress, carrying a tie that was just as large as the others.

On the evening train when I started northward, the man across the table in the dining-car looked up pleasantly when the steward seated me. After a few preliminaries he asked: "Seeing a little of old New Orleans?"

"I meant to, but I got side-tracked to Huey Long, and have spent most of my time chasing around to find out what he was really up to."

His face grew tense. "He didn't get away with any of that body-guard dictator stuff when he came up to New York. When he insulted those two girls at that night-club or whatever it was, didn't he get the beating-up of his life?"

"Just what did he say to them that could insult them?"

the man beside me wanted to know. "Anyhow, the whole thing was a frame-up."

They were still arguing when I left the table an hour and a half later to enjoy the lounge-car.

Toward midnight, when I was on my way back to bed, as I passed the dressing-room of one Pullman I overheard somebody in full voice mention Huey Long. Could it be that these two were still arguing? I pushed the green curtain aside and glanced in. No, they were another two.

"Come in and join us," a stocky man whose face was ruddy commanded me. "This is almost gone, but I've got another pint."

I told him I had heard somebody mention Huey Long's name and was only interested in what was being said.

He jumped up. "You won't drink awhile? Why, whiskies don't hurt you—at least they don't hurt me. I have ten a day, three hundred a month—that's about my average—and just feel that right arm. Hard as nails, isn't it?"

"Maybe it's just pickled."

He took a quick glance at me, decided in my favor, slapped me on the shoulder, and begged me to sit down. "Hell, it's only midnight. My friend here that I fell in with is not as good a drinker as I am, and he's almost past talking. So I'll talk to you." He laughed.

Yes! Sure! He had known Huey. That was what they had just been talking about. He had sold construction materials to the state of Louisiana while Huey was governor. And he had just been saying that he had more than once placed a little something here and there that he thought would lubricate the way to sales, but that he had no reason to believe that Huey had even profited from it personally. Of course, some of his friends might have. And Huey built the best roads in the South. "They'll stand up. They've got plenty of cement and steel in them. I know."

He turned to the other man. "But I didn't mean to hold the floor. You were just about to say something."

"Oh, I don't know whether I can make myself clear."

He shivered a little, like a boy who is chilled through, but has a strong will. "All I was trying to say was that Huey was an idealist who came upon evil days. If I can make myself clear—don't you think most people treat their idealism as an avocation? They just keep it to play around with when they're not obliged to be busy with something else. They like to have it to fall back on. There it is—safe! But Huey thought he could weave his into the texture of things. He thought it could be done. And he was soon so far from contact with most of his fellow Louisianians that he got lost." Whose fault, then, was it? Who could say? But most of Huey's crimes would be forgotten, some day, he was sure, and the eventual Huey Long myth would be that of a bright young man who had honestly wanted to be useful to his kind—and who had had some success.

The next morning as we sped through areas of rehabilitated red fields in upper Georgia, I was farther away than ever from thought of the antiques of New Orleans. What if the entire South should be awakened to new consciousness of itself and its resources? And is the human race so drugged with its own lassitude that it cannot become aware of its capacities except when jolted by some one who employs strong-arm methods?

## xiii

## Home

IT is always exciting to return from newer regions of the United States to Cambridge, Massachusetts. If I chance to come in from the west along the Charles River I begin while we are still in Newton to strain my eyes for a first glimpse of the commanding familiar bulk of Memorial Hall, with its steadily growing family of white towers and spires spreading out in every direction. As soon as I am at home I must walk some streets that I have known and see some faces that I have seen before and hear speech that I have come to like more than any other.

"Well, you see I didn't have to go back across after that job of being King," remarked the stooped, blue-eyed old Irishman who has swept our street for a dozen years, when he noticed me and thought I must be just back from somewhere. "But it does beat hell how one American woman can march right in over there and change the whole drift of everything."

The surgeons had first carved a piece out of one side of his face, and then down the side of his neck, but he declared that he was still going strong and that it was a fine day.

Something like that I encounter almost before I am out of the house. Then I wander, relaxed and at ease with the world, over miles of brick sidewalks—unquestionably the worst ones in existence—and reacquaint myself with the familiar. I must get to feeling at home once more so that I may settle down to chapter-the-next.

I walk along Kirkland Street, where I used sometimes to meet William James as I hurried to class, and recall the friendly steadiness of his eyes as I risked glancing at his face; I wander on through the Harvard Yard and Harvard Square with their high percentage of live, intelligent-looking people, and on down to the Charles, where the flashing oars of a half-dozen speeding shells ripple and rib clear water that is full of the reflection of white towers; I walk along the river and enjoy one of the Cambridge skies celebrated by a Cambridge poet; I pass a grocery store where Dean Le Baron R. Briggs one day stood backed against the rough-faced brick wall, with the front of one shoe heel lifted and hooked on the upper edge of the cement foundation and with a green bookbag full of groceries over his shoulder, and told me a story that he relished.

Cambridge is full of such memories. Cambridge is full of much else that is pleasant. Cambridge seems not to impose upon me a single disagreeable fact. I am in a haven of safety. Yet I do not long feel altogether safe. After a few days I am aware of an irritation, as if nettles were growing up here and there through the wide cracks between the bricks of the sidewalks and attaining my own height.

I always have this experience when I remain in Cambridge long enough. It recurs, I have to admit, because of my attitude toward human beings as I have known them. This attitude is nothing that I boast of; but because it seems to me such a reasonable one for anybody to hold, I sometimes reveal it when I am not trying to do so. In the abstract, it is simply this: I should like to see any person who possesses responsive native equipment possess also the livable surroundings and the freedom from inner conflict and emotional insecurity that would permit him to enjoy an enriched consciousness of life. For to me it is through enrichment of consciousness that a man comes—if at all—to the sense of harmony and fair prospect that saves him from being a lunatic or a beast.

This means more than it seems to say. For I have come to believe that the number of human beings who possess responsive equipment—who are moved to think about their own lives and to aspire to a better one of some kind, and who do aspire, perhaps up to some breaking-point along the way—is much greater than it is fashionable to admit. I know railroad engineers, oil drillers, coal miners, Pullman porters, shoe cobblers, elevator operators, potters, bricklayers, farm owners, farm wives, and farm hands whose essential gentility, humor, consideration for neighbors next door or on the other side of the earth, capacity to look at new facts and grasp their meaning, and hungerings for some unachieved satisfying life could be matched with the qualities of any group of business men, public officials, or college teachers that might be assembled for the test. I should like to see all such people, regardless of their economic rating or race or special beliefs, come into possession of whatever is required to afford them some of life's compensations.

Now anybody who lets it be known that he believes great

numbers of human beings in the United States deserve a better opportunity than they enjoy, and that he favors seeing that they get it, inevitably begets special trouble for himself in Cambridge. I ought to remember this and develop some safer technique of precaution. But each time I come back I find Cambridge at once so friendly to me as a person, and on the surface so friendly toward the world in general, that I am habitually beguiled into the necessity of learning everything all over again.

It was just so when I came back the last time. One morning when I went down to the bank to see whether I had any balance I chanced to meet an acquaintance. I had two or three etchings or lithographs from the Southwest under my arm.

"Something interesting?" he asked as he tried to peer through the thin paper.

I showed them to him. One was an artist's idealization of Tulsa, Oklahoma.

He studied it for a moment. "Now, what business have they with such buildings as those way down there?"

The next day I received a sharper, heavier impression. A friend had asked me to have a bite of lunch with him at the Faculty Club. As soon as we were seated he confessed that he had asked me because he hoped to get something out of me. I traveled, I saw the country. Now what did I think of the looks of things? Before he gave me any opportunity to tell him he told me between great choleric swallows of soup what he himself thought. The country was going to hell. Just consider his own case. He was actually worse off than he had been in the evil days of the depression. His Harvard salary, it was true, had not been reduced. But it had not been reduced in the depression either. That was just the trouble. Prices had now gone up and he could not save as much to invest as in 1931 or 1932.

I sought to comfort him. I told him that I had just returned from the Dust Bowl in northwestern Oklahoma and that, with somewhat better prices, farmers who had faced starvation only three or four years ago were now quite heroically managing to get along.

Well, yes, he supposed there might be a little something in that. But the taxes a man had to pay!

I sought to ease him along a little farther. I had seen, in the same region, how usefully some of the money collected by the government is spent. The farmers in the region had been suffering heavy losses from a certain disease among their cattle, and a government agency was the only one that could direct the war against the disease in so wide an area. I had found it reassuring to see scientific knowledge thus made a regular part of the farmer's resources.

He took larger and larger bites of cold tongue at increased speed. Then he let go: "There you are! It wasn't enough for us to feed all those Middle Westerners in the depression. We've got to be taxed so that somebody from one of their cow colleges can have the job of telling them what to do for their sick cattle. That's how much individual initiative there is left! The whole damned country is going socialistic."

He wanted resistance. So I tried not to seem merely amused. "Now, just wait a minute. Let's get the whole thing straight. On the way up from New York I sat for an hour and watched the lighthouses on every ledge and point along the Connecticut shore. Am I to understand that they are all maintained by private capital?"

"My God! You mean to say that there's no difference between the two cases?"

"Why, yes. Protecting shipping after it is in boats is

democracy, and protecting it while it is still walking round on four feet is socialism."

Since I denied him the impetus of showing any temper, he let a hot smile flash over his face while he declared that I ought to have my bachelor's degree taken away from me. How a man who seemed as sane as I did in many matters could be so absolutely crazy in economics was more than he could figure out.

As I walked homeward I stopped before a book-shop on lower Brattle Street to look at the titles in the window. A man of my years whom I have long known stopped beside me. "Just the expert I'm needing. Recommend a couple of good books to me—not tripe, but real meat."

"There they are," I said, "both by the same author." Thurman W. Arnold's *The Symbols of Government* and *The Folklore of Capitalism* were displayed together.

"Must be some God-damned Communist—if titles mean anything."

It did no good to assure him that the author held a somewhat respectable professorship in the Yale Law School. The colleges were all going to hell—Yale especially.

I kept to my work for several days and ate my lunch at Sears Roebuck's counter, a half-mile from Harvard Square.

But one afternoon I had to go down to the post-office. It was raining, and just as I entered the lobby a man turned on his heel from the stamp window with such abruptness, and brushed past two or three of us and out into a waiting cab with such an air of contempt for everybody in sight that I took a second look. As he settled back into the cab I thought I had never seen a more perfect representative of the body of New Englanders who subscribe to the Symphony, contribute to charities, entertain their friends with genuine cordiality, and drive their mill employees hard.

"Saw you noticing that fellow," the man at the wicket said. "You looked at him as if you had about the same opinion of him that I have. Somebody left some steamship reservations there on the desk in the lobby a while ago. They were for space on a boat that is sailing tonight. I telephoned to the steamship offices and gave them the numbers of the state-rooms, and they managed to get in touch with the owner. He was the bird you saw. When I passed the tickets through to him he took them as if they were money I owed him and never even grunted in thanks."

Every day I came upon some new or half-repeated variation of this strange partnership of cordiality and contempt, or cordiality and choleric rage, or cordiality and fear. One evening the wife of Albert Schweitzer lectured in behalf of his hospital in Africa. Since the evening when a waitress who is also a poet and a sensitive philosopher had first brought one of his books to me I had always regarded him as one of the great men of our time. But now, as his wife presented his case for him—talking on in broken English and showing colored slides of the suffering natives who were ready to endure any hardship for weeks or months in order to reach the hospital—he seemed not only great, but infinitely gentle in his unsentimentalized love for his kind. I understood better now how he was willing to subordinate his interest in Bach, and the building and playing of organs, and his quest of the historical Jesus, and his work on the stumbling march of civilization, to this one great enterprise of expressing in a specific way his reverence for all life. I thought I understood a little better too why he felt out of sympathy with the unthinking age in which he lived, and in consequence experienced a great isolation. Some women near us wept, and at the end of the lecture the audience contributed generously toward the hospital's continuation.

A day or two later a woman in our neighborhood remarked to me that she had seen us there—and wasn't it a wonderful thing Albert Schweitzer was doing? I spoke of having recently been down among the mountaineers of Tennessee and Kentucky, and of the need down there not only for hospitals but for something much more difficult to contribute.

A shadow swept her face as though I had announced the threat of invasion by a foreign enemy. But she recovered quickly and said she supposed that I was right. But didn't I think that giving money to people pauperized them? She had once known of an instance. She sketched it. She had actually known that instance herself. Then she wandered away into the safely vague and universal, and ended by obliging me to hear for the millionth time the story of the poor family that had been moved into a comfortable little house only to use the new bathtub to keep the coal in. I had heard some version of it in every city in the country.

I doubled my vigilance in keeping away from people who might want to know what I thought about anything except the weather. When I one day met a man just at lunch time who said that he understood I had been away and that he'd like to ask me some questions, I hastened to reply that I had to be over in the city in fifteen minutes—and then in order to make my words true, I went over. I could eat just as well over there and maybe do an errand or two afterward.

I sought out a quiet restaurant off Charles Street where one may eat upstairs. As I was about to sit down I heard somebody calling my name—my first name. Two men with whom I had had a casual Harvard Square acquaintance for years were at a table for three.

"We're giving hell to the New Deal; come over and join us."

While I waited for my order I listened in silence. But silence was not what they wanted; they wanted approval.

When they finally smoked me out I tried to make myself clear by saying that since I believed the aspirations of individual human beings were more important than anything else, I clung to no partisanships or organized antipathies, but accepted or rejected measures on the basis of whether they afforded more people an opportunity for growth.

They looked at me and at each other in consternation. "Do you mean to say then that you can find some things to accept in what this God-damned Russian dictator is doing down at Washington?"

I did not have to answer. Nor did I have opportunity to insist that my interests are not politically partisan, but only those of a man who is aware that human beings have a common destiny. For they took all the time to tell me what they thought of the President of the United States. I should like to make a record of what they called him, of what the vast majority of my pleasant friends call him when somebody's chance remark frees them of all inhibitions. Once when I was writing something on Abraham Lincoln I did print a paragraph of names that his opponents had applied to him. But the ones my neighbors apply to the President of the United States in these newer days of freedom are not printable—even in these newer days. It is only possible to record something of the point of view that friends of mine hold. One of these two—the more moderate of them—had hoped the train would run off the track when the President was on his way to the Harvard Tercentenary, but there had been no such good luck. He had been obliged to content himself with hearing one of his classmates who had had a houseful of the old crowd in for a little cheer tell one of their number who had defended the President that he was never to darken his door again.

I squirmed in protest. A man ought to be allowed to speak respectfully of the President of the United States without being accused of low motives.

Then their true state of mind began to reveal itself. "But what else could you expect? He was elected by the riffraff! Twenty millions of them bought outright!"

I suggested that the poetic spirit seemed about to flower again in New England.

"Just what the hell am I to make of that remark anyhow? Are you turning rabble-rouser yourself?"

Then I tried to grow formal. I quoted two lines of Carl Sandburg's that I had just been reading—about

> the distinction between a demagogue squawking
> and the presentation of tragic plainspoken fact.

But he found no comfort in them. Instead, he sought the harder to think of something that would express his contempt for what he called "the great unwashed" American people. "We might as well have Hitler over here. He would at least get rid of a few Jews."

I was completing the inevitable cycle. I was coming anew to see what Cambridge is like—not East Cambridge or North Cambridge, but the Harvard Square Cambridge that gives the city its name. Despite all that has been written about New England aloofness, the people in Cambridge are cordial. And they are perhaps as ready as any to tolerate the mere physical presence of a variant among them. But Cambridge is too complete in itself. This Cambridge—the Cambridge known in books—is made up largely of people who are at once endowed financially—either through private income or through salaries from an endowed institution—and blessed with the spiritual advantages of all that has been done by human beings in a long descent of years. They circulate chiefly among themselves. The people whom they know are not facing any such unthinkable disaster as starvation in a dust-storm, or civil war in an industrial city, or freezing in a blizzard, or suffocation in a mine. They therefore find it easy to believe that people who live in the world of such abject terrors and continue to suffer from them do so because of some defect of character. I have been told times without number in Cambridge that the unemployed could find employment if they were made of the right stuff. I have been told the same thing in other places—but only occasionally. In Cambridge the idea is a concentrate. It does little good to suggest that there must have been a strange relapse to laziness all at once in 1929 or 1930. The questions keep right on coming: "Why don't they stop trying to grow wheat out there?" "If they don't want to work in an automobile factory, why don't they do something else?" "Why do people want to live in North Dakota anyhow?" "I can't imagine anybody's wanting to work in a dirty coal mine. They must be pretty shiftless or they wouldn't do it."

Cambridge does not mean to be either provincial or heartless. The people who count pride themselves on being open-minded. But you have to find the side of their minds that is open. They declare they are liberals—"true liberals." And they prove their point by turning out in large numbers to hear such men as Mr. Walter Lippmann. While he employs easy-looking processes of reasoning to reduce the disquieting, shapeless facts of life to neat intellectual packages, their sense of liberality is glowing. They carry his packages away, and at dinner tables where everybody feels as they do—if he doesn't he keeps still—they have the great excitement of discovering that if you are a true liberal no action of any kind has to be taken.

This is the Cambridge that I must expect to see as long as I go away and come back. For this Cambridge derives its way of looking at human beings largely from the Harvard round which it has grown up. Not that Harvard is without excellencies. She has them, almost beyond comparison. The library is now the largest university library in the world; Fogg Museum is almost unique among the smaller museums of art; the Harvard University Press is an author's ideal publisher; the persons of distinction from other countries who are lecturing at Harvard each year are numerous enough to constitute a kind of circulating university themselves; and among the many persons in the various faculties who rank high in the world of learning there are occasional men whose feeling toward mankind in the concrete is genuinely liberal. "We keep some around," said a man who was formerly an official part of Harvard, and who does not like liberals, "just to show to people when they ask if we've got any." Whether or not this is the true explanation, these men are present, and they comfort anyone who is aware that the contemporary world exists and that some of the people in it require a better chance.

But no one who lives next door to Harvard, no matter how much he esteems the institution or how much affection he may have for the men who taught him there, can believe that the official drift of Harvard is in the direction taken by these occasional men. It is not toward any sympathetic rapid extension of democracy in the specific. The institution is too intricately enmeshed in its source of financial supply. Ralph Waldo Emerson perceived what was happening. He protested in 1861 that whereas the institution ought to be a "fountain of novelties out of heaven, a Delphos uttering warning and ravishing oracles to lift and lead mankind," it was nothing of the sort because it was dominated by State Street. In seventy-five years little seems to have changed unless it is the name of the street that may most appropriately be singled out as symbolic. Although something actually new and untrammeled seems to appear from time to time, it somehow always shapes itself to fit into a frame of reference made by somebody who was thinking of something else.

Inescapably such an environment fosters sterility in anything important to men and women who through social maladjustments are unable to enjoy an enriched consciousness of life. Investigators, instead of risking clues to what seem to be new social facts and expressions of new kinds of human need, keep to the safer practice of applying learning to compiled statistics. Instead of immersing themselves in the experience of suffering fellow-mortals until they know the feel of life as these others live it, they talk about cycles and recessions and subsistence levels and permanent relief rolls and sociological projects as if people were but matters of research to be compiled and recorded by graduate students for easier consideration—and disposition. Harvard will engage in vast and pretentious researches, make valuable contributions in such socially neutral fields as astronomy, chemistry, archaeology, and cancer, and occasionally yield minor concessions to the newer democratic spirit. But it is no more to be expected that Harvard will kick free of her restraints and lead off boldly in behalf of any economic democracy that would elevate large numbers of submerged individual men to opportunities of growth than that Duke University will launch a crusade against the use of tobacco.

Cambridge, then, comes naturally into an unshakable non-understanding of the dreams and the sufferings of diversified men and women. It comes just as naturally into its state of mistrust and fear. It sees people not as individuals craving the best they can get out of life, but as categories, organizations, masses. And masses of people have made trouble. Just look at Russia and Germany and Spain. Cambridge seems unable to know how harmless and gentle human beings are when they are treated considerately as individuals and made to feel that they are a valid and an appreciated part of the scheme of things.

And Cambridge is so engrossed with all sorts of pleasant and creditable matters that it acts as a hypnotic. I like Cambridge. Cambridge is busy with a hundred concerns that interest me. And Cambridge is home. But in this nicely conditioned atmosphere how can a man experience the chill and the heat that keep in him a vital reverence for all life? For a time I must get away.

It is not enough to walk up into North Cambridge or over into Somerville. There is still in full sight the Cambridge of towers and spires to beguile me with its bulging but unattached logic, its brightness so devoid of warmth that it almost has one believing that warmth is not necessary. I must get farther away—out among some textile workers in New Hampshire, some share-croppers' children in Arkansas, some women and grandfathers waiting in silence at the mouth of a smouldering mine in Ohio, some unemployed automobile workers in Michigan who are trying to understand the difference between a depression and a recession, some west Kansas farmers who have had three wheat crops in succession burned up by the sun but are grimly planting another. I feel the need of them.

## xiv

## Rain

VERY late I entered the dressing-room of the Pullman, and found it wholly unoccupied. The train, I noticed, was scarcely moving, and when I stepped over to the window and glanced out to see where we were, I saw nothing but water—muddy water in a limitless smooth sheet with a serpentine double row of dark green trees stretching far down across it and out of sight. A moment later we came to where dozens of stout men were working with heavy timbers and slag and sand-bags to save a bridge—the bridge that we were to cross. When rain came down on enough successive days, a little Middle Western river scarcely larger than a creek could make much trouble.

The men worked speedily, grimly, yet with a great cordiality. They had been there since yesterday—all afternoon, all evening, all night, all morning, with only a little time out now and then for a swig of coffee and a slice of bread and butter and a hunk of cold meat. They were not quarreling about working conditions, or union hours, or overtime; they were saving a bridge.

The engine crept along very cautiously. The curved high grade that was only just wide enough for a double-track road seemed thin and insecure when completely beset by evil-looking muddy water. With shovel or pick or crowbar in their hands, the men clung to the side of the embankment above the water's edge to watch us try crossing.

Very gently we came to a full stop. Then quite as gently we moved again—at a snail's pace. The engine was approaching the bridge. The engine was on the bridge. A swift, eddying current that swept across the quiet yellow sea was boiling and churning through the girders only four or five feet below the slowly turning drive-wheels. The engine was out over the middle of the stream; and then two-thirds of the way across. And now we ourselves were passing the sand-bags and slag and heavy timbers and coming onto the bridge.

But why did the engineer not hurry a little instead of going all the more cautiously, now that he was safely across himself? Did he mean to dangle us there until the abutments caved completely in? I could look directly down into the muddy waters that piled themselves with an angry swish against the steelwork supporting us, and could see in them no inviting doom. Then with a slight jerk we moved faster again. And then we were across.

With a sudden excess of good feeling for my kind, I turned to go on with my shaving. A man in clerical collar sat down beside my Irish kit-bag to enjoy a full pipe of extra-fragrant tobacco. As I fumbled in the bag for my shaving set, I saw in the flap a long, painfully written letter that had come to me the night before from a workingman, a silversmith, in New England, who had had no work for two years. He had not written about his unemployment—he had been able to live—but the time on his hands had enabled him to read and to think. He had been struggling with all sorts of books that would do credit to the reading-list of a philosopher. Just why he wrote to me he could not say. He was not writing to bother me. He was not expecting an answer. He had only seen my name in the newspaper in connection with something or other, and since there was no one else to write to, he decided to write to me. Something that had happened to him had given a tragic wrench to his understanding of all that he saw of life about him.

I ventured—as I usually do not—to begin a conversation: "Are you interested in human beings?"

"I certainly am," the priest replied as soon as he could get his pipe in hand. "That's my business."

"What do you make of this, then?"

I handed him the awkwardly written large pages.

When I was well through with my shaving, I could see in the mirror that he had put the letter down and was again smoking amiably off into space.

When I had finished I asked: "Interesting?"

"Yes—s," he replied, as if it were all in the day's work. "But what horrible English!"

Could any man who professed to be concerned with human beings thus put unimportant things first? To be sure, the letter was illiterate. But it expressed a man's state of mind—with eloquence. I suddenly felt ruffled and ill at ease in the same room with such a man. He had not been in the rain long enough. I had better get into the diner where I could sit alone and look out at the sopping earth.

The clouds did not act as if they meant to leave the sky permanently; yet the sun was breaking through now and then and giving to the hills a steamy brightness. In a pasture field alongside the railroad, a young housewife in bright beach attire was out having a swim in a little run so narrow that she could stretch her arms out and touch the willows that drooped low on either side. Two small children were speeding gaily down the hill from the house to join her.

"Seems rather inappropriate, somehow, doesn't it?" remarked the very upright, important-looking white-haired woman who sat across the table from me finishing an after-breakfast smoke.

Swimming did seem, in truth, more appropriate in languid afternoon streams than in these raging torrents that hurried onward to join forces and sweep bridges and towns away. If the farmer's young wife had been gamboling nude under the maple trees she could scarcely have been more surprising than she was among the willows in a swimming costume. Yet I argued that I could see no inappropriateness in every farmwife's taking time out from work that often is drudgery, attiring herself in bright colors, and going for a swim if she wanted to—whenever there was water enough.

"You men are all alike," she declared, and laughed a little laugh of reproof, as she arose to go. "You saw her out there and enjoyed the sight. So you argue that it is all right for her to leave the breakfast dishes unwashed, and go traipsing down across the meadow in Miami Beach style to swim in a muddy brook."

I protested that it had not seemed so muddy—there in green pasture fields.

"I hope there are water-snakes in it," she said in an effort at triumph, and smiled a bright, malicious smile as she turned to go, and left me to myself to reflect upon the general inappropriateness of floods in June. Floods ought to come in February or March or April, not in the full swing of summer. What chance had young corn in fields covered with two or three feet of water? And just how long could ripening wheat be expected to last when not even the tallest heads could be seen in low-lying fields?

All these overflowing streams seemed to be converging on Cincinnati. Would Cincinnati still be there when I arrived?

Since I could not get out of doors to see, I spent an hour between trains walking in the vast Union Station, enjoying the brightness that architects and artists had been able to create when they had a fair chance, and listening to men who were wondering if the water were going to get up into the city again. Then I took an afternoon train for Indianapolis.

Where the railroad follows the river valley for a distance just to the west of Cincinnati, the Ohio bulged toward the top of its banks. It was pressing on, irresistibly. The only thing to do was to keep out of its way.

And still the rain came down. Once, after a bright ten or fifteen minutes, there were soft white clouds in the west, then leaden ones, and then an oncoming wall of black, and lightning and thunder.

"Showers of blessing," said the white-headed old Negro porter, who saw me looking. He spoke very reverently.

"Whose blessing?"

I suppose I looked more austere than I felt. For he flinched a little, as if he had been reprimanded for telling the truth. "Oh, I don't know"—and he smiled off humbly. "But maybe somebody's."

After the first onslaught of the storm, the rain came in solid silvery sheets, and then in a steady pouring. In towns that we swept through without pausing, shade-trees sagged low as if covered with ice. Flower gardens were beaten down into unrecognizability. Cattle had abandoned pastures, and waded about in muddy barnyards as in early spring. Red roosters with their harems trailing along behind them waded over steaming manure piles with wings dressed high in disgust, or stood with heads up and tails low to let the water run off their backs—since the rain had to come down.

All Indiana was dripping. Indianapolis was only a smudgy layer of houses between streets that were rivers and skies that threatened to fall. Except for the half-hour that I spent in the barber shop, where the Hoosier barber told me who his favorite poets were, and how soon he hoped to publish a volume of verse himself, I was only so much oversensitive flesh trying to keep dry. And the next morning stiff winds had added themselves to the rain and swirled it into all sorts of protected places where it had not been before. Men did not take a cab; they dashed for one—and caved their hats in against the top of the low doorway. I darted into one, darted out again into a dry station, hurried upstairs to a waiting train for St. Louis, and then sat for fifteen minutes savoring the prospect of hours of looking calmly at a drowning world from the security of a dry train.

At Terre Haute the Wabash River had spread over unnumbered acres of fertile bottom land. "On the Banks of the Wabash!" Theodore Dreiser wasn't thinking of such days as this when he wrote that first stanza for his brother Paul. The banks were not much in evidence this morning. At any rate there was nothing romantically melancholy in the sight of them. The river was too business-like.

When I got off to change trains in Mattoon, Illinois, it was not raining. Everything still dripped, but the clouds looked as if it were only a short distance through them up to sunlight. I had an hour and a half. I would spend fifty minutes in walking, thirty in eating, and ten in pacing the station platform—since this was the last train I could take, and I did not care to miss it.

I walked eastward for twenty-five minutes—along streets where low-hanging maple branches spilled water down one's neck, and where pools stood in every slightest depression in the cement sidewalk.

When I turned back I had not gone very far before I came upon a man who was down on his knees at the edge of his lawn with a pair of shears, snipping off blades of grass that the lawn-mower had not caught.

"Pretty wet," he said, as if that fact bound men together in some extraordinary way.

"Yes," I answered, and meant to pause only long enough not to seem abrupt. But he at once sat back on his heels as if he had something further to say.

"Wet where you're from, too?"

"At least all the way to the Alleghenies."

"I just figured that you must be out for a walk between trains or something of the sort. I saw you going in the other direction a while ago."

We talked. In ten minutes—I was carefully watching my time—and without seeming to be giving me life history, he let me know the following about himself: He is a freight conductor on the Big Four railroad and works at night—till midnight—and has, therefore, plenty of time to fuss around with his lawn and hedge after he gets up in the middle of the morning. He likes to keep things slicked up and trim; has built a pleasant sun-parlor on the front of his house—a well-designed bungalow type with the end toward the street—and preferred an archway to doors through from the rest of the house; is troubled by six or eight neighborhood children who thoughtlessly break down his hedge in their play, but instead of scolding them, calls them into the house, gives each of them a piece of chocolate, and then shows them how they ought to remember to be careful themselves when other people have taken pains; has an Irish terrier that stays up every night to greet him when he comes from work, and then immediately goes off and curls up for the night; has a son who is a radio announcer—he dropped out of college because of the depression—but who wishes eventually to be a writer; does not see how the slack in unemployment is to be taken up very soon, since his freight train, with a regular crew of men, used to carry from twenty to thirty-five cars, and now carries as many as a hundred and fifteen; has measured enough cars to know that they average forty-five feet plus a few inches, so that a train of one hundred and fifteen cars is just under or just over a mile in length according to the number of extra-length automobile-cars and the like that it chances to carry; went to a little college in Effingham for a short while and taught school a little before he took to railroading, and has now been with the railroad for more than thirty years; is sixty; regretted the burning of the little college, which had been founded by two brothers and a sister who each had inherited two hundred thousand dollars, and despite the impress they left on the region, "virtually died paupers, you might say"; took his wife to Colorado for tuberculosis, but her case was hopeless and he brought her back home, where she died; was able to pay all the funeral charges in cash to one of the boys in the family that had founded the little college; feared that his Irish terrier would be run over by an automobile, since he liked nothing so much as to chase them; and he couldn't shake hands with me when I had to hurry along, because he was all covered with oil from the lawn-mower.

I saved time on my period for lunch by going into a café that invited guests to try some of its "doubt-dispelling salad served at the psychological moment."

On the train, as it rushed through the green hills of southern Illinois, I watched a steady moist breeze from the southwest lift the leaves in thousands of acres of peach orchards and reveal loads of fruit already touched with red.

At Jonesboro—I had to drive across to the Mississippi—I wished to see the spot where Lincoln and Douglas had debated. For this was "down in Egypt" where Douglas was going to trot Lincoln out and force him to say before an audience unsympathetic to "radical" abolition of slavery what he had already said before sympathetic audiences farther north in the state. We stopped in the middle of the village by a filling-station in many blatant colors and asked an old man where the debate had been held. He was deaf, and came close to my face above the lowered glass of the automobile door.

"Oh," he said when he heard. "Why, right there."

"But that is only a marker which says that the debate was held in a grove about a quarter of a mile or so north."

"Then I don't know," he answered.

We drove out to find the spot. We saw some old buildings—and a house near by—and some trees, but it was only a cow pasture. Farther on we turned in at a damp grove in front of a house. Three women sat waiting in an automobile and a young fellow of eighteen or twenty was changing from muddy shoes to clean ones in the garage. Magnificent Plymouth Rock hens and a rooster looked on inquiringly, as if they were accustomed to being pampered.

"You passed it," said the young fellow, and squeezed his other wet foot into a dry shoe. "I'll show you. See through the trees yonder—on this side of the road—that briary field? There is a stone, but you'll have to watch for it, for the weeds and the briars are pretty rank this year."

We found the spot, climbed out, let ourselves through a dilapidated farm gate into a field that was once a fairground, and while a great spotted cow breathed heavily as if she were very full of grass, and testily stripped the leaves from a young apple shoot that had sprung up among the briars, we read on a low stone—it could not have been much more than a yard high—that on this spot, September 15, 1858, Lincoln and Douglas debated.

When we were on our way again, I referred to the floods I had seen.

"Better wait till you see the Mississippi before you talk about floods," the friend who had come for me admonished me. "Then you'll be able to see what a real, life-sized stream can do when it's at itself."

And two or three days later, as I came up along the Mississippi on the train from Memphis to St. Louis, I saw. An ocean is a steady, harmless-looking thing compared with this hurrying, boiling, devastating monster when it is on a rampage. If one looks far enough, it seems only a boundless lake of muddy water. But near at hand, just there within a hundred yards of the tracks, it is whirling, seething, pouring itself into every foot of space where there is room for backwater, carrying full-grown trees along as if they were matches, and houses and barns as if they were such small toys that they were scarcely worth bothering with.

At one station the river had climbed to the road-bed, to the ties, to the rails; and then as the water had mounted, section men had put ties across the tops of the rails, other ties across these first ones, and then a third tier on which they had spiked temporary rails, so that the train "went upstairs" as it approached the station, in order to let the passengers walk dry-shod along a narrow, elevated gangway from high ground back of the station into the vestibules of the cars. Then we descended again, and the engine slithered along through backwater until the tracks slowly rose to a slightly higher elevation a half-mile up the valley.

Once, not two hundred yards from the train, I saw an entire line of trees go. They had been on the mainland, but through some wild caprice the river had started a current back of them. The current had grown. The river seemed to find some special joy in crowding over to this side of its bed and trying to go through this narrow causeway that it had cut for itself. And all the while the water had been piling against the other side of the slender island and wearing it away until the trees were toppling on a thin ledge of soft mud. Then in a flash, two dozen of them went over, and the river was at once busy tearing the last of their roots free and whirling the entire mass off southward.

Then we had miles of quiet lake on our side. Fields of ripening wheat were covered except on some well-elevated knoll. As far as one could see toward the normal river bed yonder on the other side of the wide valley, houses and barns stood in water up to the tops of doors and windows. Off there toward the river, too, were towns. Where were the people? Why, wherever people go when they are suddenly chased away from everything they possess by a river that has gone mad. Not even families can be kept intact. Families often do not so much as know where their own members are, or whether they are alive. I have known of little villages evacuated by the Red Cross or the Government whose residents were traced within a few weeks to a half-dozen states.

A man across the aisle said he did not like to look at it. He had just had the experience of going back in a rowboat with a friend who had been away from home and wanted to feel sure that his wife, who was a semi-invalid, had been taken to safety. They paddled for a long time in the darkness. Streets did not look the same when the water was ten feet deep in them. But at last they found the house. Worst of all, they found her, too.

Farther up the valley, the world seemed more secure. We could look across from the Missouri side to Illinois bluffs that had been assailed by the river for thousands of years, yet still stood up firmly like palisades. The people in the region were in a more casual state of mind. They were always within reach of higher land. Moving out every two or three years to let the river have its way for a time was more or less a part of community routine, as it is along the Ohio. A Red Cross worker told me that when she once asked an old lady how many times she had been driven out by floods, she replied: "Fourteen times by floods, not countin' high waters."

At one stop I knew that we were now out of all danger. The river was not touching anybody there too seriously. Some wag had written on the time-table blackboard on the side of the station: "This overabundance of water has resulted from the activity of the national commission appointed to combat drought."

When we reached St. Louis in the evening the rain was pouring again, and I chose to eat and loaf away two or three hours in the security of the station. When only the last hour was left, and I had watched the people milling about until I was a little weary of them, I sat and considered a situation in a story that I had in mind. Two nuns came and sat just opposite me. Soon some friends arrived to take one of them for a drive. The other—quite contrary to custom, I thought—remained alone. I arose, told her that I needed expert assistance in a story I was working on, and asked her a question about certain religious societies. She seemed to welcome the opportunity to explain. Would I not sit down—until her companion sister returned? She herself had not cared to brave the rain.

She could not have been more than forty. Yet she spoke not merely with intellectual curiosity, but with the kind of wisdom that springs only from unceasing great thoughtfulness.

She had some questions to ask me, too. What did I write? Did I by chance write poetry—ever? Did I know many poets? Did I not think that Edwin Arlington Robinson was in truth a religious man, rather than the hardened unbeliever he is so often made out to be? I sought to explain that he was a very reverent agnostic who would have been frightened if anyone had told him that he was religious, yet who was in fact more profoundly religious, according to my unorthodox conception, than most people in any church.

"Isn't it true!" she exclaimed, somewhat to my surprise. "The world is alive with such. It is foolish to pretend that only people in the Church have found salvation. The Church does not teach that, though many Catholics individually believe it."

She confessed that there was something very sad in religion for her. "When I see the different sects hating each other worse than they hate anything else in the world, when they ought to love each other, I am very sad. There ought to be much happiness, and there is so very little. How do you explain all the suffering you see everywhere? I'd have to think that God was unspeakably cruel, if there were to be no continuation of ourselves into a happier life beyond this one."

I professed surprise at her saying so.

"I know what you mean," she said. "The Church has its beliefs and I adhere to them. I prefer the Church's way. But I have to interpret the Church's beliefs for myself. We come to complete peace only when the interpretation is right out of our own searching and thought."

A man, broken and tearful and frightened, brushed my feet as he stumbled by. She looked at him with quick understanding. "Poor man! How fearful he is! But then, we all have our fears."

"Do you, Sister?" I asked.

"Yes," she replied. "My grandmother and my mother and my aunt have all died of a terrible disease, and my great fear is that I may die of it, too. I do not mind death; that is nothing. But when I think of the months of agony, maybe, that might precede death, not even my religion can quite keep me unafraid."

She had just been home, she told me, to visit her family—the first time in six years.

The next morning I was awakened somewhere in southwestern Missouri by a cloud-burst. I turned to the window, and, reclining on one elbow with my nose against the pane, watched the deluge. The wall of water was so dense that the engineer had slowed down to a few miles an hour lest he run past a signal or into a washout. A bolt of lightning leaped down and shattered an oak at the edge of the right-of-way, scarcely fifty feet from my nose. The steel train on a wet track must have absorbed the excess of the bolt, for I felt nothing beyond the surprise of being blinded for a brief second by fiery blue.

College girls in smart costumes were getting home from commencement, and the train had to make stops at flag-stations right in the downpour. I enjoyed a sense of luxury as I watched from the comfort of my berth while these young ladies in footwear that was nothing much but heels, and under umbrellas that were nothing much but color, dashed beside proud fathers in overalls through two or three inches of water on the station platform, and deeper mud beyond, to waiting automobiles.

When I was up and had eaten breakfast, and we were under bright skies, I saw boys in the woods fishing with clubs. The higher waters of preceding days had subsided somewhat, though the streams were still overflowing, and fish that had adventured into all sorts of new lagoons when the floods were at their highest were now left stranded in leafy depressions from which the last of the water was steadily sinking into the soft earth. Some of them already were gasping and floundering, and these the boys were killing.

Then we abruptly ran into another downpour and the college girls had to wade through deep water and mud again. Across the aisle, in a section piled high with Dobbs hat-boxes and other luggage, a young woman who herself looked little older than some of the college girls wondered—to me—where so many students could come from. I confessed that a greater mystery was where all the Dobbs hat-boxes came from, since I saw women and girls with them in every part of the country. Some major industrial establishment must be producing them for mass display. Hers, she assured me, were bona fide, direct from New York. She was a Virginian who lived in Texas, and when life in her home town became too flat, she packed up and visited the Atlantic seaboard. Some of these girls, she thought, seemed excessively happy. She believed a person had to be intelligent to be unhappy.

It was still raining when I took a local train from Fort Scott down to Pittsburg. The iron-gray farmer in the seat behind me in the snack-car made a remark about the weather: "Will Rogers would say that the Roosevelt Administration ought to be blamed for this." He laughed.

He and Will Rogers had lived on neighboring farms in the earlier Oklahoma days. They might have been brothers, so solid and honest did this man seem in character and speech. He drawled a little, too.

"He was al-l-ways just the sam-m-e as long as he liv-v-ed, whenever he cam-m-e back." He spoke as if he were recording an epitaph.

"But do you think he exhibited as high a percentage of funniness during the last years of his life?"

"No-o, he didn't—for a fact. My wife and I used to talk about that. I figured it out this way: he was at his best when he was taking cracks at nice, well-off people who play golf and all that. Well, you begin to live around with people like that yourself, out in California, and you get so you can't see what's funny about them. And even when you can once in a while, you're not quite so apt to say anything about it.

"But what I wanted to say was that he was just the same to his old farm neighbors. He said to me the last time I saw him, 'Now, I want you just to pack up the family and come out to California and stay a week with us. And remember you are not to pay out a penny of your own. It is to be my treat from the time you start till you get back.'

"Naturally it pleased us. But my wife and I talked it over and decided not to accept. Going on that basis, even when he did have more money than he knew what to do with—well, we didn't quite take to the idea."

I wondered how much Will had made per week in his palmiest days.

"He told me once, when I wondered about it myself and asked him, that he was raking in just about an even seventy-five hundred a week.

" 'Seventy-five hundred a week,' I asked him, 'for acting a fool?'

" 'Sure,' he told me. 'A man oughtn't to act a fool unless it's for some good purpose.' "

"Weren't you getting off at Pittsburg?" the conductor called to me. "We're right there." And I hurried from the train.

An hour later, while thunder crashed and the rain poured, I wanted to make some jottings, and discovered that in my haste I had left a note-book and some loose sheets of paper in my seat in the snack-car. I was troubled. The note-book was strictly private. The jottings in it were my honest opinions of people. I had nothing to retract, but I could see no advantage in giving some of the opinions to the world at large.

I called a cab, waded from the hotel door to the curb in water that covered the sidewalk, and hurried to the station. Could the agent telegraph ahead—with any assurance of success—and ask the train conductor to rush the book to me at my next address?

He could do better than that. He was the kind of man who ought to be made president of the company—of all railroad companies. He knew where the train would be stopping in ten minutes, and he would find out directly from the conductor himself when he went from the train into this next station to report.

Was the material safe? It was. It would be delivered into my hands that afternoon at four-forty.

The book was not much, but I experienced a great sense of relaxation and aliveness at the thought of having it returned. As I rode back to the hotel in a sudden burst of steamy sunshine, I began once again to see the world about me, to remember the state I was in, and the town. On the side of a feed-store just where the driver had to wait for traffic, a sign read: "If Kelso's egg mash won't make 'em lay, they're roosters." I was in Kansas, undoubtedly.

But the rain did not seem to belong in Kansas. It belonged in the Lake District of England. Balmy winds brought the same wet-looking clouds that one could see any day across the dark water at Bowness. The afternoon was crowded with heavy showers. In the night I was startled from my bed by a crashing bolt of lightning just outside my window in the tower-like hotel.

Could anybody tell me where I might go to escape the rain?

I had hopes when I took a night train for northwest Oklahoma—the Dust Bowl. But when I got up to leave the train at Alva the next morning—Sunday morning—the sky was overcast, and a river-bed that ordinarily was dry had water in it just as if it were as faithful a river as could be found anywhere. And countless thousands of acres of wheat covered rolling prairie, covered flat prairie, with golden yellow.

Would they be able to get into the fields to cut the wheat before it had stood too long? A strange question to ask in northwestern Oklahoma. Yet that was what I heard farmers asking one another that morning as they talked in the court-house grove, or lingered truantly outside church entrances. While four of them discussed the matter by one white little church, and bit at timothy-straws and scanned the clouded sky, a mocking-bird braced himself on the smooth knob at the top of the low steeple to keep the wind from blowing him away, and sang obliviously.

The next morning was clear, and the rolling endless fields of yellow were flashing with the steel of horse combines, of power combines, of reapers—of anything that would cut wheat. There seemed to be enough wheat in view to feed the world.

I stopped at the side of one modest field of three hundred and twenty acres. The farmer had just parked a worn-looking automobile by the fence. "I thought you had a dust-storm out here last spring," I remarked.

He smiled. "Funny thing"—and he stopped to watch the combine that sputtered to the top of slightly higher land a quarter-mile away, and then down toward us, taking a swath twelve or fourteen feet wide, and dropping bags of grain frequently—"but last April I thought everything was gone. After three or four years that were dry enough themselves, the wind began to blow the dust first one way and then another until it just sandpapered the wheat right off into the ground, you might say. Then after we had breathed dust for a month or two, it commenced to rain. And it never stopped till yesterday! The wheat stooled out, though it didn't get up very high. Some of that out yonder is not more than ten or twelve inches. But the heads are all right."

He smiled as if words were not very adequate, stooped and pulled up some straws where the combine had left a strip along the fence, rubbed the grains out of the heads in the palm of his hand, and extended his hand for me to see.

The grains were full and round and ripe.

He smiled as if to say: "There you are," and tossed the grains out into the air as if he knew how to sow wheat by hand. Then he smiled out over the field again. He was seeing something almost beyond belief.

"Gad! What do you know about that? It rained!"

# XV

# Detour

A TRUCK that had stalled on a grade crossing just ahead of a refrigerator freight-train a half-mile long and scattered cars of California fruit and vegetables all over the right-of-way, sent our train round in a sweeping detour across two or three adjacent counties. From the conductor I learned that we were to pass through the small town in which I had first attended college.

I knew what I was going to do: I was going to get off and see the place—and learn whether all the mellow stories told by old college grads at alumni meetings were based on honest feeling or mere sentimentality. For days I had been facing audiences, answering questions, meeting people at receptions, meeting people at dinner, saying for the thousandth time what I thought of the President of the United States, his wife, the Supreme Court, Russia, the current best-sellers, Bernard Shaw, and proletarian art. It would be as pleasant as settling gently into warm water or winter sunshine just to subside into the wistful oblivion of the past. I would get off as unknown as the day I entered college—more so, for on that day a man met me—wander along streets that had been familiar for four years, look as much as I liked at the townspeople and at the students hurrying late to class, and never have to bother stiffening up to say "How do you do," or to autograph books, or to express useless opinions on such and such aspects of the contemporary hurly-burly. It was to be an afternoon of complete relaxation.

I wondered if this or that old professor continued to teach. I wondered especially if "Mother," who had once been my instructor in Latin, were still alive. When I knew her, she was the kind of fluttering dry leaf of a woman of fifty or sixty who might well live on forever. But that was a good long while ago.

She had never liked me any too well. She was always slipping in little preachments on my papers—about not living up to possibilities. She had something of that kind on the last one she ever returned to me. It had been raining all morning, and when we assembled for the examination, most of the class were wearing rain-coats. We were not numerous—perhaps fifteen in all—and the room in the old bare building that somebody had christened the Sheep-pen was large enough to seat a hundred. So we were scattered about over the room in the long seats that had solid backs, and arm-rests every two or three feet for writing. The course was called Special Problems in Latin Grammar, and we had been aware for weeks that Mother had found them all. The reading of Horace the term before under a man who liked poetry and dwelt with the understanding of a

## Detour 239

great lover on the shyness of Chloe, seemed after a month or two of Mother's course to have been but facile dreaming.

Only one other person was in the long seat that I was in. She was a lusty co-ed who tried to be at the head of every organization in college, and yet seemed always able to make good grades. She sat only two places from me, and did not bother to remove her light-weight rain-coat, which had a shoulder cape. After she had read the questions through a time or two and was ready to settle down to work, she unbuttoned her coat and pushed her cape out from her elbows in the freedom of readiness.

While I reflected hopelessly on one problem that Mother —or I—had not covered well in class, I saw that Miss X had a textbook in calculus lying open under her cape and the arm of the seat to her left, and toward me. The fly-leaves were covered with fine writing which she allowed her eyes to scan every time she dropped her head to struggle in thought over the examination. She did not know that I could see through a crumple in her cape what she was doing. And I was the only person in the room who possibly could.

I found the going hard. Soon I was wondering if I could so much as pass. This was scheduled to be my last course in Latin, and I did not wish to repeat it or take another in its stead.

A week later when I went over to get my examination paper back and know my fortune, I found that I had passed —by a hair. I was pleased. But Mother was not. She held the paper in her hand as she sat at the desk, discussed its many deficiencies, and added one of her distasteful little lectures on living up to one's possibilities. "I expected so much more of you," she said.

Just why, I do not know, unless it was because Mother had been impressed by some appearance of importance in me when as a drum-major who enjoyed twirling a baton in keeping with extra height, I marched ahead of the military band on all state occasions. I had never regarded my possibilities in Latin with any feeling but pain.

"Now, here," she said. "Of course I know that Miss X is a very exceptional girl and came from a school where they had a good elementary teacher of Latin"—I had learned most of the rudiments in the shade at the ends of corn rows on hot summer days—"so perhaps I shouldn't single her out; but look at this."

She ran through the paper carefully for my benefit. Nor did she conceal the mark she had given it. It was the highest mark I had ever seen on any examination paper in foreign language.

I felt my pulse bumping in my neck. I knew that I had done poorly enough. But I wanted to say, "See here, Mother, this is too perfect. In simple justice to all the rest of the class, you should know . . ."

Yet instead, like a self-conscious kindergartener, I admitted my many shortcomings, and walked hesitantly toward the door as if I were in water already up to my chin.

"What do you expect to do?" I heard Mother asking, with an inflection that meant "after college."

I turned hopefully. She would be relieved to know that I meant to work in a field where Special Problems in Latin Grammar would have little bearing. But I received no comfort. "I should think you'd want to do well in Latin if you ever expect to be a writer."

These were Mother's words to me. Did I wish to see her, even if she should be still living? Would she welcome me as one who had turned out not specially worse than the ones who had done well in Latin? I must be deciding, for here was the station.

It did not look quite so new as it did a quarter of a century before. There was the same old cannon on the station lawn, though—still pointing in the wrong direction.

It was all just as restful as I had hoped it might be. The familiar church spires were not quite so tall as the ones in my memory, yet they were recognizable. There was a house, too, where I used to spend a little time—agreeably unchanged. A girl about whom I sometimes had thought almost seriously had grown up there and had lived there. But her name—I could remember only the first half of it. And down the street a little had lived another. They had both married somebody else. Oh, well, for that matter, I had, too.

Just ahead a bell began to ring to announce a two-o'clock class. It was the same old bell—a little the worse for wear.

Students rose up out of the earth and filled the sidewalks, as they do in any college town when a bell rings. But these ought to reveal distinction. These were my fellow-alumni-to-be. Yet they gave no special glance of kinship, but rushed together in moving clumps that bespoke the firmest bond in all human society—the bond of the generation. A glance was enough to tell them that I was not of theirs. I fell in with them, nevertheless, as they laughed and hurried and pushed along. They were carrying all sorts of ponderous tomes and bulging zipper note-books that had never been dreamed of in my day. But they were discussing the same matters—perhaps with a little less protocol—that were weighty two dozen years or more ago.

I did not care to be swept along into any class. I thought I should prefer to look at the chapel.

When I pushed through the quietly swinging inner doors, somebody was playing the organ. I dropped into a seat to listen. She was practising. But she knew how to play.

Once she leaned forward to scrutinize the music. In the bright light of the shaded lamp over the pages, her face and red hair seemed to be that of some one I knew.

I walked in the dim aisle down toward the console.

"You don't mind my listening?"

"Not at all. On the contrary, it perks me up to know that I am playing for an audience. Only I'm just finishing."

She inclined a little toward me as she rested one hand on the bench.

"But this is what I really walked down here to ask you: would you mind telling me your name?"

She gave me a swift glance as if she were not an unsophisticated person, then smiled and told me.

"I knew your father—and your mother."

"Here?"

"Yes."

"But how did you ever happen to know me?"

"Looks."

"You must have good eyes. But everybody says I look like them—both. And I don't mind. They're worth having a copy left of them."

She gathered up her music, crowded it into a portfolio, and walked with me to the door and all the way down to the street. She had the bearing of a thoroughbred. She walked as if she were alive and unafraid of the world. And she knew how to talk interestingly to a man who was not of her generation. If she were a fair sample, then the old college still must be doing pretty well!

In pleasant solitude I wandered over to a side street

where for two years I had kept a boarding-house full of boarders in order to have board myself. It did not cost much, even to those who paid money for it. On the train coming out from New England a football player from Dartmouth who sat across the table from me in the diner paid as much for one dinner as board at this house used to cost for two weeks.

I wanted to bound across the lawn, leap with a great thumping step on to the hollow-sounding front porch, rush through to the dining-room or kitchen and shout to one of the maids—also earning her board—that I was starving to death. But a certain changed appearance in the house and the sight of a dignified white-haired matron climbing into a long-wheel-base car restrained me.

Up the street a little I passed the house of one of my two favorite professors who later were colleagues in the United States Senate. This one was a large handsome man with a loud-speaker voice who was obliged by his low salary to live in a house so tiny that his students constantly wondered how he could turn round in it. He knew how to dress to advantage, but regularly he seemed to wear the same suit. Then one Monday he appeared in class late in an arrangement of clothing so unartistic that he was only half recognizable. Soon everybody learned that he had been helping his wife with the washing and that his weight, plus the weight of a tub of soap-suds, had sent him crashing through the unsteady platform of the cistern into deep water.

I wandered up to a society assembly hall that I used to sweep for a consideration when the need for money was exceptional. There were pharmaceutical laboratories on the lower floors of this building, and the dust in that hall had always had a pungent odor unlike that of any other dust. When I went up, the wide doors were standing open, and I sniffed the same odor. When I peeped in, a rangy student was at work with a broom.

He saw me and walked back. "Anything I can do for you?" He was warm from the exercise, and mopped his face. "I'm just the janitor."

"I was, once on a time," I replied.

He sized me up. "You don't look like a janitor now. Better tell me what you are. I could stand having my morale stiffened up about now."

He did not look as if he were in despair. So I told him that a free-lance author was not necessarily any better off than a janitor.

He laughed—skeptically. "Say, you didn't come up here to try to get my job away from me, did you?"

Down in the street as I walked beneath low-hanging maples, I remembered strange instances among fellow students who had lived in this house or that. Especially did I recall the man who was a mule driver along the Ohio River at two dollars a day when he was twenty-eight, but by chance came upon a college catalogue. At thirty-eight he had married the most engaging musician in the college town and was professor of engineering in one of the chief universities of the Pacific Coast.

"Why, hello here!" a blonde business-like little man of my own age called up into my face as I walked along looking far ahead. He had collected laundry and worked in a drugstore and finished photographs when he was in college. He was still in much the same business. It was pleasant to discover even this slight stability where so little remained unchanged.

"No," he had to admit, "not many of the old ones are left. But Mother is still alive—you must have had work with her."

"Is she really still around?"

"Just the same as ever. Oh, of course she doesn't teach. But she's just the same in looks. You know, she always did look as if she had turned a hundred and fifty."

"Where does she live?"

"Right down there. You ought to drop in and see her if you have time. She'll be as proud of you as a hen with two tails."

Perhaps it would not be such a bad idea. It might even develop into something that would be quite "thrilling"—one of those melodramatic stories about the man who never did so much in college, but—

I walked on—a trifle more briskly. I came up to the white house. I rang. While I waited I thought there was something unadorned about the house, like Mother. After I had waited a long time I heard somebody. Then the door opened with a squeak.

"How do you do, Mother!" I said in my most ebulliently cheerful manner. "I'll bet you don't know me"—though I was sure enough she would.

She studied my face rather passively. "I know you are an old student or you wouldn't have addressed me in that fashion. But won't you come in?"

Only for a moment, I explained. I was off between trains just to have a glimpse. In truth, she was the only person I was looking up.

The interior of the house was classically severe.

"No," she said after she was seated comfortably. "I'm afraid I'll have to admit that I don't know you."

I told her my name.

She seemed unmoved. "I don't seem to remember any one by that name. I remember"—and she mentioned my two brothers—"but I don't seem to remember you. You must be in business; you look as if maybe you were."

I told her that I was a writer—of a kind.

"What do you write—textbooks?"

"Well, no, not just that."

She was afraid she had not read anything of mine.

I went precipitately back to the subject of college. I reminded her that I had once taken a course of hers, though I was afraid I had not done brilliantly—a course on Special Problems in Latin Grammar.

Her face brightened up. That, she assured me, had been her favorite course, though she had given it only a few times.

She became reminiscent. Did I ever know Miss X, who was in college when she was giving that course? "I think she handed in the most perfect paper I ever received from an undergraduate."

I said that I did remember her, yes. Then I thought I had better be going.

She made it easy for me to get to the door without seeming ungraciously abrupt. If I had ever taught, she went on to tell me while I fingered my hat, I would understand how a student now and then along the way stays in one's mind.

I half backed down the two steps at the door. Mother, spare and unexcited as ever, stood over me so that her face was above the level of mine.

She still clung to Miss X. "So many students do not live up to their possibilities, that when one comes along who does, she stays in your memory as a kind of standard."

Of course! I understood exactly how that was. And did she ever hear from Miss X?

No; she had never heard. "She always was the kind of person who is very busy."

As I stood listening up to her, she suddenly became my

teacher again, and I felt myself shrinking into what I had been when I was a student—into the speechless dolt of the morning when she had reported on the examination. What could I say now that would alter the case? Did I wish to risk stultifying myself further by telling her that she was not judging me aright, that her "standard" had cribbed her way to glory? Mother probably would not believe me if I told her. Or she would minimize the importance of the specific offense. Had not Miss X been prominent in the Y.W.C.A. in her time—and in everything else? Who was I to expect the benefit of the doubt?

I hurried down the street toward the station, though I had more than an hour to spare. When I came within sight of the tracks, a long train stood there—pulled down by a red signal—and a conductor paced back and forth on the platform just outside an open vestibule. It was a limited train that disregarded this little town. I rushed up and asked the conductor if he would let me go aboard if I paid my fare to Chicago from the preceding station stop.

Just as the engine whistled to call in a flagman, the agent waddled out with my heavy bags.

In a few minutes we were rushing along at full speed. It was good to hear men talking about business and the President and the Senate and the League of Nations and Mussolini and Russia. Who wanted to live in the past? It couldn't be done, anyhow. One only died in the past. I was glad to be in the thick of it again—even to facing audiences who asked such unanswerable questions as: "Do you think it can be maintained that people very often shrink up as a result of truth, and that those who are untruthful become glowing and resourceful, as in Johan Bojer's *The Power of a Lie?*"

## xvi

## Ferment

IF you draw a straight line from upper Wisconsin southwest for a thousand miles to where the Red River separates Texas and Oklahoma, or a little beyond, and then make zigzag journeys back and forth across this axis for the full length of it, going out two hundred miles or more on either side, you will have traversed the region of the United States in which there is more mental ferment of original kinds than anywhere else in the country. It gives to all life a grim buoyancy, a pungent flavoring. It causes you to forget that you are making specific trips, seeing specific places, and drives you inescapably to feel a groping new spirit which proclaims with some misgivings, some resentment, and much of the bravura of youth that we can have what we require. It reminds you that all mental aliveness is one, that when a certain relation chances to be struck between stress and freedom, the fertile mind extends itself not merely in a few directions, but in many. For the region includes the locale of several political revolts, the generation of new trans-Mississippi painters typified in most people's minds by such an artist as Grant Wood, the flourishing Iowa writers, the Mayo Surgical Clinic, the beginnings of big-scale farm production, the coöperative movement, the founding of osteopathy, the large and important group of lithographers and etchers joined together in the Prairie Print Makers, such poets as Carl Sandburg, Vachel Lindsay, Edgar Lee Masters, John G. Neihardt, and John Gould Fletcher, such older novelists as Willa Cather, O. E. Rolvaag, Sinclair Lewis, and Zona Gale—not to mention the long list of younger ones—and much of the most striking in the newer American architecture.

Different elements have helped to make this phenomenon vigorous. Here, roughly, is the area where the pioneers, sweeping westward, first left the tree-covered land that stretched all the way back to the Atlantic Ocean, and were obliged to devise the machinery of an entire new civilization in order to gain a foothold on the plains and to stay there after they were once established. They are still in possession—or their grandchildren are—but they must be vigilant in ingenuity lest they be driven out by grasshoppers or weevils or plant diseases or cyclones or dust or drought. In the process they not only have developed their own ways of doing things, but have become conscious of what they have done, and are at once humble and self-assuring in their attitude. Then, too, especially in the north, they have seen another civilization—the civilization of smoke—crowd up close against them from the eastward, they have felt resentfully its impact, and they have exercised themselves in fighting off its dominance—or attempted dominance—of their lives. And then the blood that has gone into all the disturbing activity of the region is not that of any of the revolutionary, temperamental south Europeans who are supposed to threaten American orderliness, but that of good cool Scandinavians, Germans, and New England and South Atlantic Anglo-Saxons.

At the northern end of the axis the unquiet minds have been busiest with economic and social concerns. Irrepressibly they have changed the atmosphere. It is not necessary for you to penetrate Wisconsin farther to the northwestward than Milwaukee to discover that you are no longer in Michigan or Indiana or Ohio. The socialists hasten to explain to you that the good management of the city—and it has been good, compared with that of other cities—has resulted from the long service of a socialist mayor. The conservatives hasten to explain that the good management just chanced to coincide with a socialist regime—that the true causes were many. But the fact remains that there are plenty of socialists in Wisconsin, and that the conservatives of the state are themselves so different from the conservatives of—let us say—Massachusetts, that persons with variant or supposedly alien political philosophies may speak freely about them in the open. And by the time you have penetrated the state as far on the way to Minneapolis as the Wisconsin Dells, where sheer tree-covered survivals of erosion standing in soft-looking lowlands suggest nothing so much as distant ruins of feudal castles, you understand why there is today a Progressive Party there, and why there is likely to be one for some time ahead—under one name or another.

Nor need you take more than a few trips across Minnesota in order to understand why there has been a Farmer-

Labor Party there. As long as fifteen years ago some of the reasons were evident enough. One summer in the Detroit Lakes region forty or fifty miles east of Fargo, North Dakota, the rains did not come. By midsummer, crops were burning up, and farmers knew they would have little or no feed for the winter ahead. They killed their cattle and peddled the beef out to those of us who had a little pocket money at seven cents a pound—for choice parts. While they were doing this I chanced to become acquainted with an agreeable man—and a good golfer—who told me that he represented a large milling company. One day he confided to me what his business was. It was to scare farmers into selling their wheat at the lowest possible prices. Many farmers in the driest out-of-the-way corners of the Northwest, he told me, had no granaries for their threshed wheat. His business was to go about, learn where it all was, refrain from buying it until it was in danger through the coming of bad weather, and then when the farmers were afraid they were going to lose it altogether, buy suddenly from all of them before the price could start up, and have the grain rushed to safety. He was opposed to all such "socialistic" schemes as letting the farmers join together and have their own elevators, and he was sure I would find that most prominent flour men and bankers were.

The farmers assured me that this case was characteristic. And they were not going to be "told" by anybody. They were going to fight "monopolistic tendencies." All along the way there were fervid political dissenters of the type of Charles A. Lindbergh the older, Henrik Shipstead, and Floyd B. Olson. So in the course of years, especially when the Northwest professed to feel close times long before the country in general discovered the depression of 1929, and people suffered the irritation of all sorts of real or imagined grievances which they felt ought to be heard sympathetically by somebody, a definite "Minnesota state of mind" developed. It may not always be the state of mind of the majority—though sometimes it is—but it is easily recognizable.

"I suppose I am just a typical instance myself," said an elderly man in the lounge-car as he meditated the matter. "I grew up in New England—the same as everybody else— and came out here the better part of a half-century ago. All of my family were dyed-in-the-wool Republicans—you know, put the Republican Party right up there at the top with the church. And, it is God's truth, down to this present moment I have never scratched a ticket in my life.

"Well, the other day a friend of mine—we both have small businesses—handed me a pamphlet and said, 'Here, take this home with you, and tell me what you think of it.'

"I sat down in the evening to see what I had. And I'll be damned if it wasn't a pamphlet on socialism by Norman Thomas. It was the first time I had ever looked inside one. Since nobody was watching, I decided to read it. Before I was through, I said to myself, 'Why, hell, if this is what they call socialism, then I must be a socialist myself.'

"I took it back to him. 'Come on, now,' I said, 'when did you get to be a socialist?'

" 'I'm not a socialist,' he said. 'You know that as well as anybody—nothing of the kind. But just between the two of us, I thought there was some pretty good solid meat in what he said.'

"Well, there you have the whole thing. We've got our own problem out here to solve. It just keeps growing right up out of the ground at you—like weeds. We've got to keep on learning how to solve it. And any ideas that will help us to learn how, no matter who hatched them up first, or what part of the world they hail from, are good grist. I don't care—and I've changed my mind about this, too—whether they are from China, or Australia, or Russia, or Sweden, or where. If they are anything that we can absorb in Minnesota, we'll make Minnesota ideas out of them.

"And just one other thing: We don't pay much attention anymore to what some stiff-hat highbrow retained by Wall Street bankers to write pamphlets on the American way of doing things has to say about this or that in finance—unless such suckers as we are out here can see how it will fit right into what we are trying to work out. And that, of course, would be an accident. The chances are he knows nothing about what we are up against, or what's on our minds. He probably couldn't tell spring wheat from alfalfa."

Not that the coming of this new political force has been free of attendant evils! Nor would it be fair to imply that the people have given their imagination to political and economic problems exclusively. The University of Minnesota—as well as the University of Wisconsin—has shown an inclination to assume a vigorous leadership in educational pioneering; and in such Minnesota colleges as Carleton and St. Olaf—both in the town of Northfield where a Jesse James Café marks the last stand of the less orderly settlers against the more orderly ones—the impetus that has been given to liberal philosophic inquiry and to music would be difficult to parallel. But the lively political awareness which the people have developed through much battling has become characteristic. They put their energy into their battles as if they were giving the best of themselves to what they regarded as most important.

Late that same afternoon I asked the farmerish-looking man across the table from me in the dining-car what a certain unusual building was that we had just passed.

"Then you don't live in these parts?" he asked, after he had answered my question.

"No—I live in New England."

"In New England?"

"Yes."

"Hunh!" he said as if he had made a very amusing discovery. "You're the first one of 'em I ever bumped into that spoke first."

We were still talking an hour later when the train rolled close past the Mayo Clinic in Rochester.

"Now, why haven't more surgeons in other small towns developed places like this? But it's funny the way the human race doesn't think—till something tells it to. I'm making a trip tonight that I ought to have made twenty years ago. For we've waited just that long out where I live to have the power company electrify our rural community. Then one day last year somebody said, 'Why don't we do it ourselves?' And now it's done. I'm on my way down to Chicago to settle up the last detail. Think of the women having to pack oil lamps around with them wherever they go while they are doing the housework, and grinding away at cream separators and all that sort of thing, year in and year out, when they might just as well have had electricity!"

Down in Iowa the activity of mind is not so completely concentrated in one direction. Nobody could say that the Iowa farmers refrain from the kind of rebellious thought that has brought Minnesota the attention of the entire country. But the Iowans come nearer to having a racial solidarity. And they brought a firmer political front from Ohio and the other states east of the Mississippi and north of the Mason and Dixon line. In substantial percentages, too, they were the kind of good Methodists, good Presbyterians, and good Lutherans who are not supposed to boil over very much with unorthodox ideas. So the basic ferment of the region, seasoned by some total effect of their inherited culture, has brought them to a more diversified expression of their unquietude than merely revolting against mortgage foreclosures in time of depression, or striking for livable farm prices.

Instances are everywhere. At the University of Iowa John T. Frederick thought it affectation for young writers to busy themselves with subject-matter foreign to their own experience. He established *The Midland,* which for years published stories and poems out of the life of the people as the writers had lived it. Critics sometimes referred to it as a magazine of barnyard literature. But it had the greatest of all artistic qualities—honesty. And it offered encouragement. Either as a result, or as some exceptionally well-timed outcropping of the same fundamental unrest that produced *The Midland,* or as a combination of the two, sturdy Iowa writers—well represented early in most minds by Ruth Suckow—have appeared. Grant Wood rose up to say, in effect, "If we want to imitate the old masters, why don't we paint the world in which we live, as they painted the one in which they lived?" And Henry A. Wallace saw as the right basis for the most secure civilization of the future a body of free men on the soil, and had to kick out of all entanglements that would prevent him from going forth and battling for that idea—for a strange new order in which the Sermon on the Mount was to be substituted for the law of the jungle.

All the while, just over in Nebraska, where William Jennings Bryan had too early championed bimetallism, the abandonment of the imperialistic ideal, the government ownership of railroads, and an effective neutrality when other nations warred, Senator George W. Norris had been growing into a more and more dangerous man to the unethical and undemocratic. He believed that government ought to help make it possible for a people to experience the high self-realization about which they persist in dreaming. He has been long on a lonely crusade.

And just over in the opposite direction in Illinois Vachel Lindsay one day set forth on a crusade of a different yet related kind. He went forth to proclaim the beauty that is in life. Edgar Lee Masters startled a self-satisfied, skeptical literary world by proving that there is just as much comedy and tragedy in a Spoon River community as anywhere else. And Carl Sandburg cried out with an originality which could be at home only in the Middle West, and which has not lessened, that the new world of the plains was dramatic, that greedinesses and uglinesses invaded life, and that the people who suffer from these invasions may some day wreak vengeance—"the people, yes."

Within twenty or thirty miles from where Sandburg was born and from where Allen Crafton established the Prairie Playhouse in an old abandoned saloon to prove that new things could yet be done in the theater, I went to see the sculptor Ben Cable. I had been interested in two of his best-known pieces—"Maternity," the mare humped in the storm over her new colt, and "Homeward," the old man supporting himself by holding to the mane of his old horse as they plod along. I found him to be a farmer—not a dude farmer, but a "dirt" one. When I went up to the house—where small bronzes of these two pieces adorned the posts of the front steps, I was told that he was back at the barn somewhere. His studio was back there, too.

"Oh, I don't have much time for my sculpture," he said, "with the work to do. And you know how it is when I don't see anybody very often who is interested in such things. But I fuss around with it a little—on material I know about." Then he seemed hesitant. Then he decided. "Here's something I haven't finished yet. Do you know these hawks that sit so much on fence posts? I've seen them all my life. So I decided to do one."

With these the time is the present and the place is where we are now. They are proud of George Washington and Thomas Jefferson, but are sure that they themselves know much more about the hybridization of corn and the combatting of grasshoppers than either of those heroic ones. They suppose Tennyson and Longfellow must have been poets of some importance, but of course they never knew the feel of life in the reaches of the Mississippi Valley, never saw a spring sunrise across the boundless plains.

John G. Neihardt was stirred in this region to see something epic, and thought he had better go at once—or at least soon—to the writing of it. Willa Cather never wrote with more power than when she was busy with the Nebraska of her youth. Grant Reynard, after years in the sophisticated centers, went back to Nebraska for the subject-matter of his best work in black-and-white. Down in Missouri where Mark Twain once was accused of using unorthodox native material, Josephine Johnson saw the possibilities around her before she got away, and Thomas H. Benton came back and settled down to work as if he now knew that he was at home. And on south still, John Gould Fletcher returned from his self-imposed expatriation and wrote with a new energy in honor of the pioneer spirit. T. S. Eliot has not yet returned.

"It is a world that leaves men enough alone to develop

an initial self-confidence. "Why is it so good?" I asked the director of the Kansas City Art Institute, as he showed me through the Midwestern Exhibition.

"I've tried to figure that out myself," he replied. "To one who has lived chiefly in another part of the world, it seems to be about like this: these youngsters do not know too much technique. But they can get along. Then they see something right before their eyes, right outside their own doors, that they want to paint; and they just crack into it and paint it."

Not all the wild ideas have had origins of approved respectability. A physician named Still who had seen his children die of spinal meningitis, despite the best medical attention he could secure for them, and who remembered how he used to cure his own headaches by lying on his back on the ground with the back of his neck resting on a swinging pillow made of a suspended rope and a blanket, after much experimentation arrived at the unacceptable conclusion that such diseases as typhoid fever, diphtheria, rheumatism, sciatica, gout, croup, colic, and the like were not things in themselves, but only different expressions of a partial or a complete failure of the nerves to conduct through the body the sustenance of a full bloodstream. He proposed to give the blood a chance to provide all the remedy required right out of its own drug-store, and not resort to a drug-store of any other kind.

The Methodist college that he had helped to found—he was the son of a Methodist preacher—refused to let him explain his theory in its halls. He had been regarded as an able physician and a valuable citizen. But when he professed to be able to use the bones of the body as levers and, by twisting the patient up in just the right way, cure flux and colds and whooping-cough, the people in the east

Kansas town joined in praying that he be saved from the insane asylum and the tortures of hell's fire. After casting about long enough without being lodged in an asylum, he found a town—Kirksville, Missouri—that was willing to have him stay. Not all conventionally trained physicians are yet ready to admit that a lesion at the right point along the spinal column will result in sexual sterility, but they are ready to admit that osteopathy is here, and might as well be tolerated or even looked into. And in Kirksville the old man's statue occupies one of the places in the courthouse square that most towns reserve exclusively for major-generals.

Other heresies of the thoughtful have gained place. When men who had something at stake and their hired propagandists tried to tell the farmers that consumers' coöperatives were un-American, the farmers said in reply, "Well, they won't be if we all adopt them. Maybe they're not, anyhow." So the idea has steadily been put into practice. It has withstood all effort to make it out communistic or Swedish or British. North Kansas City has become the headquarters of a retailers' wholesale coöperative that reaches out into as many as eight or ten states.

And there to the westward Kansas has a full complement of her own originalities. Kansas is not just a commonwealth; Kansas is an institution, a condition of mind—a condition of split mind. The Puritan spirit is strong in Kansas, as it well might be. For that is where the Puritan spirit went—to make Kansas a free state and to keep it free. The New England qualities make themselves known, too —a firmness that will not be stampeded, persistence, self-denial, a hard attitude toward industrial labor, profound conviction, traces of flaming intolerance, a settled love for the things long known. There are stone walls in east

Kansas—flat stones—and attractive residential streets lined with elm trees girdled against moths that look like nothing so much as the tree-arched streets of Cambridge, Massachusetts, back at the turn of the century. Yet in this seemingly undisturbed atmosphere, ideas of great force smoulder. Sooner or later they break forth like sun-spots, create at least as much local disturbance, and then frequently are absorbed by the public mind as a regular part of the state's operating energy, until they seem as much at home there as William Allen White and the Emporia *Gazette,* or Senator Arthur Capper and the *Household Magazine.* I have been told very privately by more than one Kansan that if all uninviting labels could be discarded, Earl Browder would come nearer than Alf. M. Landon to standing forth as the political representative of the true Kansas spirit.

"Do you know why all the region between the Mississippi and the mountains is radical politically—that is, according to the standards of the older parts of the country?" a Republican politician in Kansas asked me as we sat together in the train.

I glanced out at the window as I considered—into a bulging, rapidly changing wall of steamy smoke that a wintry wind from the northwest rolled off alongside the track from the two heavy engines that were carrying us comfortably at a mile a minute. The vaporous smoke was as soft in the late afternoon sunlight as if it had been a cloud in the sky a mile above our heads. A section-hand who had stepped back to let the train pass and stood with his mittened fist on the grip of a shovel that rested on the frozen turf looked, in the fraction of a second while he was in sight, like a gentle old professor of philosophy I had known in college.

"Because," I queried, "the two major parties out this way are shrewd enough to carry on a continuous borrowing from the 'wild' new parties that spring up?"

"Exactly. William Jennings Bryan swiped so much from the Populists that they all had to vote for him in order to keep from voting against their own principles. Republican legislatures in Kansas have helped themselves in more or less the same way."

He laughed. "So who needed the Populist Party any longer?"

Kansans have gone in heavily for native art, too. They publish their own literary magazine—with very exceptional illustrations—so that people inside and outside the state may see what Kansas writers—such substantial and emotionally honest writers as Kenneth Porter, for instance—are doing. And the state is alive with etchers and lithographers, and makers of block-prints both in black-and-white and in colors. The Atlantic seaboard may hear only of such Kansas artists as H. V. Poor and John Steuart Curry when they take high place in some international exhibition. But there are others—many others.

The artistic mind has been quickened; yet other minds have been too completely occupied with the hard facts of life to make wide interest in the work of the artist easy. So the artists, in addition to doing their own work, have sought to lend aid and comfort to their kind. C. A. Seward, for instance, not only has made lithographs and block-prints and etchings of Kansas plains and hilltops, and the Cimarron Canyon, and the pueblos of New Mexico, that have gone to all parts of the United States and to Europe, but has acted as a godfather in the region of Wichita to a group of distinguished younger workers in the same fields.

And he has done so without imposing his own style upon them. E. L. Davison and his wife, while giving their chief time to their own painting with the sure devotion of artists of greatest sensitivity, have yet found it possible to encourage contemporaries in the most substantial of ways. Up in Lindsborg, Birger Sandzen, known chiefly as a painter, has fostered another interesting center. In yet more isolated places there are such workers of clear originality as Arthur W. Hall and Norma Hall. Few people outside the state had ever heard of Howard, Kansas, until Norma Bassett Hall's colored block-prints found favor, and Arthur W. Hall's etchings began to find their way into international exhibitions. Other artists have likewise been good incidental crusaders.

And right on southward from Kansas the restive mind has expressed itself in an art that is quite as much at home in the region. Just across in Stillwater, Oklahoma, Doel Reed, a native of another state, has caught the feeling of the Southwest as if he had always lived there. Young natives have contributed distinguished murals to many Oklahoma public buildings—such artists as Mopope, Auchiah, Asah, Hokeah, and Acee Blue Eagle. In other places there are artists who ought to be named. Right on southward, too, those who work in the arts have sought to encourage other workers and promote a better understanding of good work. At Norman, Oscar B. Jacobson not only has convinced men and women with eyes that the landscape in Oklahoma is as sheer and red and purplish as he has painted it, but has fostered some of the very men who have done the interesting murals in the state institutions. Such writers as Stanley Vestal and B. A. Botkin and their colleagues have provided a kind of rallying ground for all writers of the state. And the University of Oklahoma Press has published interesting books in typography and format that would invite anyone to read.

The architecture, too, in this part of the region seems less away from home than the architecture in most sections of America outside of New England. It is not to be forgotten that Frank Lloyd Wright grew up at the northern end of this regional axis and that Bruce Goff grew up at the southern end, and that both have recorded their genius in Oklahoma.

Down through the whole of the region too—all the way down from the homeland of Charles A. Lindbergh the younger to that of Will Rogers and on into Texas—the people have created institutions of learning based upon their needs in their own environment. The state universities in some instances have kept nearer to traditional education. But in such institutions as the State Colleges at Ames, Iowa, Manhattan, Kansas, Stillwater, Oklahoma, and College Station, Texas where heavy percentages of the students are from the farms, and where many of them expect to go back to farms, the education has been adapted to the very immediate purpose of making life in the region as livable and as interesting as possible.

"Do you know me?" a towering gray-haired man of forty-five or fifty asked me when I was spending two or three days in one of these institutions.

Yes, I knew him. But what was he doing—twenty-five years after college?

He told me—with honest pride. For not everyone in college in his day had expected him to do great things. In Oklahoma, he explained, the dry weather is likely to catch the corn—when anybody grows any—just when it is coming out in tassel and before the ears have developed. It is risky to try to grow it. Yet in a proper diversification of crops on

Oklahoma farms, corn ought to be used. Well, he had developed a short-season corn that this year was coming out in tassel by Decoration Day instead of the first of July.

"You may bring about some great social changes in the state," I suggested.

Well, yes, he thought if enough people worked at the job of helping the soil do its best, something yet undreamed of might be done.

Some of these direct-action educational institutions have almost outgrown their sister state universities. And down in the northern edge of Texas a related institution—the Texas State College for Women—has almost outgrown itself. Scarcely forty years ago it began as a woman's industrial college. Today it is a flourishing institution of twenty-six hundred students—larger than either Smith or Wellesley—that makes available both the practical and the liberal arts. Students are busy with the economy and the art of the household; with painting, and black-and-white, and pottery, and wood-carving, and music, and drama, and poetry, and economics, and all sorts of problems that must be faced in an enlightened society. When they graduate many of them go far over a state larger than France to supervise art in the schools and to help the wives of second-generation settlers plan a better-looking world.

How swiftly human energy may speed through the entire cycle to fitness for such activity I saw one lazy afternoon in February at this institution. I went to the new arts building to look at some pottery. Somebody directed me up one flight too far. A sandy-haired girl was down so close over a block of wood at which she was working that her hair hung loose about her head and completely obscured her face—to me. For five minutes I stood unobserved and watched her work with great deftness at the face that was slowly emerging from the block. Finally, to rest her back she straightened up—and saw me.

"Hello, there!" she said as if she had been calling to some neighbor along the road. "I didn't see you standing there."

"Don't stop!" I begged of her. "Go right ahead. I like to watch you."

"Oh, it can wait. I just came up here to put in a few hours extra on it this afternoon when there weren't many others around."

I studied the face in the block. It was rather stunning.

"How long have you been working in this course?" I asked.

"Oh, just since September."

"But didn't you have practice at this sort of thing before you came here?"

Her smile broke into a little laugh, as if I did not know much.

"No, never tried it before."

"And never saw any?"

Her smile broke into the same kind of little laugh. "No, never saw any, either. I never saw much of anything till I came here. If you live on a ranch out in the Panhandle, there isn't much to see."

While she spoke I remembered something that Governor Alfalfa Bill Murray once said to me. We were sitting in his office in the state-house when work for the day was about over. He had his hat on—a broad-brimmed black crumpled hat—and he had slipped down in the large office chair until he was half reclining on a leather pillow, with his heels resting on the edge of the executive desk. He wore high shoes that needed a shine, and white cotton socks that were down over the tops of his shoes. His mustache and hair looked as if they had never been trimmed, and a growth of stubbly gray beard was showing all over his face. But his eyes were keen.

"What are you reading?" he asked me after he had told somebody over the telephone that he would see that the state provided fruit-jars to some needy persons if they would grow what was to go in them.

"Oh," I replied, remembering the libraries he had read when he was working on a constitution for Oklahoma, "not so much. My guess is that authors read less than most people."

"Most people," he said, "read too damned much. If they'd go off to a mountain somewhere and think . . ."

"What do you expect to do?" I asked the girl.

"Oh"—and she threw her head back and shook her hair into place a little—"I don't know; teach, maybe."

And this institution's approach to life which is doing so much in a state as extensive as a good-sized nation to enrich the taste of the people right where they live every day is the approach characteristic of the entire region of ferment. Whether we like it or not, whether or not it seems to lack the bouquet of traditional culture, it provides the interesting spectacle of men and women trying in some degree to make their philosophies out of the new facts of life, instead of trying to bend and distort the facts to make them fit into categories long ago conceived for other purposes.

# xvii

## Sunlight

IT was a strange preparation for the sight of a region—the mere fact that on a train out of Kansas City into the Southwest I had to take an upper berth. In the middle of the night, long after I had gone to sleep, I became drowsily half-aware of voices that penetrated the steady roar of the train. As I grew a little more sharply conscious I thought they must be near me. And by the time I was wide awake I knew that they were in the berth beneath mine. I could not hear what they were saying, but one of them was the voice of a man and the other that of a woman, and the tone of their speech was serious. Just when I was ready to press the button and request the porter to have quiet, the train came to a stop, and I could hear what the two were saying. They were an old man and an old woman, and their voices expressed great resignation.

"It wouldn't be so bad," the old man said, "if you could

see anything. But just to go roarin' along through the dark like this—"

She held out little comfort. She supposed they would have to make the best of it till daylight.

"What time do you suppose it is, anyhow?" he wished to know.

"Oh, some 'eres around two o'clock, I shouldn't wonder."

He was silent for a time. Then he asked: "Do you suppose they'll be there to meet us?"

"They said they would."

Thus they talked together as if some mutual mighty awareness reduced all else in their lives to inconsequence. As soon as I knew that they expressed no unfriendly intent, I dropped off into the soundest of slumbers that lasted until late the next morning.

When I came back from breakfast the porter had made up the section and they were sitting together in the sun—two kind, drooping old people whose faces and hands recorded long struggle. They were so oblivious of their immediate surroundings that I could not bring myself to breaking in upon them and claiming my half of the section. Conveniently, the one across the aisle was now unoccupied.

In a chance word now and then, plus an occasional glance into each other's face when they referred to something that they were ready to hurry past, it all came out: they were on their way home from a famous hospital up north, and it seemed that there was little or no hope for either of them.

"Anyhow," the old man said after a long silence in which they both had looked distantly out at the window, "it's good to have some real sun once more." Then after another silence they smiled at each other like two very unworldly-wise lovers.

"That sun!" he said again, as if she might not be fully appreciative of it.

Something of their overpowering sense of life's tenuousness swept across to me as I watched them. I, too, had to look away into the distance. And almost before I knew it, the sun was making me aware that he was newly important. We were getting down into the Texas Panhandle where the sun is a great sun, and where most of the time there is nothing much in his way to prevent him from displaying his full power on the earth's surface. Down here his light gives new character to everything; it touches everything with wonder. It makes the sky a bigger, clearer sky. It brightens up the landscape until you not only feel the vastness, the limitlessness of the plains, but in the high visibility discern all sorts of detail that give the distance an unbelievable kind of depth and solidity. In ordinary sunlight, that long silk thread of a dark line just at the horizon would have been only an undistinguishable part of the general vagueness, but in this brightness it was a freight train a mile long creeping on its way from Memphis to Los Angeles. What loomed as large as a small city in the far distance turned out to be when we came up to it only the buildings and the clump of planted shade-trees on a ranch. But what was that —there was a city, was there not? It stood up high—almost too high—just beyond a shimmering lake. It was my first mirage. The city was there, undeniably. But it was many more miles away than it seemed. And there was no lake. And the buildings, I found when I was ready to get off the train, though high enough, were not so high as the ones in the phantom city I had just seen.

The sun had awakened me to a large-scale drama. And when I fell in with a painter from New York who was spending his first days in the region, and whose awakening by the sun had amounted to an intoxication from which he experienced no let-down, I was soon seeing yet more than my own eyes had seen unaided. He had to stop in the middle of the street in Amarillo to sketch an effect of light that he had never observed before. He had to pull up at the roadside to catch a wheat-field of billowing gold with a man sitting high on a combine that marched irresistibly across the field. He had to follow for a half-hour a broad man who bulged out over the seat of a mowing machine behind two stout bay horses plodding lazily along the grassy edge of the road—following, driving up close, sketching; falling behind, driving up again, sketching, until the man, despite the noise of the mowing machine in thin grass, detected him and good-naturedly wanted to know "just what the hell."

Fortified by a Texan who had lived in the Panhandle for twenty-eight years, and who could not be induced to live anywhere else, we roamed the region, just to feel the vastness of a world under a bright sun. We sped beside wheatfields that promised to be without end, yet did end; then through fields as large as townships dotted with cattle, cattle, the white faces of Hereford cattle everywhere—and everywhere in the fields with them jack-rabbits that stood high on their hind legs, their eyes full of inquiry, their long ears so erect that light showed through them, and then quickly squatted close down to the ground in the hope that they had not been seen; then more fields of precisely the same kind, and more thousands of cattle—big cattle soon to be ready for market, young heifers and steers, and tiny white-faced, innocent-looking calves—the cow-puncher's "dogies"—tugging at mothers that acted as if giving milk should not be the entire business of life; and yet other fields here and there that had been overpastured until the cactus and the yucca had crept in and taken possession.

And right in the middle of this flat Panhandle country we came suddenly out above the Palo Duro Canyon. Most people seem to think that there is only one canyon in the world. Few have ever heard of this one here, and fewer still have ever seen it. Yet it is one of the earth's beautiful wonders. In this seemingly flattest of all flat regions, in the course of enough tens of thousands of years, a prairie streamlet—the headwaters of the Red River—in a constant effort to keep to its clearest course has meandered back and forth across miles of terrain, and broken and swept the fragments away until it has cut its way deep down through multicolored rock of unbelievable brightness. Into the hazy purplish-yellow distance as far as you can see are points and domes and cathedrals and cliffs and giant toadstools in maroons and yellows and greens and whites and grays and mauves too bright to be accepted at first view. It is so many miles long that you are not troubled about whether it has an end or not; yet somehow it is not so large but what the mind can encompass it.

It is a canyon worth talking about. For on a well-kept road it is possible to descend into it, and enjoy the quiet that seems somehow colored by the rocks everywhere above one's head, and breathe the late afternoon coolness, and come back up to the starting-point, and linger there, and become again as rapturous as one wishes over the yellows and blues and violets—all within the limits of a few hours.

The sun does not let anything in the region seem ordinary. Least of all is the sun's own afternoon decline an ordinary sunset. It reaches the horizon without any of the accompaniments of mountains or forested valleys and old ruins that are supposed to give sunsets the significant touch.

It is big enough in its own name to go down. As I watched it the first evening I ever spent in the region, the prairie seemed to extend solidly from where we stood right out to the very edge of the sun.

"Wait a minute," the painter commanded when he saw one of his first.

He rushed off like a boy and came back in a moment all ready to make a water-color. He worked with a wild sureness.

"I can put that old windmill in tomorrow," he said when it was no longer light enough to work; "but I wanted to get the proportion of that black line of earth and the big sky. Did you ever see a sky as big as that one?"

Nor does the sun leave the spirit of the people untouched. They express something of its bright expansiveness. From the Panhandle on down through the western side of the state through the Staked Plains area the best of the early American memories have fused with the spirit of the western pioneer in an alert, hopeful, friendly people. Life has not been easy. In truth, it would be difficult to imagine anything more disheartening than the march into this Panhandle region when there was nothing there—not even a decent hill—to invite one with an assurance of protection. The open prairie with a thunder-storm coming on can fill one with a sense of helplessness not to be paralleled anywhere else. Constantly when I went into shops, I was imagining that I heard echoes of the people's loneliness in the manner of their invitation to come again: "Well, hurry back!" "Don't stay away long!" "Sure will be glad to have you come again!" For these lonely days were only a few decades ago—within the memory of men still living. Many a face that one sees bending over a ranch-house kitchen bears the marks of hard days still present—but also the softer lines implanted by hope.

And their children are a kind unto themselves. Ever since they were able to do anything that might be called work—and that was early in their lives—they have labored in the faith that things were sure to be better if only they persisted long enough. Life was to be something progressively expansive—naturally, for they have never lived where anything was on a small scale. After enough winters and summers on a ranch, they pack up and drive a few hundred miles to college—to learn more about agricultural life, to prepare to teach, to gain less utilitarian knowledge and points of view that in some way they have come to believe worth having. The boys are rangy fellows of cheerful disposition who have not the slightest doubt about their ability to do whatever they decide to undertake, and who say constantly in their looks, "All right; but no kidding." And the girls suggest some strange and uncontemplated union of the romance of old Virginia with the enforced self-reliance of the pioneer West. I should be willing to risk the dagger words of women in other regions to say that there is a higher percentage of naturally beautiful girls in west Texas than in any other area of the United States.

The painter was exclamatory about this part of his discovery of the region, too. "Say! They know how to walk! They walk on their feet! None of this pitching and clattering along of the girl who has been propped up on high heels all her life! And no piano legs, either! They are slender without effort, what? And liveliness of motion—did you ever see anything quite like it? And beauty of face! And genuineness—in the boys, too, the same as the girls. I didn't know it existed anywhere in the world any longer—like that. I walk around here in the evening just to see these young couples strolling together. It makes me feel better toward the race."

Here are people who have not been prevented by the presence of their fellow-beings in too great numbers from developing their own originalities. They have had solitude. They have thought things over. They have considered the world where they live. They have wondered just what they were about.

They have become intelligently concerned, too, with preserving an adequate record of what they have contributed to civilized life. Men whose chief and outward occupation has been to keep an eye on cattle or to make semi-arid land produce more wheat have been busy also with unearthing journals kept by their fathers and mothers—or grandfathers and grandmothers—at the time they came into the region, making collections of all kinds of firearms, cooking utensils, crude agricultural implements, and all sorts of hand-made household means of livableness that were not so long ago a part of everyday existence but are already more or less forgotten, and building museums where all this material may be safely preserved. The museum on the campus of the State Teachers College at Canyon, fostered by men and women scattered over the Panhandle area, makes vivid the history of the region. Even the sculptors who contributed to the external beauty of the building felt the importance of using the life of the locality as motif.

Nor have the people contented themselves with the immediate past. They have preserved the record of what they found there. They have gone far back. Not only does a mural record the coming of Charles Goodnight into the Palo Duro to establish the first Panhandle ranch in 1876; another records Coronado's expedition leaving the canyon in 1541.

And now they are busy with the geologic past. Something in the dry atmosphere—and dry earth—has helped to preserve in unusual state the skeletons of mastodons and other more ordinary fry of ages long gone. In this museum I saw men working on one almost perfect tusk more than ten feet long that had just been unearthed in the vicinity. One of the college buildings is faced with stone split from the remains in the region of a petrified forest in which trees six feet in diameter have been found. The more imaginative of the people contemplate nothing less stupendous than some day having trees on the plains again—and perhaps a more productive rainfall.

Southward across west Texas, life has much the same color—the sun is much the same sun. If you go two or three hundred miles east from the central Panhandle region, you run into the rolling long-range red hills of Oklahoma where cottonwood and elm down deep in canyon-like gutters and all sorts of draws and stream-beds rise just high enough to produce meandering billowy ridges of lush green above the level of the fields and make into rhythmic patchwork vast areas of land that receives enough rain to meet requirements. If you go east a little farther down, out into the body of Texas, you run out of the flat land and the half-desert-looking undulations covered with yucca and cactus and mesquite into greener levels and, eventually, more timber and all sorts of tangled vines—and more fruit trees thriving in gardens. Or if you go in the other direction over into New Mexico, you enter desert country that is unmistakably dry and hot. But for the hundreds of miles down through west Texas you are just in between. You have brightness without being quite in the desert, and vegetation without being in frequent danger from downpours.

Or if you prefer, you can go off southwest through New

Mexico to the tip of Texas—it must be remembered that El Paso is farther west than Santa Fe—and enter the southern end of the region from the west. But by whatever route you proceed, you come into the same surprising and little-known country. In truth, it is yet more surprising than the region farther north, for here you are in a vast area of mountainous country two hundred and fifty miles or so in length and almost as wide. Just to discover that there are so many mountains in Texas, and that one of them rises well toward ten thousand feet above sea level, is in itself rather breath-taking. It is more breath-taking to discover the kind of mountains they are. For they are not the ordinary mountains that everybody visits, and camps in, and uses as a base from which to mail post-cards. They are a dreamer's mountains: long ranges of so many points and levels that they seem without number or end; areas of isolated volcanic peaks rising high above the plateau; great bulks of rock looming ponderous in the sky like gigantic castles; vast stretches of palisades in flutings and columns—all these in sunlit pink-grays and pale green-grays and yellow-grays which near, farther away, and so far away that they are just visible make endlessness something easy to accept.

For a week I found time to make trips out from Alpine, a little city forty-four hundred feet up on a spreading plateau, and a center for the mountain region. I explored to the north, or northwest, in the Davis Mountains—the Jefferson Davis Mountains, from the Fort Davis of pre-Civil War days—and found a peacefulness that invited me to linger. The plains between mountains were covered with cattle, and frequently antelope were enjoying the pasture with them. From the top of Mt. Locke, where the MacDonald Observatory of the University of Texas stands sixty-eight hundred feet above sea-level, one can see the clear gray outlines of the mountains stretching away eighty or a hundred miles.

I had a bird's-eye glimpse of the people of the region, too. A legal interlude in Alpine enabled me to have it. A man and wife from some other part of the state had decided to make a home for a thirteen-year-old boy. They took out a five-thousand-dollar life insurance policy in his name. Then they came to the mountain region—after due time—for a vacation. Late one day the "father" and "mother" came to town with the boy's mangled body. They said he had fallen from a three-hundred-foot cliff. He was buried rather promptly. And rather promptly the "father" was arrested and charged with having thrown him to his death.

The trial was on. From all over a county as large as a small state the people had come to hear and see. Here was something real enough to be interesting—a clear-cut issue of life and death. The movies were neglected; the classes at the state college for teachers shrank in size. Men and women and boys and girls crowded into the large courtroom and filled every seat and every added chair; they stood close about the judge's bench; they filled every aisle; they stood high in the windows.

I soon lost interest in the proceedings. For before I had been present an hour—wedged in among shorter people far down one of the aisles where I could see well—I decided that the man was guilty. His efforts to be casual and nonchalant and confident were not effective. He forgot to keep up appearances and occasionally bit his nails in great nervousness or obliviously dropped his face to the table with his hand clutching his forehead. So I watched the people—men now a little rotund in their slacks and work-shirts, with their good-sized light-colored felt hats crushed under their arms; men in down-to-the-minute clothes who were stealing a little time from store or bank; women fresh from ranch kitchens with their hair sleeked back; town women who could afford to have Mexicans from south of the railroad do their housework for them; boys and girls who silently flirted while the life-or-death trial proceeded; small children who squirmed and wiggled in their mothers' arms and wondered when they were ever going to be through with whatever it was they were doing. The entire assemblage who watched radiated great cheerfulness and good-will. They were not hostile toward the defendant. But they seemed to think that if he had been keeping anything back that he could say for himself, it was about time for him to be telling it.

The next afternoon when the jury returned a verdict of guilty and the man was sentenced to death, the people suddenly became more interesting than ever. The sentence was what they had expected, yet it terrified them a little. It was too bad for the man to have to go to the electric chair. But then men should not be throwing little boys from high cliffs for life insurance money. Anyhow this fellow had given their mountains a bad name. He had caused numberless press despatches about a murder to go out all over the country dated "Alpine, Texas." They were glad he was from somewhere else. And in relief and content they went off to the stores to buy a few things before they hurried back to their workaday lives.

These people express much the same blending of the old South and the new West that one finds all the way north to the Panhandle. They have awareness of the common destiny of their kind, and of the continuity of civilized life. Like their neighbors farther north they are interested in preserving the record of their regional past. I found them busy assembling in a new museum every kind of household

## Sunlight

and outdoor object that had been used in the first struggles toward orderly life. But also like their neighbors to the north they live chiefly in the present and the future. Life must go on, must it not? Life must be made more livable. If money must be scarce, then ways of getting along in good style without much money must be devised. On a campus that is steadily growing into a larger and larger spot of green at the base of a dry-looking mountain, in attractive cottages of native stone which the teachers' college has erected, a student can live coöperatively for an academic year on what many a student in socially important colleges spends in a month. Did people quit trying just because there was more sunshine than rainfall in a region?

It seemed not. For a week all my spare time was taken by students who slipped down to the hotel to talk over something they had been thinking about. And they were thinking about everything but crassly utilitarian projects. One, a tall young woman of thoughtful manner, came in behalf of some one else, a young man on a ranch—her fiancé perhaps. On a ranch he had plenty of solitude in which to think. He had been trying to put something down on paper —something of his immediate world. He would never have ventured to suggest that she bring any of his results to me. But she had arranged some of them in a loose-leaf note-book, and would I take a glance? They were more than the pleasant but harmless little verses which college students too often write. Here was the drama of the range—the drought, the bulls fighting, the spiritual vagabonds who happened along and touched the current of his life, his own way of looking at things. It was something fresh from an active mind. It partook of the region. It was poetry.

From Alpine, too, I went on down to the Rio Grande— to see some mountains of special interest. The president of the college at Alpine is a dreamer of dreams. These mountains, isolated by act of nature, must be set aside as a great park. But they must not be made into any ordinary state or national park. They look right across to neighboring extraordinary peaks in Mexico. In at least one place the Rio Grande has to squeeze through a canyon so narrow that a bridge would readily tie the two mountains and the two countries together. The park must be an international park, devoted to friendship. It is something well on the way. And soon I was to see it.

All the way down I experienced a special preparation of mind. The biological scientist in charge of the survey of wild life in the region pointed out every neighboring range and peak—the Glass Mountains, so pale and so seemingly translucent that their name was obviously appropriate; a darker range off in another direction with sawteeth of some very light formation distinct against its side from one end to the other; isolated peaks with dark traces of volcanic ash streaking their sides; stretches of desert in which we stopped for the ripe fruit of the cactus. From nine-thirty in the morning till four in the afternoon we saw only six automobiles.

Hawks sat undisturbed in the sun when we passed within thirty feet of them; turkey buzzards that fed on the carcass of some jack-rabbit that had been too careless of the occasional automobiles on the road, scarcely circled out of our way, and then were back again; road-runners that evidently had found enough choice lizards and young snakes for the day scarcely moved out of the road at all, and once when we stopped to watch, and made a peeping noise, one of three became so curious that she had to come peering and ducking in strange feints of movement all the way to the front fender; an occasional red racer four feet long or so paused and protested in angry, harmless disgust that his leisurely progress should be disturbed by an overtowering vehicle; mocking-birds sang on tall stems of yucca that leaned over the road, and never changed their tempo at our passing.

And then after a long steady climb that heated the engine, we were in the mountains: the Chisos Mountains—unworldly in their cragginess. Five thousand feet above sea level in the wide mouth of a canyon we stretched out under a gnarled piñon tree that the botanist said was probably from four to six hundred years old, and ate our sandwiches, and lounged, and felt the cool breeze sweep our faces, and listened to the flood of bird music that came from everywhere, and let our eyes range over the bright red crags that rose three thousand feet or so above us. Then we pushed on, climbing higher and higher until we were over a pass and beginning to have intimations of something far beyond the Gothic-like bulks that shut out most of the distant view. Here high in the sunlight was as appropriate a place as any to consider the journey at an end. For over there to the south, on and on and on, the same kind of mountains rose peak beyond peak until in the bright sunlight they faded into the palest of luminous ethereal grays.

## xviii

## Novelty

IT was just the trip I had long dreamed about but had never taken: a great swing-around down out of the Plains into the desert Southwest, up along the Pacific Coast to the Canadian boundary, and back through the mountains into the Plains again—all in a swift succession that would enable me to feel the differences between one place and another.

Contrasts were not slow in arising. In one afternoon a stream-line train carried us flying close against the earth down from St. Paul and Minneapolis through the untamed lushness of southern Minnesota into the cleaner-looking fields of Iowa, across Iowa, across a portion of Missouri, and into Kansas City. The people in this train were matter-of-fact in appearance, and they busied themselves with matter-of-fact concerns—with wheat, and the prices of beef, and the evils of tenant-farming, and whether the family had done well in breaking up the old home-place when they might have gone on together farming it as a unit. Such workaday matters they discussed as we swept down across the country to the accompaniment of a broadcast of a Minnesota-Michigan football game. But in Kansas City I stepped into another world—into a seemingly endless extra-fare train of stainless steel from Chicago that was filled with somewhat swanky people apparently bound for a destination where there were no matter-of-fact concerns to trouble anybody.

This was a train guaranteed to take people somewhere in a hurry. By the next morning the last of the productive-looking farms of the region of sustenance had vanished, and we were in a desolate land—somewhere in eastern Colorado—where nothing much was growing except some half-famished cottonwood trees along gravelly stream-beds that had no water in them. Before the morning was old we were down among dry-looking mountains in New Mexico. Cattle roamed over rocky foot-hills among runty trees and boulders as if they were finding a spear of grass now and then that ordinary human eyes could not see.

The train stopped at a station—perhaps it was Las Vegas—and a gray man in leather coat but with plenty of money in his pocket for extra fares and full meals said in the silence: "There's something all right, all right." Railroad workers had erected a memorial bearing an inscription that began: "Lest we forget . . ." The monument consisted of three or four old-fashioned coupling-links such as brakemen had to lift into place as the cars bumped together—sooner or later at the expense of a hand or arm—back in the nineties before the installation of automatic couplers was required. "Maybe I don't remember those old meat axes!"

I asked him about the cattle. Just what did they find out there that could possibly result in beef?

He smiled. "Takes just exactly one section of that land to keep one steer going—if he don't run himself to death getting from one blade of grass to the next!"

We talked.

And then I was in Lamy—and in Santa Fe. In a short twenty-four hours I saw something of the bright picturesqueness of the surrounding mountain country—including the rounded peak where I was told the ashes of Mary Austin had been scattered—and caught something of the spirit of the community. Santa Fe is active—a trifle self-conscious and overanxious to live in the older New Mexican tradition—but none the less unafraid and productive.

In Santa Fe there were still threads of life running back eastward—and binding Santa Fe a little. But the next day before I had gone far on my way I was aware that we were in a world that bore no logical relation to what goes on in the Mississippi Valley and along the Atlantic seaboard. The detachment had become complete. We were surrounded by a dry-looking picture-book unreality. The farther we traveled the drier-looking the rock-piles of mountains became—and the narrower and farther apart the watered strips. Out here people live in a great scantiness of everything—including human associations—as if life were in fact a game in which you win if you can still prove that you are alive.

"It's an interesting spectacle," I remarked to a conductor who bore as much gold braid as an admiral.

"Yes, but who would want to live in a spectacle?"

He, too, watched out at the window while great sheer buttresses of red rock to our northward moved by in snail-like procession. "People ask me every day just what this country down here is for, and I've been making this run now for twenty-odd years, but I've never been able to tell them." Later when he came through he said, "We're right on top of the Continental Divide, if that interests you. There's one of the markers—7,248 feet up."

By daybreak the next morning we were across Arizona into southern California, and the rock-piles of mountains that rose up out of a desert which seemed only a rock-pile flattened out were complete in their magnificent suggestion of eternal death.

In the dressing-room a hectic young fellow who glanced out from time to time as if he were in familiar country asked me if I had ever been out there in summer weather. He had tried it. "I spent three months once over there about forty miles just beyond that mountain, right when it was hottest—June, July, August. Midday temperature anywhere from 120° to 135°. Many a day I've left a cup of coffee standing on the table at breakfast and by the time I came back in the afternoon half of it would be evaporated. Some people say they like such a life, but I'd rather be dead than to go out there and spend another three months."

I was limp at the thought of so much desolation. Men might survive here, they might prove life possible, but the life which results in any cumulative resource must be lived where a more generous earth helps its children away to a running start. These men who pant in the desert will be important to the race only if the entire earth turns so dry that everybody has to learn a dry technique. Then I felt myself restored, and discovered that somewhere between Barstow and Pasadena, in fields that were well irrigated, grass grew as if it were actually growing. The mountains, too, had taken on a slightly less lifeless appearance. They seemed to block our way—high, massive ranges, with scant vegetation, and at the base of them great slabs of smooth white, as high as hills, turned up edgewise in the sun. Then, after a swift descent through a narrow valley and some ugly smudges of smoke, the green of the earth widened into orange groves, and palm trees lined streets of houses of some semi-tropical looking architecture that seemed specially appropriate in the bright sun.

Many somewhat oversleek-looking people began to get off at suburban stations which were alive with people of the same kind—people who were dressed up a bit beyond the requirements of an ordinary day, and who moved about as if they expected to stay dressed up. From inside a train that had recently been in Kansas City and Chicago, everything seemed foreign. I was startled to hear close outside the train window snatches of the English language. I seemed to be entering a vast dreamland retreat for people who wish to settle down to something that is neither physically nor mentally too difficult.

People in Los Angeles tell you that the city is the greatest thing of its kind on earth. And it is. It has a very great interest. But its interestingness is that of any other good show. Those who declare that Hollywood and motion pictures have given to all Los Angeles a reputation that belongs to only a part of it speak falsely. For there is about the entire city a piquant unreality as great as that of any movie. Nowhere is the tempo one which suggests that here we have the sweat and pain and waiting and renewed struggle of men who have settled into a natural stride.

I was invited—by men in gold braid—to see Beverly Hills and "the homes of famous movie actresses." The tour did not actually admit one to the stars' houses, no; but one was likely to see some of them walking with their dogs. I was invited to go to Santa Monica, for there I could see "the seaside homes of movie stars." I was implored to make an all-day tour of "the great City of Make Believe," where I would see nothing but studios and other "homes of famous movie stars" without number, and would be the "privileged guest" —just whatever that might mean—of one of the largest producing companies on earth. The trip included luncheon at Studio Café, where movie stars positively dine, and where by all the laws of chance one might see three or four. Through somebody's subtle feeling for unity, this tour— so I was assured—ended with "a visit to Aimee Semple McPherson's million-dollar Angelus Temple." And then if I had not seen enough, I could make a Los Angeles Night Club tour guaranteed to be "more daring" than anything put on in New York or anywhere else in the world. The fare itself included three full-sized cocktails, and a midnight supper that positively would not be served before midnight.

I preferred to go out unguided. I wanted to see the fundamental Los Angeles. I went to a ten-cent store—one that stretched from one street to the next. It would be reassuring to see "the people." But all the people there looked as if they belonged somewhere else. They did not act as if they had been there long, or as if they expected to stay. I asked fifteen of them if they minded telling me where they were from, and seven of them were from Iowa. What were they doing out there? Oh, nothing much—just acting as supers in the greatest show on earth.

I followed them to a two-story cafeteria—one of the best ones I was ever in—and by "ordering" a second time I managed to sit at two different tables. But my sense of unreality was only heightened. One man with a strange new eagerness in his eye assured me that life begins at sixty-five. This discovery he had but recently made. He had lived in one place or another more or less—in Iowa, in Texas, in Hawaii—but he had now lived in Los Angeles so long that he regarded himself as one of the early settlers. He talked interestingly while I sat for an hour and enjoyed an ornately decorated stage set with men and woman at tables all about me eating food that looked substantial enough, and talking about apartments and agents and studios and somebody they knew who had just sold picture rights.

Sooner or later I had wandered in all directions—south, west, and north. But I never quite escaped the feeling that everything was make-believe. There are earnest, solid people of all sorts at work in Los Angeles—in business, in the schools of the city, in the universities—of course I know that. One modest philosopher in Los Angeles who would be speechless in the presence of a movie star has recently said something more important in the history of the world than all the highly advertised products that have come out of all studios of the region. But such conscientious people, slithered over by the rough-shod life everywhere about them, have not yet become powerful enough to save the city from its unreality. Who are they? Why, the people who take prominent rôles in the great show never so much as heard of them!

"Tell me where to find the most characteristic thing in Los Angeles," I begged of people, "the thing I ought not to get away without seeing." And they directed me to Hollywood, to the studios all along the edges of the region, to the houses on Beverly Hills. I did not mean to go out at all; I preferred time at the Huntington Library or the Zoo. But the library was closed for a period, I was told. And there seemed to be no time when one could not see "the houses of famous movie stars."

Eventually I was out there seeing some of them. And

some of them were so beautiful that they almost made me forget the billboards and the buildings painted over as if all life were a street carnival. But never quite. The tawdriness had been too much exalted. Everybody was advertising something—studios devoted to the development of speech, agencies guaranteed to sell picture rights, dentists pledged to straighten unattractive teeth, beauty-parlors fully equipped to make good whatever nature had carelessly left undone. And everywhere—so it seemed—were institutions devoted to the developing of the full personalities of dogs —and cats.

"Am I overimaginative," I asked a man when I was passing a studio devoted to "the clipping and boarding of dogs —bathing and defleaing," "or are there lots of places here for the care of dogs?"

"You're not overimaginative," he replied, the least bit grimly. "There are more damned dogs in this place than on all the rest of the Pacific Coast. Eight of them have insulted me already today while I've stood talking with people about real estate." He smiled a faint smile. "I'm thinking of running for Governor and doing something about it."

It was toward the end of a warm day when I was in the region of the Hollywood Bowl. Pressed together were cramped houses announcing board and lodging; blocks of undeniably beautiful houses with well-watered shrubs and flowers that were beginning to give the new houses a settled-in appearance; and billboards with premature nighttime luridness flashing their invitations to buy cigarettes or gasoline or a pleasant lot in a distinguished cemetery. Places of business did not have names above entrances; they were painted all over the front of the building. Right ahead of me when I turned one corner was a spacious illuminated sign which begged to say: "Motion pictures are your best entertainment. Go to a movie to-nite." Nowhere was anything inappropriate, for there was no standard of congruity.

But here was something to see. A sunset behind the hills was lighting up broken clouds all over the sky—gorgeously. And there on another hill was a great cross in the reflected glow. It was an unbelievable spectacle. Yes, that was just what it was. It was an arrangement—a movie. The sunset seemed overdone as if it had been devised by somebody who was desperately trying to attract attention.

And then just as if it had been prearranged by the man in gold braid down at the hotel, my trip back to town took me past the Angelus Temple. I saw the bright name; I saw an illuminated cross slowly revolving; I saw neon letters announcing when Aimee Semple McPherson was next to appear, and who was to assist her. The man who arranged tours was right, it was a perfect ending for an afternoon in the world of make-believe.

There was something of the same unreality in the tough districts when I wandered through them at night. True enough, I encountered men who looked me over, suspected that I might be an undercover person of some sort, and would have been pleased to bump me off if they could have done so without raising questions about their own identity. But most of the men were out of Bret Harte's stories. With the trace of a romantic flourish, the ones who drank at the bar pushed their hats back on their foreheads and put a foot on the brass rail as an accepted preliminary, just as Mr. John Oakhurst might have done. And roomful after roomful of them sat at tables and drank and played for modest stakes and made remarks designed to incite the women to braggadocio, just as if they were out of the same book— or on the stage; and the women looked sacrificial as if a thousand of them might be the legitimate daughters of Mother Shipton.

Nothing in Los Angeles was dull. But I never was without the feeling that the whole place had been made up. I thought I had better go to a movie. I wanted to see something real.

But San Francisco—I must have been prepared by a night on a Coast train to appreciate San Francisco. At quarter to two I was awakened by a woman in the aisle just outside my berth who persistently declared, "I can't! I can't make it! I p-positively can't!"

"Then I'll go first," a man said. "Watch me. I can shoot right past him—just like a meteor."

I peeped out. Just ahead a gray-haired man in his pajamas stood reaching into an upper berth as if he were getting something out of a bag up there. The man by my berth said again, "Now watch me." And he was able to get past. "See! You can make it! There's plenty of room! Come on!"

Heads appeared all along the aisle. And the old man smiled in the pale light of berth lamps as if he did not mind.

She laughed a little; then she shrieked a little, as if she faced some such feat as swimming the English Channel. Then she plunged. But the old man multiplied just as she came up, and she crashed right into one of him.

She had to try again. It was fun. But some man who had been awakened late in the show wanted to know "What the hell?" And a woman ordered the porter to call the conductor, who came.

It all took time. Then somebody had to talk when he got off the train at five-thirty. And a business man who sat opposite me at breakfast insisted on talking about the department-store strike in San Francisco when I wanted to enjoy the trees of Palo Alto. By the time we were approaching the water-front, my nerves were enough alive to enable me to see what San Francisco is like.

As soon as I was established in a hotel I went out to enjoy the clear views and the invigorating air. I climbed the nearest hill, and I had glimpses of the bay and the great bridges. But I wanted a more complete view. For here was poetry.

I picked out the highest building I could see, made my way to it, found the administrative offices, and told the efficient-looking woman in charge that I wished to view the city. Would she be good enough to let me go to the roof of the building? She seemed to decide that I had no bombs in my pockets, drew a key from a drawer, handed it to me, and said that the elevator boy would show me the stairway that led on up to the door which the key unlocked. I felt as if I had the key to the city—and I had. The door opened out to a view not to be matched in America: plenty of well-kept city covering many hills, gigantic bridges suspended over vast expanses of clear water, and yonder on Treasure Island the outlines of new World's Fair buildings that express an unaccustomed appropriateness.

When I was back in the street I had to climb a hill again —just to enjoy the experience. High above most of the city I came upon a half-finished cathedral. I wandered in. A genius in glass had contributed windows that were alive with the spirit of poetry and religion. I seemed to be finding the right things in San Francisco.

Back down in the busier streets I enjoyed a strange rush of good feeling—without knowing just why. Then I was aware of music. It seemed to be in Union Square.

People filled the paths, stood in the shade of low-arching palms, lounged on the grass in the warm sun. A band that had just finished one number and was beginning another spread out like a fan at the base of the monument in the center of the park, and above the heads of the musicians was some new scaffolding where a workman regilded painstakingly the record of Admiral Dewey.

The music had taken hold. Well-tailored men away from business for a moment of luncheon rest stood with lighted cigars or cigarettes between relaxed fingers while they listened. Office girls everywhere on the grass in bright clusters looked away as if there were still some distant golden haze in life that they had all but forgotten. Down-and-outers with days of stubbly beard on their unhealthy-looking faces who had come early in order to enjoy the park benches looked blankly at something indefinite. It was Sibelius's *Finlandia*. I shared the great sensitivity of the crowd. I did not know that any music could be so profoundly moving.

"Who are they?" I whispered into the ear of the man close beside me.

"Reliefers," he explained. "W.P.A."

In the intermission after the prolonged applause had died away I went down and talked with the conductor—a distinguished American musician. "I did not know anything could be quite like that," I said, having largely in mind the absolute silence of the people feeding on something which they very much needed.

"They are the finest musicians in San Francisco," he replied.

Two or three of the numbers they played were the compositions of members of the band. And—near the end of the program—one was an arrangement of several of Stephen C. Foster's best-known songs. Four brasses stood and carried the melody of "My Old Kentucky Home." How appropriate that a band of intelligent musicians in need of a living should play Foster! He would have been on relief himself if there had been relief. My dream city of San Francisco was becoming more literal. San Francisco was only carrying out the great American tradition of treating saviors of various kinds as if they deserved to be paupers.

But San Francisco had become a magic city again by the time I left it. For I crossed to Oakland on the ferry to take a train for the north. As we pushed out into the bay, out into water that pressed through the Golden Gate from the Pacific—from Hawaii, from China and Japan, from Samoa, from Australia—men stood about on the crowded forward deck in clumps of four and played pedro. But there were others who saw with fresh wonder the disappearing sun, the intervening purple mountains, the miraculous spans of the "eight-mile bridge" far above our heads where trucks scooted along in the open framework like beetles on a wire, and later the faint blinking of thousands of lights against the darkening hillside in Oakland.

Yes, it was all new—a thing unto itself. That was what explained pretty nearly everything on the Coast, a white-haired stout man assured me that evening. He stood leaning back against the wash-basin in the dressing-room with his coat off, and smoked cigarette after cigarette and talked to me while I enjoyed the long upholstered seat.

There was the labor problem, for instance. In most places the employer-labor fights arise after society has hardened into unsympathetic classes. But in California the troubles have arisen because society has not hardened enough. California had pretty nearly always had a leisure class—for somebody got the gold. And in the past two or three decades this class had grown until a man sometimes thought everybody belonged to it. Yet always California had had roving migratory workers in overabundance who picked hops or grapes or lettuce or whatever there was to pick. People out of work in Kansas or the Oklahoma Dust Bowl or the Twin Cities seemed always to head for California. "Why, I know of one project in this state that is going to require men, and right now before there is anything for any of them to do, seven thousand have drifted into the community—from everywhere. Maybe that isn't a mess for the local authorities! And when all these people see everybody else who comes to California taking it easy, they begin to demand all sorts of things themselves. Maybe we'll—"

He stopped in the middle of the sentence, and I noticed that he had grown pale and seemed to be about to topple over. I jumped up and offered to help him to the seat. "It's my heart," he said, and began to fumble in a vest pocket for something as he slumped into the corner by the window. "I'll be all right—as soon as I can swallow one of these 'high-power explosives.'"

When the color was returning a little to his face, he explained: "My heart is just no good—and never will be, now. I have to carry these capsules with me all the time to keep her from stopping completely."

He had to tell me how it was. He was sixty-eight, and within a year and a half had lost both his wife and his daughter. There was no special reason why his heart should go on beating. And added to all that, he was overweight, and so gave his heart too much to do. He had consulted a specialist who promised to tell him the truth—and who told him that he had never known a heart as badly wrecked as this one that lasted longer than two years. If he smoked plenty of cigarettes it would not last that long. Well, he was still smoking. A few months more or less—it was just a detail.

But what the doctor told him set him to thinking. What

could he do in two years—at a maximum—that he'd really like to do? After turning the matter over, he decided that the only thing which seemed worth while at all was just to be friendly to people who might have more than two years ahead—or less.

He began with the black woman who had devoted her life to his wife and daughter. He went down to the house where she lived and gathered together the children and an old black mammy who was well past ninety. "I told them that we were going to have a little picnic—with plenty of ice-cream. Well, sir, I never knew that anything no more important than doing that could make people so happy that they'd shed tears and say 'God bless you' till they embarrassed you."

He became so completely warmed to his narrative that he had to stand up again and lean against the edge of the wash-basin and light another cigarette. "I felt as if I had gone somewhere and got religion—and maybe I had. I would go right on doing pleasant things for other people—maybe for two years. That would be something—or as near something as anything is.

"Well, the next morning as I went down the street I passed a man I'd passed before, though I didn't know him. 'Why not speak?' I said to myself. 'You're just a couple of humans.' So as agreeably as I knew how I said, 'Good morning!'

"He gave me the stoniest stare I ever met up with—and walked straight on without a word.

"'Then go to hell!' I called after him.

"He turned. 'Didn't you say something?' he asked.

"'Yes, I told you to go to hell.'

"'But didn't you say something before that?'

"'Yes, but it was something you couldn't understand.'"

He laughed, then in sudden pain clutched his chest and held his breath. "Ooh-h-h. Just like going down through there with a curry-comb." He waited a little. "I suppose I had better try to get some sleep." Then he came back to what he had laughed at. "You know, there are some things that you just have to go slow with, even in California."

I was awake at five o'clock the next morning. The train was laboring along a narrow canyon. Once, as we took a curve, I could see towering fir trees that looked as if they had always been there and a thin sliver of a moon that was growing pale in the coming light There could be no doubt: this was Oregon.

At Eugene something of the strangeness of the Coast had disappeared. Students in the state's university there were youngsters fresh from new cities and new farms, but they had habits of mind which suggested that their fathers and mothers had not long been out of Ohio or New England.

And even more of the strangeness had gone by the time I had reached Seattle. Here people grew apples, not citrus fruits. Here there was rain—and fog, too. Here there were people who had come in easy stages in two or three generations all the way from Minnesota and Michigan and Indiana and Vermont. There had been no break. Down at the foot of the campus of the University of Washington the new theater that had just opened—a model for experimental theaters—was called the Show Boat, and it stood white at the water's edge as if it were afloat on the Mississippi. Here something perpetuated was being employed in fresh pioneering. And near each other in a non-commercial theatrical area that is much to the credit of Washington and Seattle the Wesley Players produce religious drama, and the young political radicals of Independence Hall produce plays of the proletariat—or at least controversial plays. Other groups in the city are active. In a stable setting, all sorts of ideas are jockeying for place.

One morning I watched as we were coming eastward across the neck of Idaho.

"Highway?" I asked the conductor, indicating some even embankments of fresh earth far toward the top of the mountain across the canyon.

"Highway? That's where we go. We do twenty miles to travel four. And we do a hair-pin turn up here right in a tunnel."

When we were at last up there, and through a pass, and going down on the other side, I had a strange nostalgic feeling that we had left the last of something bright and new behind. Down toward Missoula—at least it seemed down— there were inviting grassy mountains of great roundness that might have been in the north of England—almost.

And over in South Dakota the next day passengers who were getting on the train talked about Atlantic seaboard football scores as if their interests were back in that direction. And when we passed through a town called Groton and immediately afterward through one called Andover, and a wag in the observation-car said that a St. Mark's man who had owned real estate farther north had named them in the hope of putting a curse on the region, the people who heard understood the joke. There were bleached skeletons of cattle in the fields along the way, and occasionally steers' skulls hanging on a wire fence. Men and women who looked as if they had never received more than they had earned discussed the price of wheat, and wondered if they were going to be able to go out to the Coast to see the World's Fair next year—the Coast, off yonder just as definitely as that.

# xix

## Panorama

HAVE you ever tried to see the entire United States of America at one look? It is an unforgettable experience. For there is no denying it: the United States is something amazing.

It is difficult enough, first of all, to accept the simple fact that the United States continues to exist. Why does it not fly apart into a half-dozen self-sufficient entities? Once on the train when I had listened to two men who were trying to decide whether the country was too big to be one nation, and we came suddenly out several thousand feet up just east of a northern sector of the Continental Divide where there was nothing in view except the haze of distant plains, I tried to imagine that I was viewing the whole country. And the first result was a feeling that the continued existence of the United States was only some miraculous accident. What geographical reason, for example, is there for the nation? The distance from the extreme limits of one coast of it to those of the other is as great as from North America to Europe. One of the chief mountain systems of the world cuts directly athwart it, and, supported by a desert, does what it can to isolate the west-coast area from all that is to the eastward. The Great Plains region with a vast river system directing thought north and south instead of east and west is ready-made an empire in itself. And yet once more a mountain system cuts down across the country and invites the people on the eastern seaboard to go north and south instead of east and west. The men with whom I had been traveling who proposed that the country was too far-flung to be administered as a unit had some geographical arguments on their side.

Neither is the continued existence of the country less to be marveled at when one sees the diversity—and often the conflict—of economic interests. The Pacific Coast has its natural front door toward the Orient; the Middle West is busily concerned with producing for anybody who will buy, and wishes no outside competition lest its cherished civilization of free men on the soil pass into obscurity; the great industrial region of Smoke stands forth as a dominant yet unstable feudalism in the heart of a country dedicated to democracy; the central Atlantic area of powerful financial concerns would make itself still more powerful by dominating the rest of the country, including the feudal industrialists; in the old South an oversupply of human beings would be glad to have the New England mills move down to them; and in New England, geographically out of the current of national life, people who know England and France better than their own country quite reasonably fear that the South will take what New England must keep.

Nor does national unity become anything less to be marveled at when one views the hodge-podge of races covering the landscape in these diverse geographical and economic regions: everywhere a first coating of English; and then Italians and Irish and French Canadians in New England; Irish and Jews and Negroes in New York; millions of more or less unwanted Negroes in the old South; Mexicans in the Southwest; all sorts of Europeans in Michigan, Wisconsin, and Minnesota—one country school in the Upper Peninsula of Michigan had seventeen nations represented in it; Indians scattered here and there west of the Mississippi; and on the Pacific Coast, representatives of all these races, with some Japanese and Chinese thrown in. Where is the unifying homogeneity?

And there are other fundamental diversities—such as religion and political prejudices. When religious feeling is confused with denominational feeling, the result is enough hate to menace the most substantial national unity. I have been in towns where the chief business of the Catholic and the Protestant clergy seemed to be to keep members of each other's faith out of political office. I have heard Catholic and Protestant mothers declare fervidly that they would rather follow their children to the grave than have them marry anybody of the other faith. In some regions political partisanship takes on a religious-like character strong enough to break up business partnerships and families. And in many places if a man chances to hold to some specially distasteful political faith, he may be pursued and set upon as an outlaw.

Not even the least serious approach makes the existence

of the United States seem any more logical. Everywhere people vainly trying to recapture their pasts, people trying to leave their pasts behind them, people desperately in pursuit of reality, people just as desperately trying to escape reality, people who are reducing, people who are trying to put on weight, people rushing to Miami, people rushing to Reno, people reading the *New Yorker* and sniffing at people who read the *Atlantic Monthly,* people reading the *Atlantic Monthly* and blasting with silence the people who read the *New Yorker*—where in all this is there anything that explains why the people are nationally one?

Yet something does. If one rides long and hears people when they are not on parade, has glimpses of them when they are absorbed in enterprises that they put above all others, and catches something of the feel of their lives as they live in their own special solitudes day by day, it is possible—even quite easy—to know why the United States is a very close unity. One discovers that the people are bound together by something more potent than geography, more potent than any cold-blooded balancing of economic interests, more potent than any elemental feeling of race. For they are bound together by a dream. And it is the mightiest of all dreams—something that parallels the sense of biological growth. It says that the individual human beings who make up the United States shall enjoy the sense of freedom that is to be found in growing into an existence that is undeniably expansive; that they shall feel that they are experiencing an increase of life rather than a decrease. Day after tomorrow must be better than day before yesterday. They have made the extension of self-feeling, the freeing of the spirit, and consequently the developing of mental power and the enlarging of life, the one great national romance. No matter how much they may disagree on many matters, they are in overwhelming general accord on this: that the extension of self-feeling into the world roundabout is at once the most fruitful experience that the individual can have, and the most useful, the "best" contribution he can make to the world. It is a tenuous dream, sometimes confusedly merged with others, sometimes shrewdly perverted by the unscrupulous and made to yield financial dividends, sometimes shamed out of sight by those who talk loosely about it as if it were only a sentimentality. But always some remnant of it is left, always the whole of it reappears intermittently to view.

A means of expressing the dream, of perpetuating it, of multiplying it toward realization, must be at hand. So the people have given themselves to the creation of liberalizing institutions. This means of expressing the people's dream has exceeded anything known in history. It has become so completely a part of every community that there is always the danger of regarding it as a commonplace. But lift it up a little into relief and it becomes to all eyes what it really is—a thing without parallel: Millions of children, from Maine to Texas, from Key West to Seattle, every morning marching off in the exuberant style of the unafraid to centers within easy reach—or being hauled in school buses if the centers must be too far away—to spend the day with older trained persons in coming to new understandings and new skills, not only in the more strictly utilitarian fields, not only in the fundamentals of subjects that are to be explored more maturely later, but in music and drawing and dancing and poetry and other imaginative worlds that offer fresh joys to a child's daily living; and then older millions going to high schools that are better equipped with laboratories, machine-shops, working libraries, experimental theaters, and facilities in music, in practical design, in the arts and economy of the household, than most of the colleges were as recently as thirty years ago; and then still other hundreds of thousands occupied—sometimes lightly, often seriously—in higher institutions of learning with man's past and man's mind and man's world, and all sorts of schemes of life that might be adapted to the needs of man in the future. Although there were efforts in some quarters to preserve the higher reaches of education as a kind of intellectual sanctuary where only the elect should hold forth and reproduce their kind, the entire world of higher education has been more or less invaded by the hungrier youths who have swarmed everywhere from the high schools. If they have not been "prepared" to enter, to work within the strict limits of the sanctuary, they have stormed the doors until the sanctuary has been adjusted to their essential needs.

Now more significant nationally than anything else in this scheme of education—and in its inclusiveness and idealistic character it is truthfully without parallel—is the fact that it has become not only a means to greater freedom of spirit for those who participate in it directly, but a kind of high standard by which everything else in the nation's life—and everything proposed—receives the most nearly impartial measurement possible. Especially do the millions who have been directly touched—it may be very superficially, it may be profoundly—insist on determining whether what takes place in the United States furthers or hinders the great dream of individual freedom.

That is why there are many stirrings in the country. That is why there seems to be a fight on. All those who write about "the growing arrogance of the proletariat," the increasing power of all sorts of "subversive influences," the display of "class feeling" where it had not been noticed before, have a certain surface rightness in what they say. But to attribute the general disquiet to people's supposed unintelligence or their supposed low motives is to confess blindness to what has been taking place right under our eyes. We have seen and are seeing the rise of the educated many in a democracy. They want as much freedom—both the inner feeling of freedom and the manageable environment—as possible, and many of them know that despite their conscientious effort they are having little, and may have less. They are troubled because they see elements at work in our life that do not seem to parallel the dream of a nation of free men. They fear that something else has been lifted up for adoration until the one thing least thought about in many quarters is the state of the individual human beings who live there. They invite you, many of them, to ride through their part of the country and compare, for instance, the sheltering of human beings with the sheltering of mill machinery and decide for yourself which of the two the United States has come to accept as the more important. They ask you to make a collection of the programs proposed in this city or that for the restoring of good times when times have been bad, and see whether you would care to be thought of as only so many consumers who might be kept around to use up things and thereby keep the wheels turning and the dividends coming and the price of stocks mounting. Here is why they are discussing remedies—not a few of the ragged proletariat, as some would like to believe, but all sorts of substantial citizens: farmers, skilled craftsmen, railway conductors, school-teachers, shopkeepers, judges, mill workers, the unemployed young, the insecure old, university professors, ministers, social workers. Here is why they are ready to hear about any wild scheme that anybody begs to propose. Here is why some of them wonder regretfully if a revolution of some kind will be required to extend democracy into fields where it can produce results. "All right," the more impatient say; "we've learned how something better can be had; so why aren't we all having a little more of it?"

It would be pleasant to say that these fears are groundless; that as one travels over the land one discerns no hindrances to indefinite extensions of the democratic principle; that with enough faith in something or other, everything must come out for the best in the end without anybody's special thought. But I believe nothing of the sort. To pretend that I did would be groveling dishonesty. For after seeing the country three or four times a year for a decade and a half, and living among all sorts of people, from coal miners and ditch diggers to business executives, I am convinced that the extension of democracy confronts formidable obstacles.

The greatest of these is high-pressure industry. It is the sore spot in our national body. I do not refer to the fact of mass production; I do not decry the development of the machine—I encourage it; and I believe that anybody who directs the production of anything needed, or invests his capital in production, should have as fair a chance of financial return as human beings in general have. But the spirit of the contemporary industrial world—with notable exceptions—is quite another matter. It does not fit into a democratic scheme of life. Its functioning is avowedly monarchical; it is ruthless; it is arrogant in its attitude toward other human productivities; and it arbitrarily takes from men fundamental freedom by telling them where they shall live, when they shall live somewhere else, when they shall work and when remain idle, what work it shall be, and whether they and their families shall eat.

If the democratic ideal in the United States is not to be

swallowed up sooner or later by some totalitarian ideal, then the people who operate factories must own them. I do not mean any scheme in which the government would be the direct owner and the people would hold only an indirect ownership by being the final arbiters in maintaining the government, but an ordinary direct and full ownership in which the workers and the managers of the factories —the people who together know how to run them—would accept an owner's hazards and receive his profits. The time will come when some such democratic participation in industrial production will be accepted as so right and inevitable that the present feudal monstrosity will then seem immeasurably more fantastic to the public mind than this suggested democracy does to the most dogmatic industrialist today.

The case is simple enough when one looks. A man feels substantially related to his fellows when he possesses enough of the means of production to give him as much control over his destiny as people in general have over theirs. From being in undisputed possession of a piece of the earth from which all things have sprung, a man derives, too, a primal, half-mystical steadying that is important. Here are reasons why even the smallest of farmers who own their land—and face hazards from the weather alone that make the risks of the wholesale millinery business seem like absolute security —have an independence of character quite out of proportion to that of the mill workers who receive the same income or more. Here are reasons why the men who work in factories and the men who manage them must own them. If it is good for farmers to own their farms and band together in the production of milk and grain and fruit, and we have evolved an industrial scheme in which vast numbers of people may not own farms because they work for life in a factory, it must follow that if they are to derive from a sense of ownership the self-respect and sense of freedom about which the biggest owners speak more worshipfully than anybody else whenever any kind of collectivist state is mentioned, they must derive them from ownership in the factory. They cannot have them if they have nothing to sell except their labor and somebody else can tell them whether or not they are to sell that. If they shared ownership in the factory they might then own the houses that sheltered them and express individual preferences in making them livable, as they cannot well afford to risk doing when an industry owned by somebody a thousand miles away may pack up and move somewhere else next week and render houses valuable only as kindling for the unfortunate last-to-leave. There would be risks, and they would be for the good of the men—infinitely better than the simple formula: "Do this exactly as I tell you and see that you put lots of personal initiative into it"; or the simpler formula, "Do nothing at all."

And as if this sore dislocation in the democratic scheme of life were not enough of an evil in itself, the czarist type of executive mind which it exacts insists on injecting the high-pressure profit aims and techniques into all sorts of activities where they do not apply—into the church, into the arts, into education, into government. After years of casual and intimate acquaintance with men who have "alien" social and political philosophies to promote, and with every kind and grade of business man and business philosopher, I have come to believe that the greatest menace to orderly and satisfying life in the United States is not any group who champion a supposedly alien political philosophy, but a certain type of man who through persistence plus good luck comes into financial power, and then immediately wants to apply his oversimplified philosophy pig-headedly to the whole complex problem of other people's existence. For he does not want to depend on thinking; he depends on power. He believes in telling people what to do. Too many of his kind among people who have grown more sensitive through education might in fact result in an upheaval. In the interests of democracy we must think about him.

A second great hindrance to the extension of democracy that the traveler eventually sees is our out-dated attitude toward poverty. We shall have to quit treating poverty as if it were only something pitiable to be kept out of sight, and begin thinking about it as something that bogs down the entire experiment in individual freedom. We speak in lofty phrase about how a democracy increases the general welfare—how it "lifts the life of the people to higher and higher levels." Very well. In some degree, it can. But if the lifting is to be done—done at all—how is it to be done? Is it not in some such manner as this? Certain exceptional heads —by superior endowment plus good luck—get up above the others, see farther, do more original thinking, open new ways, and in some degree—according to the capacity of the general level—have their better ideas accepted and absorbed until the level is actually brought up ever so slightly. The exceptional minds that spring from this slightly lifted level have a somewhat better start, and a somewhat better level to deal with in the spreading of their more original ideas. They lift the level—eventually—once again. Thus the process may go on. Thus we may come to have much improved levels—in the long course of time. If ever we should be lucky enough to have a general level quite receptive to direct new ways of thinking, it is even conceivable that the process might become swifter, that what today is still unimagined improvement might finally result.

But just how speedily can that process be carried on if

twenty or thirty millions of people in a nation with a population only four or five times that large are made a millstone on the neck of the others by being constantly dependent, constantly humiliated, constantly baited into doing their worst instead of their best? By all the laws of chance, any potential leaders among them will have a harder time achieving their own development. And if they do in smaller numbers or in lesser degree succeed, how much effect will their own fertilizing ideas have on a general level that has been so extensively deadened? For it must be remembered that in a democracy the humbled, the embittered, the passively inert have quite as much to say about what shall be adopted and put into practice—or not—as the more healthy-minded have.

I was in a state where fifty thousand children who had nothing to wear to school were being provided with clothing by the government. The number of children of different ages had been ascertained, and the clothes had been provided according to age. There were many exclamations of "How terrible!" when the news got abroad that much of the clothing was too large because undernourished children were below normal size for their age. I saw some of these children. But what impressed me more than mere evidence of undernourishment was the feeling of inferiority, the consciousness of being on the outside when nearly everybody else was on the inside, that was already marked in their faces.

Now multiply this great army many times into the total army of the young who are growing up with the feeling that they have been left out, and then ask if there could be any greater stupidity than to let this army go on accumulating into a substantial percentage of the voting population of the country. Here is a problem so stupendous and so full of social dynamite that it makes all such supposedly important concerns as balancing the budget or preventing inflation seem like the merest trivialities. For the presence of the poor in large percentages thwarts all near approach to the democratic ideal, and in the end may obliterate it wholly.

A vague hypocritical knowledge of this clutches us now. The poor talk about their fear of another depression, when as a matter of fact they have become aware that the "depression" for them is something that will last as long as they do. The more fortunate desperately proclaim their disgust that some magical recovery has not been brought about, when the real trouble is that they are caught up by a great fear lest their own present abundance be required in the unending struggle to feed the permanently unemployed. So nobody is in a right state of mind to do his best work or to find the greatest satisfaction in living.

But suppose we were to become honest with ourselves. Suppose we were to recognize poverty—poverty that did not result from sub-normal mentality unmistakably—as a national disease, and were to admit that we were under obligation to find cures for it, if for no other reason than that if we did not destroy it it would destroy us. Suppose we were to set to work with the best intelligence we could concentrate, as nearly untrammeled as possible by political or economic preconceptions, to discover a scheme of productive life large enough to include everybody, and rid ourselves of such a cancerous disgrace as hunger and consequent slow spiritual destruction for millions in an age that can produce plenty. This we would do not merely out of good feeling for the unfortunate, but as a means of improving the entire social climate. After all, such pompous affairs as nations and eras and civilizations, when reduced to their lowest terms, consist of hesitant, fearful, hopeful human beings.

And hope carrying promise of any degree of fulfillment would soon give large numbers of the poor—the young among them, at least—a positiveness of attitude that would help at once to rehabilitate their lives. They would not only cease to be a millstone on others; they would soon be energizing these others through their own new-found dynamic. Through their own freedom they would help to set everybody free. We could in this way have a renewal of the sense of common enterprise that we have somewhat lost—and that totalitarian states do have, and profess to monopolize. We would have it not by surrendering our personal freedoms, but by increasing them.

Other hindrances are in the educative process itself—the process designed to increase the people's acquaintance with the art of democracy. The press, for instance, has now come to be owned by what we conveniently call the capitalist class—the class that has money to invest in any business that promises profits. Naturally the press reflects the point of view of the owners. Yet these capitalists attempt to provide mildly restive non-capitalists with the news. They must seem to be concerned with the people's rights in order to have readers; yet they dare not champion the people's cause lest the people decide to take things in hand and in some frightening process of revivification take away some of the capitalists' power—that is, their money. So a very large part of the press has taken its cue from the press in the regions where the economic battle is acute, and publishes news that will be exciting without having economic significance, stories and articles that entertain without bestirring thought or contributing too much basically enlightening knowledge, and important-looking editorials and special columns that do not conflict with the economic interests of the predominant class of newspaper publishers.

The result is one of the spectacular ironies of the age: people by the millions reading the parts of newspapers that interest or amuse them, and then acting and thinking and voting in disregard of the newspapers' expressed convictions.

All groups and blocs should have full newspaper representation—including the capitalist bloc. But the people ought always to be able to read with enlightened discrimination. "Somebody," a young executive who is interested in newspapers and education said to me, "ought to write up in accurate detail the complete life history of every important newspaper in the country, so that readers could know specifically who owns it, what its financial and social connections are, and on what basis it prints or excludes news." More important still, there must be many newspapers—many of them—owned by large numbers of the people who read them, so that the great diversity of stockholders would make it not only reasonable but safe for the staff to publish all the successes, all the failures, all the aspirations, of democracy at work. The great body of participants in our enterprise must have their own voices, their own advocates. They must have the assurance that the news is printed chiefly by those who are in sympathy with full extension of the idea of democracy, rather than so exclusively by those who often give the impression that they would rather see the United States disintegrate than have it succeed in ways not proposed by them.

So, too, does the radio fall far short of what it could do in the interest of the national dream. No one can make a sweeping turn of the dial of a radio today without wondering if Americans have become a nation of imbeciles, so overwhelmingly is the "air"—which of all things should be as open as possible to everybody—used by those who have axes to grind. It may be a trifle far-fetched to suggest just yet that a manufacturer of dentifrice or a distributor of gasoline should confer bachelor of arts degrees. Yet we content ourselves with depending upon them to set standards in music and speech. Even the Lord's Prayer over the radio is preceded and followed by the more positive voice which assures you that this great privilege comes through the generosity of some soap manufacturer or cigarette-maker or meat-packer or druggist. The radio—which, after all, is the result of disinterested men's long sacrificial inquiries—should be unrestrictedly at the service of institutions of learning and the arts, not merely because they can offer vast audiences of people something worth having, but because they are as nearly disinterested as any agency in the country.

Nor can the traveler fail to see how democracy is confronted by the hindrance of partisan interpretation. Putting people in pigeonholes or on sides saves all the trouble of new thinking. When anybody has once been pigeonholed and labeled—even if incorrectly—everything he thereafter proposes is regarded as having a certain bias, a certain second motive which is assumed to be in truth the primary one. It may be years before partisanships have been shifted, or certain of them completely obliterated, so that the country in general is able to see just what was of value in all that once had been so bitterly fought over. This partisan interpretation of many matters not only slows down the extension of democracy, but helps to create doubt as to whether we are making any headway whatever.

Such hindrances are real. Sometimes they assume the aspect of menaces to the entire national dream. We cannot ignore them. We cannot escape them by seeking refuge in some highly idealized past. They constitute an incontrovertible fact. Yet they are not the chief fact of our national life. The chief fact is that not even the most formidable hindrance deters the people altogether in the pursuit of their dream. They only move a little confusedly. They need to have their sense of enterprise sharpened—their sense of high enterprise. The democratic idea at work must be made visual, rendered vivid. Few people in the United States—relatively few—have even the slightest conception of what all the people in the country together are bringing to pass. Few people have any image of the country itself. Few can draw a map of the United States that shows with even roughest approximation the state lines, the regional topography, the products of the different wide areas.

Likewise the people need a non-partisan symbol that will stand for their total aspiration. In England, it is the business of every good Britisher to denounce many things, as cabinets come and go. But all Britishers can get together on the king. No other kind of king will do. If he stutters a bit, what matter? He represents everybody. He stands for the whole people. We admit the need of a symbol whenever we concentrate on a transatlantic flyer, or child actress, or philosopher from the cattle-fields of Oklahoma. Perhaps from time to time some living symbol, free of all confusing ties, will rise up, like a kind of democratic messiah, and be content to do nothing but keep the people sharply aware of their dream. Perhaps they will create out of their own dreaming an ideal man who will always be there ahead in the future to beckon them and keep them from turning aside.

However that may be, here they are, deeply engaged in a spectacle quite unlike anything we have record of: providing themselves with bread and fruit and clothing, blasting coal from the hills, drawing oil from the depths of the earth, building bridges that span unbelievable stretches, building skyscrapers that touch the clouds, exploring the air, studying the distant heavens, investigating God, detecting how sun-spots affect the radio in their houses, attempting to explain stock-market values, predicting the weather, performing operations on the brain—even on the heart—establishing coöperatives, combatting dust, combatting floods, building more highways than ever were built before—yet all the while with a dream in the back of their heads that it is possible for individual men to achieve a certain freedom, that they should be as free as possible, that their children must be freer than they themselves have been. The presence of the dream makes the people more interesting to see. The presence of the dream is somehow greatly to their credit.

Nor is it to their discredit that they are ever ready to hear the spell-binder who promises them some overcomplete realization of their dream. They like to dwell upon stupendous possibilities. They have come to the view of the man who proclaimed a new interpretation of the song of the sirens; they know that the politician is not luring them to their destruction, but only stirring them to try new dangerous ways toward the poetic unknown which they are dead in earnest to discover. The rhapsodic politician adds to the romance of their lives by pointing out something yonder ahead. They may laugh at him—they do often enough —but they wish that all he says might come true.

They are no longer "the monster, the people," "the unthinking masses" who are supposed not to be able to understand civilization and therefore would destroy it. They have come to understand it too well, and know that changes in it—rapid changes—must be made. Although not one of them in a hundred—perhaps not one in a thousand—has yet received an education that opens the way to anything approximating full growth, they have received enough to know that somewhat enlightened beings can be helpful to themselves, and that they can try new ways of helping themselves without losing their balance. As one sees thousands of them in all corners of the country, in every condition, in every temper, the total seems to say: "See here! Just why is there any big joke in dreaming of something magnificent enough to be worth having? Did anybody ever dream of anything so wild but what somebody sooner or later came along and made it all come true? Haven't we seen light and heat and power come in over a dark, cool, silent wire, and wagons run without being drawn, and men descend and travel under the sea, and men rise in the air and fly, and men's voices and their photographic likenesses flash from the other side of the earth on the wings of nothing, and slaves go free, and yellow fever disappear, and other ills lose their deadly import? So what is so impossible about having enough food to eat, and pleasant places to live in, and a little time for enjoyment, and mental light for anybody who has a mind —all in the protective climate of a government which we ourselves constitute and can change whenever we choose? We are on to that old wail that all this would be very nice to have, but that it is useless to begin talking about wanting it until we know exactly how we are going to get it. If we want it enough, we'll find a way of getting it. And if we can't get it in one way, we'll try another. What are minds for? We might hit upon something. Or if we don't, maybe our children will."

Something that has shown them how reasonable and how available the "utopian" may be has made the dream into a mightier one than ever, that will not let them go.

(1)